Designing Personalized Learning Experiences

Designing Personalized Learning Experiences offers theoretically grounded and pragmatic approaches to designing personalized learning initiatives for higher education and organizational contexts. With current research concluding that a multitude of variables can enable learners to direct their own experiences and achieve their goals, new guidance is needed to hone the range of instructional approaches, activities, and interactions available to support adult learners. This book offers practical strategies on how to design and implement effective personalized learning interventions, advance learning and engagement, encourage ownership over the learning process, and decrease attrition.

Professionals in instructional design, learning and development, organizational development, consultancies, and beyond will be emboldened by the work to leverage a mix of technology-enabled social and content interactions.

Dr. Helen Fake is a Lead User Experience Researcher at The Motley Fool and serves as an Adjunct Professor in the Division of Learning Technologies at George Mason University, USA.

Dr. Nada Dabbagh is Professor and Director of the Division of Learning Technologies in the College of Education and Human Development at George Mason University, USA.

Designing Personalized Learning Experiences

A Framework for Higher Education and Workforce Training

HELEN FAKE AND NADA DABBAGH

NEW YORK AND LONDON

Designed cover image: © Shutterstock

First published 2024
by Routledge
605 Third Avenue, New York, NY 10158

and by Routledge
4 Park Square, Milton Park, Abingdon, Oxon, OX14 4RN

Routledge is an imprint of the Taylor & Francis Group, an informa business

© 2024 Helen Fake and Nada Dabbagh

The right of Helen Fake and Nada Dabbagh to be identified as authors of this work has been asserted in accordance with sections 77 and 78 of the Copyright, Designs and Patents Act 1988.

All rights reserved. No part of this book may be reprinted or reproduced or utilised in any form or by any electronic, mechanical, or other means, now known or hereafter invented, including photocopying and recording, or in any information storage or retrieval system, without permission in writing from the publishers.

Trademark notice: Product or corporate names may be trademarks or registered trademarks, and are used only for identification and explanation without intent to infringe.

Library of Congress Cataloging-in-Publication Data
Names: Fake, Helen, author. | Dabbagh, Nada, author.
Title: Designing personalized learning experiences : a framework for higher education and workforce training / Helen Fake and Nada Dabbagh.
Description: New York, NY : Routledge, 2023. |
Includes bibliographical references and index.
Identifiers: LCCN 2022061938 (print) |
LCCN 2022061939 (ebook) | ISBN 9780367638566 (hardback) |
ISBN 9780367631864 (paperback) | ISBN 9781003121008 (ebook)
Subjects: LCSH: Individualized instruction. | Instructional systems–Design. | Experiential learning. | Education, Higher. | Vocational education.
Classification: LCC LB1031 .F35 2023 (print) |
LCC LB1031 (ebook) | DDC 371.39/4–dc23/eng/20230221
LC record available at https://lccn.loc.gov/2022061938
LC ebook record available at https://lccn.loc.gov/2022061939

ISBN: 978-0-367-63856-6 (hbk)
ISBN: 978-0-367-63186-4 (pbk)
ISBN: 978-1-003-12100-8 (ebk)

DOI: 10.4324/9781003121008

Typeset in Garamond
by MPS Limited, Dehradun

Contents

Preface   *vi*

1 The History of Personalized Learning   1
2 Approaches to Personalized Learning   17
3 Designing Personalized Learning Experiences Using the PL Interaction Framework (PLiF)   44
4 Designing for Learner–Content Interaction   60
5 Designing for Learner–Learner Interaction   87
6 Designing for Learner–Small Group Interaction   106
7 Designing for Learner–Mentor, Coach, or AI Interaction   128
8 Designing for Learner–Social Network Interaction   145
9 Evaluating Personalized Learning Designs   169
10 Empowering Learners to Engage in Personalized Learning Experiences   186

Index   *209*

Preface

What you will find in the reading of this book is a multi-level interaction framework of personalized learning. We will explore how expert research has suggested that by building upon Moore's Interaction Framework, we may be able to support lifelong learners in cultivating and creating selfsustaining ecosystems of learning that leverage Web 2.0 and even Web 3.0 learning technologies (Fake & Dabbagh, 2018, 2020). We will delve into the history, research, best practices, and expressions of personalized learning. And we will provide a framework that you can implement within your organization to support your learners in developing personalized learning strategies that encourage and scaffold lifelong learning practices. We hope that the implementation of this framework will not only measurably impact the lives of the individuals that adopt these interactions, new behaviors, and life skills, but also positively transform the organizations they seek to serve.

Why is this important? Well, it comes down to the need to support the reskilling and retooling of a global workforce that's facing unprecedented levels of change (Donovan & Benko, 2016; Pelster et al., 2017; Thomas & Brown, 2011). According to Deloitte's 2020 Global Human Capital Trends Survey, 53% of respondents indicated that more than half or all of their workforce would need to change their skills and capabilities and skills in the next three years (Schwartz et al., 2020). This is echoed in the World Economic Forum's "Future of Jobs 2020 Report" with COVID-19 only enhancing the need for a workforce that can adapt to constantly changing conditions (Schwab & Zahidi, 2020). The Future of Jobs also projects that 40–50% of currently needed skillsets will change over the next 5 years. These studies espouse that Workforce Training and Development Programs have a critical role for individuals and organizations to maintain a competitive edge in the modern age (Donovan & Benko, 2016; Pelster et al., 2017; Thomas & Brown, 2011).

The ethos of continuous development continues to be an important initiative when according to Thompson et al. (2018), the challenge ranked the second most difficult by training and development professionals surveyed (N = 500) was "getting employees to make time for their personal training and development". Given that US Corporate Training budgets hovered around $82.5 Billion in 2020, the market need and demand for training begs questions of why employees are not engaging with current Workforce Training and Development Programs.

This book offers practical guidance and strategies on how to design and implement effective personalized learning interventions, advance learning, increase engagement, decrease attrition, encourage ownership over the learning process, develop employees, and retain talent within workforce environments. Specifically, this book provides a personalized learning interaction framework that could be leveraged for a range of use cases.

References

Donovan, J., & Benko, C. (2016). AT&T's talent overhaul. Harvard Business Review, 68–73. Retrieved from https://hbr.org/2016/10/atts-talent-overhaul.

Fake, H. (2018). A delphi study on the dimensions of personalized learning in workforce training and development programs. [Doctoral dissertation, CRC Press]. Proquest.

Fake, H., & Dabbagh, N. (2020). Personalized learning within online workforce learning environments: Exploring implementations, obstacles, opportunities, and perspectives of workforce leaders. Technology, Knowledge, and Learning, 25(1), 789–809. DOI: 10.1007/s10758-020-09441-x.

Pelster, B., Johnson, D., Stempel, J., van der Vyver, B. (2017, February). Careers and learning: Real time, all the time [Research Report]. Retrieved from Deloitte Insights: https://www2.deloitte.com/insights/us/en/focus/human-capital-trends/2017/learning-in-the-digital-age.html?id=us:2el:3dc:dup3818:awa:cons:hct17#endnote-4.

Schwartz, J., Denny, B., Mallon, D., Durme, V. D., Hauptmann, M., Yan, R., & Poynton, S. (2020, May 15). Beyond reskilling: Investing in resilience for uncertain futures. Deloitte Insights. https://www2.deloitte.com/us/en/insights/focus/human-capital-trends/2020/reskilling-the-workforce-to-be-resilient.html.

Schwab, K., & Zahidi, S. (2020). Global competitiveness report: Special edition 2020. World Economic Forum.

Thomas, D., & Brown, J. S. (2011). A new culture of learning: Cultivating the imagination for a world of constant change. Lexington, KY: CreateSpace?.

Thompson, L., Pate, D., Schnidman, A., Lu, L., Andreatta, B., & Dewett, T. (2018). 2017 workplace learning report: How modern L&D pros are tackling topchallenges. Retrieved from https://learning.linkedin.com/resources/workplace-learning-report-2018?trk=lilblog_02-07-17_WLR-announcement_tl&cid=70132000001AyziAAC

The History of Personalized Learning

1

Personalized learning is not new. In fact, one might argue that historically, personalized learning has roots that reach back to the time of Aristotle. In the interest of brevity and despite the inherent appeal of understanding personalized learning's ancient Grecian origins, we will begin our exploration of personalized learning in the 1900s.

The history of personalized learning has taken many forms and approaches. From learner-centered teaching strategies to machines, personalized learning has taken many perspectives over the years. In fact, previous research suggests a multitude of variables that could be used to personalize the learning experience including (a) who should conduct personalized learning, (b) what can be personalized, (c) where it can be personalized, and (d) how personalization should occur.

To explore the history, we describe two approaches to personalized learning in the following paragraphs: learner-centered teaching approaches and the efforts of teaching machines.

Personalized Learning Through Learner-Centered Teaching Strategies

We begin the exploration of learner-centered teaching strategies with John Dewey's paper titled "Democracy and Education" (Dewey, 1916; Watters, 2017). In this paper, Dewey advocated for an approach to education that placed the student in the center of the instruction and emphasized individualized learning experiences.

DOI: 10.4324/9781003121008-1

2 The History of Personalized Learning

Dewey's ideologies and approach to education were embraced and experimented with by Helen Parkhurst in the early 1900s. As an educational researcher and a contemporary of both Montessori and Dewey, Parkhurst developed the Dalton Plan which started as a field experiment in Dalton, Massachusetts. Parkhurst was a proponent that students should be given ownership and support over their learning process (Lager, 1983). According to the Dalton Plan, each student's learning program should be personalized and adapted to every individual, as well as their needs and interests. As Dewey (1922) states, "The very set-up of the school program enlists the cooperation of the children. By giving them real jobs, their wills become an active force in the learning process" (p. 2).

To support student learning, the Dalton Plan relied on a variety of interactions within defined structural pillars to personalize the learner's experience (e.g., the homeroom, the assignment, and the lab). More specifically, the Dalton Plan included four of the five interactions offered by the Personalized Learning Interaction Framework: the learner-mentor, learner-learner, learner-content, and learner-small group as described in Chapter 3). As mentioned before, the homeroom, the assignment, and the lab offer structured pillars of the Dalton Plan. We present the alignment of these structures, the interactions they enabled, and the purpose of each pillar in the table below (Table 1.1).

Table 1.1 Interactions Enabled by the Structural Pillars of the Dalton Plan

Dalton Plan Structural Pillar	Purpose of Structural Pillar	Interaction Enabled by Structural Pillar
Home Room	Supported the socio-cultural interaction between teachers and parents. Examined potential to extend the learner-mentor relationship beyond the classroom.	Learner-Mentor/ Parent
Assignment	Described as where the learner defined learning goals based on goals and interests according to a short and long timeframe negotiated with a mentor.	Learner-Mentor Learner-Content
Lab	Examined as a place where students could work with other learners to build upon and provide feedback about their learning.	Learner-Learner Learner-Small Group

As you can see in the table above, the house or homeroom supported the socio-cultural interaction between teachers and parents. Next, the assignment served as a negotiation between the learner-mentor where the learner defined their interests and learning goals while collaborating with the mentor to set short-term and long-term timelines. Finally, the Lab, or one-on-one and small group sessions, provided opportunities to field feedback from other learners or a small group about what is being learned throughout the assignments (The Dalton School, 2016).

The program's popularity grew and eventually expanded the Dalton schools to an audience of learners worldwide. Dalton Schools could be found in Australia, Germany, the Netherlands, the Soviet Union, India, China, and Japan (van der Ploeg, 2013). In 1923 there were thousands of Dalton Schools in England and between 100 and 200 in the United States (van der Ploeg, 2013). Currently, there are still over 40 Dalton Schools internationally (Dalton International, 2016).

The decline of Dalton Schools may be associated with the loss of Helen Parkhurst in 1973, but many critics of the program cite difficulties with the sustainability of the Dalton Plan's resource-intensive structure. Other detractors uphold that the Plan's approach to personalization was unrealistic and unscalable (Lynch, 2014). Despite the success and impact of the Dalton Plan's approach to learning, Parkhurst's understated legacy and influence is explored by Lager (1983) in her dissertation.

Personalized Learning with The First "Intelligent Machines"

To address issues of scalability, researchers began to explore how machines or educational technologies might support personalized learning. According to Benjamin (1988), the first documented effort to build an "intelligent machine" can be traced to Sidney L. Pressey in the early 1920s. Pressey's wooden apparatus allowed students to receive immediate feedback on the answers to a set of multiple-choice questions. A further description of the machine reveals both a "teaching mode" and "learning mode" setting that would change the behavior of the machine (Benjamin, 1988). In the "teaching mode" setting, students would not advance to the next question until they answered a multiple-choice question correctly. In the "learning mode", students' answers would advance regardless of their accuracy and the final score would be calculated and reported back to the student at the conclusion of the session. Thus, students were encouraged to experiment and find answers through the "teaching mode", where they were able to get answers through a course of trial and error. Afterward, they could check their knowledge in the "learning mode". As the development of the tool evolved, the design awarded candy to students who achieved minimum scores (Benjamin, 1988; Shute & Psotka, 1994).

While Pressey was the first known to develop intelligent machines, Skinner is better known for his experiments in this domain. Frustrated by the pacing of his fourth-grade daughter's math class, Skinner conceived of ways to individualize instruction to better accommodate student needs. Two complaints of the current method of instruction were that students were instructed at the same pace regardless of their knowledge and understanding and that there was a lag time between individual performance and feedback on class assignments. To address these problems, Skinner developed a "teaching machine" grounded in his theories of behaviorism and designed to instruct learners by introducing new material in small steps (Bates, 2014; Benjamin, 1988; Skinner, 1983). This allowed students to complete exercises at their own pace and advance to updated content once key concepts had met minimum requirements. In doing so, the machine was able to provide immediate feedback and allow the learner to advance at their own pace based on their performance.

Both Pressey's and Skinner's instructional systems allowed for a personalized learning experience by providing immediate and individualized performance feedback while facilitating opportunities for advancement based on the learner's performance. Meeting the minimum criteria would allow a high-performing student the opportunity to advance to more difficult questions and exercises. For those who did not meet the minimum criteria, the teaching machines were adapted to provide increased practice opportunities. Ultimately Pressey and Skinner's machines were replaced by electronic-based teaching systems, which overcame many of the mechanical constraints of their designs which provided more flexibility.

While there were major advantages to scaling by leveraging these tools, there were also limitations. For example, machines were excellent resources when the rules for what is "right" and "wrong" are well defined. Certain domains, such as math or science, tend to be well-suited to teaching machines. The advantages of "teaching machines", or adaptive path systems, may be best leveraged when the learning task is well structured (e.g., when there are rules that constitute right and wrong answers). The development of teaching machines continues with the innovation of electric-based systems which we explore in the paragraph below.

The PLATO Project. The scalability of learning machines continued its trajectory throughout the 1960s to the 1980s reflecting and expanding the possibilities of "intelligent machines" as they evolved from mechanical apparatuses to electrical systems. This transition facilitated increased opportunities for learning outside the classroom since no instructor was needed to operate the machine or maintain the machine parts. PLATO, or the Programmed Logic for Automatic Teaching Operations, is often cited as the first generalized Computer Assisted Instruction (CAI) system. It was initially developed by a team headed by engineering professor and physicist Bitzer at the University of Illinois, who conceived of the project upon learning that 50% of all high school graduates were functionally illiterate (Encyclopædia Britannica, 2016; Seattler, 1990).

Personalized learning was described as characteristic of the PLATO system's content offerings. As detailed in the PLATO User's Guide, individualized instruction (e.g., frequent testing, frequent feedback, detailed feedback, alternative learning paths, mastery learning, and objective-based instruction) is the most common feature in the PLATO system because its presentation capabilities are broad enough to support these demanding instructional methods (Control Data Corporation, 1981).

The PLATO project lost steam due to costs, inability to scale, a backlash against "kill and drill instructional strategies", and technological affordances provided by more flexible micro and personal computers. While the project eventually lost support, it is important to note that many advances were made in the PLATO project that facilitated the development and refinement of many of the information communications technologies we embrace today, including modern-day computers, chat rooms, community boards, online testing, multiplayer games, and more (Hart, 1995; Woolley, 1994).

A Continuum of Personalized Learning

As noted, so far, these two approaches to personalized learning (i.e., learner-centered, or machine-enabled) represent a dichotomy of thinking surrounding personalized learning which Gallagher and Prestwich (2013) represent in Figure 1.1.

The figure demonstrates that personalized learning ranges on a continuum from adaptivity to autonomy that can be described, framed, and designed using several dimensions (Gallagher & Prestwich, 2013). Here we see personalized learning as a broad construct. On one extreme end (Macro), PL encourages a learner's complete agency and ownership over the learning process. At the other end (Micro), a machine or system makes the decision for the learner based on its evaluation of the learners' aptitudes or

6 The History of Personalized Learning

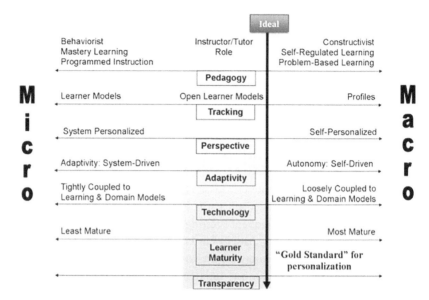

Figure 1.1 Continuum of Personalized Learning.

performance. Within the continuum, you can see there is a mix of machine-led and learner-led PL approaches.

Gallagher and Prestwich (2013) encourage organizations to go beyond the method or technology used to personalize learning and to consider the different approaches from a pedagogical perspective to help define which learning technologies to use and when. For instance, Gallagher and Prestwich (2013) argue that adaptive path and systems-based approaches are optimal when the learning objectives are outcome-based or observationally driven. The types of personalized learning approaches are best leveraged when the aims of the learning are behaviorist or objectivist and the "rules" of a domain are clear (e.g., grammar, elementary school mathematics, learning the contemporary and defined laws of physics). In this approach, there are right and wrong answers that can be defined by the system and are most suited for learning outcomes associated with remembering and understanding.

Not all learning tasks, however, have clear "rules". It may also take time and resources to program and set up "rules" within systems-based implementation in emerging and constantly changing operational environments. When it comes to establishing clear "rules" for systems-based implementations, they may be difficult, if not impossible, to define. For example, while there may be clear insights into how best to collaborate with others, it is harder to define an instance wherein someone's actions are "right" or "wrong". Here, adaptive path technologies or systems-based approaches may be less effective in accounting for the contextual and cultural dimensions of the learning task at hand. Hence, learner-based personalization may be better suited to such situations.

Of course, this exploration discusses the extremes of purely systems-based and purely learner-based personalization. Each approach has its own advantages and disadvantages. On the one hand, system-based PL can scale and is easily measured based on successful adherence to the defined performance metrics. The disadvantage is that developing these tools may be time-consuming and resource intensive to code. On the other hand, learner-based personalization empowers the learner to take ownership over their learning process, allows for flexible learning based on constantly changing operational environments, and can respond to ill-structured problem spaces without the need of defining and coding for constantly changing parameters. The disadvantage to this approach, however, is that it requires high levels of motivation, and the success of learner-driven initiatives may be harder to measure or define.

What is important to note is that neither approach to personalized learning is fundamentally right nor wrong. The best answer toward how to design a personalized learning experience likely requires a mix of strategies that take into consideration learning theory, learning models, instructional strategies, learning tasks, learning outcomes, learner maturity, and technology, and to ensure that these factors are pedagogically aligned. As learning leaders, leveraging these dimensions enables us to develop personalized learning approaches from a strategic rather than tactical position.

Next, we will explore the theory of affordances and its implications on technology and the design of personalized learning.

The Role or Influence of Technology in Personalized Learning

To understand the role of technology in personalized learning, we explore the concept of affordances and its implications on the evolution of technology-based learning environments from a pedagogical perspective (Dabbagh, 2004; Dabbagh & Reo, 2011). Gibson's theory of affordances is an ecological approach to psychology that emphasizes perception and action rather than memory and retrieval. Gibson (1979) proposed that objects and artifacts

8 The History of Personalized Learning

(e.g., technologies) have certain affordances or possibilities for action that lead organisms (e.g., people) to act based on their perceptions of these affordances. In other words, action and perception are linked through the affordances present in each situation and the abilities of an agent to act upon these affordances. This leads to the construct of pedagogical ecology that emphasizes the non-neutrality of the learning space and characterizes the linkage between pedagogy and technology and consideration of the expectations and interaction potentials that each learning medium brings forth to the teaching and learning process (Dabbagh & Reo, 2011; Jaffee, 2003). Supporters of this view (e.g., Frielick, 2004; Kozma, 1994) argue that each learning medium, setting, or context, has a unique set of characteristics and that understanding the pedagogical affordances of these characteristics is essential to understanding their ecological influence on teaching and learning.

For example, pre-Internet technologies such as broadcast technologies that focus on transmitting information or one-way provision of content (e.g., PPT presentations, video lectures, film, TV) "afford" pedagogical practices that are primarily behaviorist or objectivist in nature. These include direct instruction, individualized learning, self-contained curricular units, and drill and practice activities resulting in predetermined technology-based instructional systems or adaptive systems such as programmed instruction (PI) and computer-assisted or computer-based instruction (CAI/CBI) (see Figure 1.2). Learning interactions supported with pre-Internet technologies were confined to learner-instructor and learner-content interactions. Types of interactions are defined in Chapter 3.

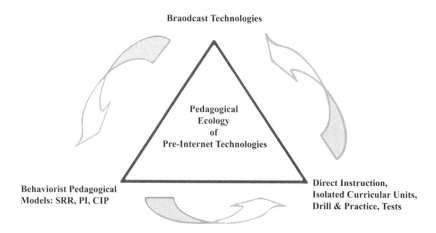

Figure 1.2 Pre-Internet Technologies.

As the technology evolved from static and unidirectional to dynamic and participatory with the onset of Information Communication Technologies (ICT), the Internet, and the World Wide Web, or what has come to be known as Web 1.0 technologies, learning interactions and teaching practices also evolved enabling open and flexible learning spaces and affording multiple forms of interaction. Such interactions included learner-learner, learner-group, learner-content, learner-instructor, and group-group allowing teaching and learning to be distributed across time and place synchronously or asynchronously (Dabbagh & Bannan-Ritland, 2005). These technology-based learning interactions led to instructional strategies that are constructivist in nature, such as collaboration, articulation, social negotiation, exploration, and reflection to name a few (see Figure 1.3).

Technology evolved again in the 21st century leading to a new wave of ICT known as Web 2.0 technology. Web 2.0 technology possessed many of the inherent technological and pedagogical affordances of older computer-mediated communication tools but also represented a qualitative shift in how information is created, delivered, and accessed on the Web (Dabbagh & Reo, 2011). Web 2.0 became a concept that embodied themes such as openness, personalization, customization, participation, social networking, social presence, user-generated content, the people's Web, read/write Web, and collective wisdom leading to its characterization as the "Social Web" (Alexander, 2006; Davis, 2008; Jones, 2008; O'Reilly, 2005). The social side of Web 2.0 and its implications on the education sector was emphasized in the 2014 NMC (New Media Consortium) Horizon Report (Johnson et al., 2014) particularly as this

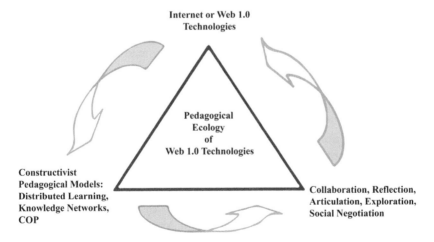

Figure 1.3 Web 1.0 Technologies.

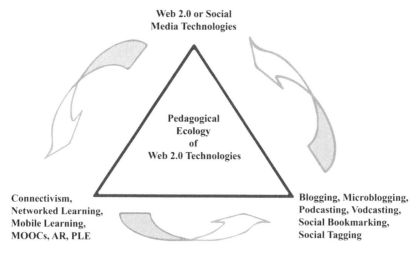

Figure 1.4 Web 2.0 Technologies.

relates to social media use and how this is changing the way students and educators interact, present information, and judge the quality of content and contributions. For example, blogging, microblogging (tweeting), podcasting, social bookmarking, social tagging, and social networking became the new affordances of Web 2.0 technologies and as a result, new teaching approaches, theories, and constructs evolved such as connectivism (Siemens, 2005), networked learning, MOOCs (Massive Open Online Courses), mobile learning, augmented reality (AR) experiences, and Personal Learning Environments (PLEs) (Figure 1.4).

Unlike Web 1.0 technology where use was limited to only 14% of the adult population, most of which were programmers and tech-savvy individuals (Aggarwal, 2014), Web 2.0 technology use grew to 90% of the U.S. population and 65% worldwide (Hootsuite, 2021) because of its read/write affordances. The new activities that grew out of Web 2.0 technologies (e.g., blogging, wikis, creating and posting videos) moved web-based learning activities away from having to be teacher-centered to the possibility of being more learner-centered. First, Web 2.0 technologies made it possible for learners to engage in high levels of dialogue, interaction, collaboration, and social negotiation through social networks and provided learners with the ability to generate and share knowledge across learning networks. Second, Web 2.0 technologies deflected control of learning away from a single instructor or expert by distributing learning among all participants in the learning community, promoting agency in the learning process and enhancing an appreciation of diversity, multiple perspectives, and epistemic issues. And third, Web 2.0 technologies enabled learners to personalize their learning environment by selecting the technologies they wish to use (e.g., apps on mobile devices), accessing and organizing information sources, customizing the user interface of technology, and building personalized learning and professional networks (Dabbagh et al., 2019).

The approachability and promise of Web 2.0 platforms did not escape the notice of the educational community. The interactions and increased communications enabled by Web 2.0 technologies prompted leaders like David Miliband, England's Minister of State for School Standards, to call for increased personalized learning experiences within England's school systems (Miliband, 2006). In his speech, he expressed his support of personalized learning technologies as expanding the influence of the teacher. New educational technologies, accountability frameworks, and streamlined and simplified internal processes could support "what the most successful teachers do best … (which was) create an education system with personalized learning at its heart" (p. 2). Despite the promise of these tools, Miliband also acknowledged how relying too heavily on the "silver bullet" of technology could result in poor student outcomes. In this, he promoted the synchronicity of technology, teacher, and social support to effectively integrate personalized learning into England's school systems.

The role of Web 3.0 technologies in personalized learning is also evolving and merits its own course of study. Web 3.0 technology is the next iteration of the World Wide Web and is sometimes referred to as the "semantic", "spatial", or "3D web" (Evans, 2021; Roy, 2022). As Evans describes, rather than seeking information by keyword, activities, or interests, users will be able to define their preferred means of information seeking. Enabled by blockchain technologies, the Web 3.0 movement has been characterized by embracing the principles of "open, decentralized, censorship-resistant, immutable, trustless, and permissionless" interactions (Eshita, 2021). These platforms cut out the middleman of the larger corporations so that the user can control their own data analytics, set their own rules, and obtain the full monetary gain from their efforts online. For example, a user getting a cut of profits from their offerings on Medium.com may be able to leverage Web 3.0 technologies to gain the full profit using blockchain technologies like Mirror.

Web 3.0 also promises interoperability so that end users do not need to create multiple accounts for multiple services. Web 3.0 also promises users voting rights that regulate the governance of overarching communities' roles as opposed to relying on the dictates of bigger platforms like Twitter,

Figure 1.5 Affordances for Web 1.0, Web 2.0, and Web 3.

Google, or Meta. Given the promised interoperability, Web 3.0 may enable personalization across platforms, yielding a cryptographically-backed digital identity to be represented across the web and resources that connect better to the end users based on their interests and powered by machine learning (Evans, 2021). These extended capabilities, however, are in their nascent stages and beg questions about privacy, security, bias, and censorship. Figure 1.5 demonstrates the fundamental affordances of Web 1.0, Web 2.0, and Web 3.0 technologies which result in different implementations of PL.

As can be seen from the discussion above, there is a reciprocal, recursive, and transformative interplay between technology and pedagogy. The co-evolution of technology and pedagogy suggests that technology can no longer be perceived as a tool that may or may not be used for teaching and learning. Rather, technology is an enabler of virtually every teaching model or strategy and an empowering agent for its users. Patterns of technology use across the decades have shaped our teaching and learning experiences, and consequently, our learning theories, models, and strategies. As technology continues to evolve, pedagogical processes and practices will also continue to evolve. This is where "the relativistic nature" of the ecological view comes into play. A mutuality exists between our tools and our intentions, and while our tools are the product of our intentions, they also shape our intentions in turn (Beston, 1948 in Popova, 2015). Fawns (2022) refers to the relationship between technology and pedagogy as "entangled pedagogy" or an "entangled relationship" where (a) purpose, context, and values act as drivers of method and technology; (b) technology is perceived as part of entangled pedagogy; (c) agency or control is negotiated between elements (teacher, tech, students, policy, infrastructure, etc.); (d) outcomes are contingent on complex relations; and (e) skill equals relational design and orchestration.

While there is a symbiotic set of interrelationships at play with "the relativistic nature" of technological affordances, experts continue to battle the prevailing tendency to limit conceptions of the 'social' to interactions between persons rather than between persons and things (Malafouris & Renfrew, 2010). Gibson's theory of affordances is one of those attempts. The theory of affordances has direct implications on how we may understand the evolution or ecology of personalized learning and the technology-based design of learning activities and interactions. For example, pre-Internet technologies played a major role in ushering adaptive learning systems that personalized learning based on the learner's performance outcomes. Web 1.0 technologies enabled flexible learning spaces that allowed learners to learn at their own pace formally and informally and increased the level of interactions from learner-instructor and learner-content to learner-group and group-group interactions. Web 2.0 technologies allowed learners to generate their own content, select the technologies they wish to use for learning, and build personalized learning and professional networks prompting more learner control and agency in the learning process. Web 3.0 technologies are enabling even more learner control and agency through access to personal data analytics and interoperability.

The Importance of Lifelong Learning and the Role of Learner Agency

As our technologies evolve, the pace of change continues to accelerate. The rapidity of change requires workers to be constantly reskilling and retooling their skillset to adapt in the face of operational, social, contextual, and ecological changes (Donovan and Benko, 2016; Pelster, 2016; Thomas and Brown, 2011). Given this dynamic and the constant pivoting of the operational environment, it becomes increasingly important for an organization's future success to develop programs that support workers in cultivating lifelong learning skills.

Learning leaders understand the strategic importance of training in sharpening their company's competitive edge, decreasing employee attrition, attracting, and retaining top talent, increasing productivity, and addressing the pace of change inherent in a globalizing world where technological disruptions accelerate transformational changes. Competitive organizations share the perspective that continually investing in skill-building, expanding competencies and skillsets, cultivating awareness about changing operational environments, facilitating, and empowering learning relationships, and refining project and people management skills will be key to survival for organizations in the modern age (Donovan & Benko, 2016; LinkedIn Learning, 2021). Attracting top talent may also be won or lost based on a company's dedication to training and development opportunities (LinkedIn Learning, 2021). The key to survival and success for individuals in this environment is contextual awareness, flexibility, and continuous learning (Knowland & Thomas, 2014). As Alvin Toffler, author and futurist said, "The illiterate of the 21st century will not be those who cannot read and write, but those who cannot learn, unlearn, and relearn".

The challenges of being in a continuous learning mode require empowering the learner to develop agency in lifelong learning. Personalizing learning and the framework described in this book, the Personalized Learning Interaction Framework, is an effective and sustainable solution to addressing this challenge. With historical, theoretical, and pedagogical foundations set, we will continue to explore Personalized Learning by looking at what researchers have discovered in K-12, Higher Education, and Workforce Training contexts.

References

Aggarwal, R. (2014, March). 25 years after its birth, the World Wide Web becomes appified. Wired Magazine. Retrieved from http://www.wired.com/insights/2014/03/25-years-birth-world-wide-web-becomes-appified/.

Alexander, B. (2006). Web 2.0: A New Wave of Innovation for Teaching and Learning? *EDUCAUSE Review*, *41*(2), 33–34.

Bates, T. (2014, December 10). A short history of technology [web log post], Retrieved from http://www.tonybates.ca/2014/12/10/a-short-history-of-educational-technology/.

Benjamin, L. T. (1988). A history of teaching machines. *American Psychologist*, *43*(9), 703–712. doi: 10.1037/0003-066X.43.9.703.

Control Data Corporation (1981). PLATO user's guide [pdf document]. Retrieved from http://www.mirrorservice.org/sites/www.bitsavers.org/pdf/cdc/plato/97405900C_PLATO_Users_Guide_Apr81.pdf.

Dabbagh, N. (2004). Distance Learning: Emerging Pedagogical Issues and Learning Designs. *Quarterly Review of Distance Education*, *5*(1), 37–49.

Dabbagh, N., & Bannan-Ritland, B. (2005). *Online Learning: Concepts, Strategies, and Application*. Pearson/Merrill/Prentice Hall.

Dabbagh, N., Marra, R. M., & Howland, J. L. (2019). *Meaningful Online Learning: Integrating Strategies, Activities, and Learning Technologies For Effective Designs*. Routledge.

Dabbagh, N., & Reo, R. (2011). Impact of Web 2.0 on higher education. In *Technology Integration in Higher Education: Social and Organizational Aspects* (pp. 174–187). IGI Global.

Davis, M. (2008). *Semantic Wave 2008 Report: Industry Roadmap to Web 3.0 & Multibillion Dollar Market Opportunities (Executive S*ummary). Washington DC: Project 10X. Retrieved June 16th, 2008 from http://www.eurolibnet.eu/files/REPOSITORY/20090507165103_SemanticWaveReport2008.pdf.

Dewey, E. (1922). *The Dalton Laboratory Plan*. London: J.M. Dent & Sons.

Dewey, J. (1916). *Democracy and Education: An introduction to the philosophy of education.* New York, NY: Macmillan.

Donovan, J., & Benko, C. (2016). AT&T's talent overhaul. *Harvard Business Review,* 68–73. Retrieved from https://hbr.org/2016/10/atts-talent-overhaul.

Eshita (2021, September 9). *Web3: In a nutshell.* Mirror. https://eshita.mirror.xyz/H5bNIXATsWUv_QbbEz6lckYcgAa2rhXEPDRkecOlCOI.

Evans, B. (2021, December). *Three steps to the future.* Helsinki; Finland: Slush.

Fawns, T. (2022). An entangled pedagogy: Looking beyond the pedagogy – technology dichotomy. *Postdigital Science and Education.* 10.1007/s42438-022-00302-7.

Frielick, S. (2004, December). Beyond constructivism: An ecological approach to e-learning. In *Proceedings of the 21st ASCILITE Conference* (pp. 328–332).

Gallagher, P. S., & Prestwich, S. (2013). *Developing a personalization strategy for online learning environments.* Unpublished manuscript.

Gibson, J. J. (1979). The theory of affordances. The ecological approach to visual perception. *The people, place and, space reader* (pp. 56–60). New York, NY, USA: Routledge.

Hart, R. S. (1995). The Illinois PLATO foreign languages project. *CALICO Journal, 12*(4), 15–37.

Hootsuite, W. A. S. (2021). Digital 2021: Global Overview Report. *DataReportal–Global Digital Insights.*

Jaffee, D. (2003). Virtual transformation: Web-based technology and pedagogical change. *Teaching Sociology, 31*(2), 227–236.

Johnson, L., Becker, S. A., Estrada, V., & Freeman, A. (2014). *NMC horizon report: 2014 K* (pp. 1–52). The New Media Consortium.

Jones, B. (2008). *Web 2.0 Heroes: Interviews with 20 Web 2.0 Influencers.* United Kingdom: Wiley.

Knowland, V. C. P., & Thomas, S. C. (2014). Educating the adult brain: How the neuroscience of learning can inform educational policy. *International Review of Education, 60*(1), 99–122.

Kozma, R. B. (1994). Will media influence learning? reframing the debate. *Educational Technology Research and Development, 42*(2), 7–19. 10.1007/bf02299087.

Lager, D. (1983). *Helen Parkhurst and the Dalton Plan: The life and work of an American educator* (Doctoral Dissertation). Retrieved from http://digitalcommons.uconn.edu/dissertations/AAI8317707 (AAI8317707).

LinkedIn Learning (2021). *2021 Workplace Learning Report.* LinkedIn. https://learning.linkedin.com/content/dam/me/business/en-us/amp/learning-solutions/images/wlr21/pdf/LinkedIn-Learning_Workplace-Learning-Report-2021-EN-1.pdf.

Lynch, M. (2014). Personalized learning in K-12 schools: How did we make it happen? Retrieved from http://www.huffingtonpost.com/matthew-lynch-edd/personalized-learning-in_b_6315402.html.

Malafouris, L., & Renfrew, C. (2010). *The cognitive life of things: Recasting the boundaries of the mind.* McDonald Institute for Archaeological Research.

Miliband, D. R. (2006). Choice and voice in personalized learning. In *Schooling for tomorrow. Personalising education* (pp. 21–30). Paris: OECD.

O'Reilly, T. (2005, September 30). *What is web 2.0.* O'Reilly. https://www.oreilly.com/pub/a/web2/archive/what-is-web-20.html.

Pelster, B., Haims, J., Stempel, J., & van der Vyver, B. (2016, February). *Learning: Employees take charge*. Retrieved from Deloitte Insights: http://dupress.com/articles/fostering-culture-of-learning-for-employees/?id=us:2el:3dc:dup3026:awa:cons:hct16.

PLATO. (2016). In Encyclopædia Britannica. Retrieved from https://www.britannica.com/topic/PLATO-education-system.

Popova, M. (2015, November 16). Henry Beston's beautiful 1948 manifesto for reclaiming our humanity by breaking the tyranny of technology and relearning to be nurtured by nature . *The Marginalian*. https://www.themarginalian.org/2015/11/16/henry-beston-northern-farm/.

Roy, N. A. (2022). The Seasonal Tokens Podcast - Crypto Investing, Not Gambling. *The Seasonal Tokens Podcast with Polar*. other.

Seattler, P. (1990). *The evolution of American educational technology*. Eaglewood, CO: Libraries Unlimited, Inc.

Shute, V. J., & Psotka, J. (1994). Intelligent tutoring systems: Past, present, and future. In D. Jonassen (Ed.), *Handbook of research for educational communications and technology* (pp. 570–600). New York, NY: Macmillan. 10.21236/ADA280011.

Siemens, G. (2005). Connectivism: A learning theory for the digital age. *International Journal of Instructional Technology and Distance Learning, 2*(1). Available from http://www.itdl.org/Journal/Jan_05/article01.htm.

Skinner, B. F. (1983) *A matter of consequences: Part three of an autobiography*. New York, NY: Knopf.

Thomas, D., & Brown, J. S. (2011). *A new culture of learning: Cultivating the imagination for a world of constant change*. Lexington, KY: CreateSpace?.

The Dalton School (2016). *Philosophy: The Dalton Plan*. Retrieved from http://www.dalton.org/information.

van der Ploeg, P. (June, 2013). The Dalton Plan: Recycling in the guise of innovation. *Paedagogica historica, 49*(3), 314–329. 10.1080/00309230.2012.725840.

Watters, A. (2017, June 9). The histories of personalized learning [web log post]. Retrieved from http://hackeducation.com/2017/06/09/personalization.

Woolley, D. R. (1994). *PLATO: The emergence of an online community*. Retrieved from http://www.thinkofit.com/plato/dwplato.htm.

Approaches to Personalized Learning

2

Overview of Personalized Learning Approaches

So much has been said and written about personalized learning (PL) starting with describing it as a one-to-one computing model or One Laptop Per Child (OLPC), to couching it as a pedagogy, a learning approach, a technological concept, a new canopy for blended learning, e-learning, individualized learning, differentiated instruction, or an adaptive learning system pushed by ed-tech software companies. As research suggests, PL is an idea struggling for an identity (McRae, 2015; Shemshack & Spector, 2020).

Given this ambiguity, it is important to consider why we are studying PL in the first place. This chapter provides evidence-based research that demonstrates the effectiveness of PL across multiple contexts, including K-12, Higher Education, and Workforce Training and Development Programs. Before presenting this research, we begin with efforts to define PL.

Efforts to Define Personalized Learning

As with any new construct, PL has different definitions that emphasize or deemphasize aspects of how instruction is personalized for learners. Debates arise about what personalizing learning means. For example, **what is personalized** (e.g., content, interface, delivery mechanism, etc.), **who facilitates the personalized learning** (e.g., the individual, a manager or supervisor, the instructor, the training department, a collaborative network of peers, or the learning system itself), **or how personalized learning should occur** (e.g., implicitly or explicitly referencing user behaviors or inputs, referencing the

DOI: 10.4324/9781003121008-2

characteristics of associated peers or segmented groups, or employing a hybrid mix of implicit and explicit feedback). It's important to note that the types of data sources used to personalize include implicit or explicit feedback. These may be based on the learner's role, learner tasks, individual proficiency (perceived or performance-based), learner preferences, or learner goals (Fake & Dabbagh, 2019; Fan & Poole; 2006; Kwon, Cho & Park, 2010; Kwon & Kim, 2012).

In reviewing the definitions, one can see that each context changes the emphasis on these variables. As Shemshack and Spector (2020) state, the lack of a unified definition is one of the most critical problems with PL. To encapsulate the differences, we've included definitions from the different contexts, including K-12, Higher Education, and Workforce Training and Development Programs below.

For K-12 Learning, we borrow from the U.S. Department of Education definition which states: **Personalized Learning** refers to instruction in which the pace of learning and the instructional approach are optimized for the needs of each learner. Learning objectives, instructional approaches, and instructional content (and its sequencing) may vary based on learner needs. In addition, learning activities are meaningful and relevant to learners, driven by their interests, and often self-initiated (U.S. Department of Education, 2017). While the socio-technical relationships are not stated explicitly here, they are implied. This implication may account for the blended focus of most K-12 PL implementations (Fake, 2018).

Another definition from the American Institute of Research (AIR) emphasizes a number of ways teachers in K-12 contexts can personalize learning for students, including the way their day is structured, the ways they engage with content, and even how interactions between teachers and students can facilitate personalization. In this, AIR describes many different aspects of who can personalize, what can be personalized, and how one can personalize learning. There is also a recognition that alignment between approaches may be necessary as PL programs scale. This is reflected in the following definition from Division 15 of the American Psychological Association (APA) (Walkington & Bernacki, 2021):

> **Personalized Learning (PL)** refers to a broad assortment of approaches and programs for adapting instruction to learner characteristics to achieve learning outcomes. The range of possible PL approaches is quite diverse and includes (but is not limited to): the use of technology for individualized instruction, rotation models where students move between different instructional formats, learner profiles that assist teachers' decision-making, student-driven academic goal setting,

project-based learning, social-emotional learning, and competency-based learning where students master concepts at their own pace.

PL in K-12 contexts is often implemented at the school, district, or even state level when stakeholders come together around a particular set of PL approaches and thus definitions surrounding PL seem to espouse a blended approach.

Definition of PL from Higher Education

In Higher Education, researchers' emphasis is given to the learner-centered approach of PL emphasizing flexibility and student agency as reflected in this definition by Dede, Richards, and Saxborg (2019, p. 3). Personalized Learning is defined as having four fundamental attributes:

1 Developing multimodal experiences and a differentiated curriculum based on universal design for learning principles;
2 Enabling each student's agency in orchestrating the emphasis and process of their learning, in concert with the evidence about how learning works best and with mentoring about working towards a long-term goal;
3 Providing community and collaboration to aid students in learning by fostering engagement, a growth mindset, self-efficacy, and academic tenacity; and
4 Guiding each student's path through the curriculum based on diagnostic assessments embedded in each educational experience that are formative for further learning and instruction.

Zhong (2022), however, examined current design trends of PL in higher education through a systematic review of the research literature. This study found that despite high interest, there was a low level of maturity in the field of PL as evidenced by a lack of structure and sequencing for PL learning materials as well as acknowledgment of learner readiness. The review also indicated that implementations, definitions, approaches, models, and terms associated with PL in Higher Education vary greatly. Of the existing studies, most focus on structuring and sequencing learning materials for adaptive path systems by adjusting instruction to learning traits such as cognitive and learning styles, personality, and prior knowledge. This last point also underscores a focus on adaptive or systems-based approach to PL.

Other definitions from workforce training and development programs focus on learner-centered personalization. For example, the results of a Delphi study

(Fake, 2018) revealed that experts conceive of personalized learning as characterized by **new teaching roles and practices**, *flexible learning pathways*, *flexible learning assessments*, a focus on creating a **learner-driven experience based on their defined needs**, and where *technology is integral to learning*. In this definition, PL is seen as learner-driven and facilitated through a variety of socio-technological interrelationships extending beyond content (Fake, 2018; Fake & Dabbagh, 2020; Fake & Dabbagh, 2021).

Another definition from the workplace learning literature that emphasizes the use of technology posits that "personalized learning technologies attempt to create different experiences for different learners (or for the same learner) at different points in time" (Folsom-Kovarik, Chen, & Mostafavi, 2019, p. 181). The authors go on to say that this approach to PL involves using technology to customize settings for the learner based on individual preferences resulting in differentiated instruction. This system can be continuously adjusted based on incoming data (analytics) to adapt to users – often touted as "the benefits" of PL.

While this definition can be interpreted as adaptive or systems-based personalization, modern technologies are increasingly supporting learner-based personalization by allowing learners to leverage transparent analytics to search within a curated and targeted set of learning resources and select learning tasks that best suit their individual goals, prior experiences, demonstrated knowledge and performance, environmental conditions, and/or social contexts.

Despite the multitude of aforementioned approaches and the lack of maturity of the PL as a defined strategy, studies across contexts have shown positive and tangible results and learning outcomes associated with PL. These include PL initiatives cultivating a sense of ownership, developing skillsets, scaffolding lifelong learning practices, reducing time spent on learning tasks or locating relevant materials, or navigating information overload (Bersin, 2017; Dabbagh & Kitsantas, 2012; Leone, 2013; Valtonen, et al., 2012). The definitions provided above also offer a variety of approaches to implementing PL, with three approaches that seem to clearly emerge: the **systems-based approach**, the **learner-based approach**, and the **blended approach** to PL. In the next few pages, we will explore the research in each approach to PL for each context (K-12, Higher Education, and Workplace Training and Development).

Research on Systems-Based Personalization

Systems-based personalization refers to a learning experience where the system makes the choice of what, how, when, where, and why learning is personalized. Similar to Pressey and Skinner's historical learning machines, systems-based personalization seeks to offer immediate feedback on the students' performance based on predefined tasks (Fake, 2018; Watters, 2021). Depending on the sophistication of the system, it may even recommend other tasks that support learners to achieve specific learning goals and achieve a certain level of competency (Skinner, 1958).

For the purposes of this book, **systems-based personalization** also includes recommendation systems that may reference static learner profiles, preferences, or styles that are not revisited, but are collected within the first or first series of interactions with the learner. In the next few paragraphs, we will explore existing systems-based learning in K-12, Higher Education, as well as in workforce and informal learning contexts.

Systems-Based Personalized Learning in K-12

Domenech, Sherman, and Browns (2016) define PL from a systems perspective when they say "we envision a transformation in how children are taught and how the system organizes for learning" (p. 6). They go on to say that each K-12 child or student will be treated as a unique individual requiring a personalized education plan. Each student will be assessed on the subjects to be taught, and based on the results of the assessment, personalized lesson plans will be developed that build on what the student already knows and provide scaffolding through the use of instructional strategies that are aligned with the student's ability level. This personalized instructional approach will also take into account student interests and learning profile as well as emerging workplace and postsecondary competencies or what is known as 21st-century skills such as self-regulation, metacognition, collaboration, problem-solving, critical thinking, creativity and innovation, social responsibility and cultural environmental and global awareness, and social-emotional and physical development to name a few.

In order to achieve this level of breadth and depth of PL, technology will need to play a major role in this approach in order to monitor student progress and adapt instruction accordingly. Domenech, Sherman, and Browns (2016) add that students will have the freedom to work independently as well with teachers and peers to design personalized approaches to mastering competencies to include online, self-paced courses, a range of multimedia-driven options for interactivity within the learning environment, mastery-focused skills and concept progression via technology-enhanced modules, adaptive digital content accommodating varying readiness levels, student interests and learner profiles, game-based learning options, and embedded assessments using different learning progressions and pacing (p. 96). The ultimate goal is to use technology to address the unique needs and talents of every learner by allowing technology to act as a recommender system that offers suggestions and instructional programs and resources based on the student profile, knowledge, likes and dislikes, educational and professional goals, and motivation.

In terms of traditional systems-based personalization, computer-based adaptive learning programs have been around for a long time in K-12 public schools (Wang & Liao, 2011). Researchers have attempted to study how computer-based adaptive learning programs provide access to learning in rich, engaging, and interactive environments in which students acquire new skills (e.g., Hooshyar et al., 2021; Puntambekar & Kolodner, 2005; Quintana et al., 2004). The underlying assumption of researchers' efforts is that computer-based adaptive learning programs provide students with an infinite supply of personalized one-to-one attention that a teacher in a traditional classroom could not provide in today's highly diverse schools or simply due to a large number of students in each classroom. Computer-based adaptive learning programs can be loaded with scaffolding functions that observe students, interact with them, interpret their learning behavior, and scaffold their learning to allow teachers to focus on face-to-face classroom instruction (Bimba et al., 2020; Graesser, & McNamara, 2010; Hannafin, Land, & Oliver, 1999; Zulfiani, Suwarna, Miranto, 2018). In addition to scaffolding, computer-based adaptive learning programs can capture and analyze learners' interactions and provide an abundance of data to teachers and administrators. Such data can provide a lens for educators and researchers alike to understand how students learn (Romero & Ventura, 2010).

In recent a study, Amro (2019) examined the effect of different types of scaffolding on student achievement as measured by an end-of-year (EOY) benchmark assessment in a middle school mathematics computer-based adaptive learning program. The findings showed that soft or dynamic scaffolds followed by frequent hard or static scaffolds were the most significant predictors of students' achievement scores. More specifically, the instructional strategy of probing and diagnosing used by online instructors who were available to address student questions and understanding as they completed the computer-based adaptive program was the most effective soft scaffolding strategy in supporting students' problem-solving tasks. The study also revealed that students' performance levels impacted the frequency of soft scaffolding strategies. Specifically, students in the below basic and far below basic groups may not have the adequate skills to interact meaningfully with online instructors. These findings should be taken into consideration when designing systems-based personalization to support students' problem-solving skills in K-12 settings.

Systems-Based Personalized Learning in Higher Education

In Higher Education, research on systems-based personalization focuses on learner preferences and learning styles (Fake, 2018; Zhong, 2022). For example, in order to evaluate the impact systems-based personalization had on online learning environments, Milicevic, Ivaonic, and Budimac (2011) conducted an experiment (N = 440) to measure first-year undergraduate student perceptions and performance in an online Java course using a learning recommender system called the Programming Tutoring System or Protus. Designed to adapt to students' individual learning styles and knowledge levels, Protus collected student interaction, behavioral, and log data to identify learning styles and patterns as well as user habits through data mining and interaction analytics.

Based on the information gathered, students were clustered into groups using Felder and Silverman's Index of Learning Styles and an algorithm recommended content to the student based on their learner profile and PL parameters. The results of this intervention revealed that students who had access to the recommender system were able to complete a course in less time than students in the control group. Also, seventy percent of learners using the Protus system found it to be convenient and were pleased with the accuracy and speed of the system's recommendations. Despite the enthusiasm learners expressed and the potential time savings, the Protus system did not demonstrate significant differences in student learning outcomes. Additional research is needed to determine if Felder and Silverman's Index is an effective means of personalization for improvements in learning outcomes.

In another higher education systems-based personalization study, Chookaew, Panjaburee, Wanichsan, and Laosinchai (2014) developed a personalized basic computer programming course for undergraduate students (N = 23) to measure the learner's performance in a pre and post-test experiment. The system created by Chookaew et al. (2014) personalized instruction based on the individual's learning preferences and performance on a pre-test assessment. The pre-test assessment sorted students based on their aptitude at low, medium, or high levels. Low performance on the pretest indicated to the system that further remedial or support content was necessary before the student could advance to more challenging topics. These topics were assigned a preordained order so one could not advance to a new topic until the student performed at a minimal level of competency. In addition to adapting to the students' performance, content in the course was presented based on the students' learning preferences according to another index created and researched by Felder and colleagues, the Felder and Soloman Index of Learning Questionnaire.

A post-test analysis of the basic computer science course demonstrated a normalized gain in conceptual knowledge, and ad hoc feedback from students indicated favorable views of the system.

Overall, while there has been excitement surrounding systems that personalize instruction based on learning or cognitive preferences with results that suggest these programs increase user speed and satisfaction, there have been mixed findings regarding the effectiveness of systems that personalize based on user performance. In an experimental study, Griff and Matter (2013) split 587 anatomy and physiology students from six different colleges and universities into an experimental and a control condition. Participants in the experimental group were assigned chapters from McGraw Hill Higher Education's (MHHE) LearnSmart, an online study tool that adapts quiz questions to learners based on their previous performance. Participants in the control condition were assigned online quizzes from the question bank supplied by MHHE's textbook. Results between the two groups showed no significant differences in pre/post-test performance, grade distribution, or retention (Griff & Matter, 2013). The researchers did notice, however, that there was a positive effect on pre/post-test performance and grade distribution for two out of the six institutions. Inquiries into what factors may have influenced the differences in results, however, were inconclusive.

In follow-up feedback sessions, instructors reported that learners assigned to the experimental condition asked more challenging questions in classroom sessions and seemed more engaged than users in the control condition. In addition, instructors reported that MHHE's LearnSmart program did not take much time to integrate and implement into their current courses. The mixed results of this experiment suggest that the LearnSmart tool may not have been aligned with the course objectives at the respective institutions (Griff & Matter, 2013) further supporting the argument that for PL interventions to be successful, it will be imperative that designers align technologies, strategies, and learning outcomes to ensure success.

Systems-Based Personalization in Workforce Training and Development Programs

Given that there are so many learning opportunities online, many workforce learners complain about feeling overwhelmed by the amount of information available (Kulkarni, Rai, & Kale, 2020; Pelster et al., 2017). Despite the number of opportunities online, it becomes difficult to evaluate what might help advance the learner's goals or what might support their continued learning. Therefore, many of the systems-based personalization efforts in workforce training and development programs have focused on recommender systems.

For example, Skillsoft and IBM analyzed data from over 32,000 learners to optimize a recommendation system for users. Leveraging insights from user feedback, consumption patterns, and user behaviors the new system generated recommendation emails based on student web log data. According to a Skillsoft press release, personalized recommendations based on past user behaviors resulted in a 128% improvement in user engagement when compared to their baseline (Skillsoft, 2014).

It is important to note that this particular study measured whether student visits to learning content would increase with systems-generated email campaigns based on previous behavioral student usage trends and content consumption. This study did not measure the effectiveness of personalization based on the ultimate educational outcomes, but rather site visits to learning content. Therefore, future studies are needed to ascertain the impact such efforts had on learner outcomes.

An important aspect to consider in the design of recommendation systems (RS) is how to generate learner profiles for recommendations. These types of recommendations may be based on implicit (behavioral) or explicit (user-generated) feedback (Kulkarni, Rai, & Kale, 2020). As machine learning evolves, new algorithms focus on a variety of variables in order to create user profiles.

Previous research has revealed that learners are often not as aligned with their actual interests as they perceive. Lavie, Sela, Oppenheim, Inbar, and Meyer (2010) found that RSs that tailored content based on explicitly described personal interests in static learner profiles were not always consistent with the actual interests of the user according to log data and other behavioral analytics. For instance, users tended to rate their interest in Lifestyle and Leisure and Science and Technology articles significantly higher than their actual interest level (measured in the number of articles read). The researchers additionally found that timeliness was significantly more important in topic areas focusing on politics, sports, business, and finance than in the domains. Finally, users in this experiment tended to be interested in more general topics than specific ones.

This particular finding suggests that any personalization system will need to strike a balance between over-personalizing RS to provide too narrow a topic scope and providing relevant content that meets the interests of the learner. It will also be important to consider how to motivate users to go beyond their comfort levels and dig deeper into content that is new and challenging. Since the users' espoused interests and actual interests could be different, a combination of user-generated, network-generated, and behavioral data may be key to determining the actual wishes of the learner. It may also offer the system the opportunity to inform the learner of differences in their professed interests and actual behaviors which begs questions about whether or not the learners' goals are consistent with their actual espoused interests.

The literature shows that the results associated with systems-based learning initiatives have been mixed. Based on this synthesis, systems-based personalization has shown encouraging results in learning domains that have well-defined rules like basic computer programming or beginning language learning courses. There is also evidence that systems-based PL may drive positive results in user satisfaction, performance when specifically applied to structured tasks, engagement, perceived cognitive load, and completion times. Other studies suggest that how educational technology is implemented may impact the success of the PL initiatives. As we have previously discussed, it is critical that a pedagogical alignment exists between the choice of PL technology, the instructional strategy, and the learning outcome (Dabbagh & Fake, 2016; Gallagher & Prestwich, 2013). Consideration of these variables is key to implementing PL effectively.

Many of the systems-based attempts at personalization focus on content as opposed to other learning interactions. This may present opportunities for future researchers to explore how systems might personalize other facets of the learning experience. Despite the gaps, the results indicate that systems-based personalization merits further exploration, especially in consideration of how to encourage the best learning outcomes.

Research on Learner-Based Personalization

For the purposes of this chapter, **Learner-Based Personalized Learning** refers to a learning experience wherein the learner drives the choice of what, how, when, where, and why the learning is personalized. A common approach that captures user-based PL in the literature is through the technosocial construct of Personal Learning Environments or PLEs (Dabbagh & Castaneda, 2020). PLEs embody the socio-material entanglement with which people learn as well as an approach that enacts contemporary ideas about how people learn. PLEs are built by the student using social media technologies to support the accomplishment of individual learning tasks and goals (Dabbagh & Kitsantas, 2012).

Learner-Based Personalization in K-12 Contexts

A study by Drexler (2010) examined students' construction of a personal learning environment (PLE) in a 7th-grade science class to study poisonous and venomous life forms. Students (N = 100) used social media technologies such as Google Scholar, science-specific search engines, videos, blogs, articles, and books, as well as API widget technology, to access, organize, and synthesize content into a PLE using Symbaloo as an aggregating tool. The study examined the processes students go through when using technology to construct a PLE in a middle school science class. Findings revealed that students applied the processes of practicing digital responsibility and digital literacy; organizing content; collaborating and socializing; synthesizing and creating; and taking responsibility and control for learning. These findings are supported by higher education research on PLEs that demonstrates the pedagogical affordances that social media have in supporting and promoting student self-regulation learning strategies by enabling the creation of PLEs (Dabbagh & Kitsantas, 2012; Kitsantas & Dabbagh, 2010). It is important to note that Drexler's research also took into consideration student readiness to accomplish the learning objectives by scaffolding the construction of PLEs using appropriate instructional strategies and gauging the level of support based on student needs. The processes the students used to construct the PLE informed a model of the networked student that will serve as a framework for future instructional designs involving learner-based personalization.

In another study (Verpoorten et al., 2010) based on learner-based personalization using the construct of PLEs, nine 14/15-year-old students used Web 2.0 technologies in a formal learning context to access, collect, and organize resources on a specific topic by finding and tagging relevant digital resources in their PLEM (Personal Learning Environment Manager) and to look at the evolution of their tags cloud. PLEM is a rich tool that allows the organization of a personal collection of Web resources. The findings of this study through self-reported student data revealed that the action of finding and tagging resources affected four dimensions of their learning experience: satisfaction, feeling of learning, effects on memorization and understanding, and personalization of the learning sequence.

In a study by Crompton (2013), fifteen (N = 15) boys from a single-gender, preparatory school, enrolled in grades 8–12, volunteered to participate in a research project aimed at exploring the concept of a PLE within a formal school environment in order to understand potential reactions to the concept by students and to generate ideas for possible larger-scale implementation within a particular environment. The participants were trained in the use of a number of Web 2.0 tools that formed their PLE. They were encouraged to base the construction of their PLE and PLN (Personal Learning Network) on a single personal interest. Their interests ranged from film to food to soccer to musicals. The results of this study revealed that while there was enthusiasm from students toward creating their own personal learning environment using these technologies, activity was at its peak when a new tool was introduced. Most students also found it difficult to integrate building a PLE into their daily routine and commented that it would be easier to make the use of these tools a habit if there was an ecosystem of PLEs within the school that all members of the community used. This research suggests that in K-12 contexts, there needs to be a certain momentum, both internal and external to the student, for the implementation of this kind of learner-based personalization. Specifically, K-12 students need to learn how to learn and develop self-regulated and metacognitive skills so that they can tailor their learning around specific interests, and learn to a point, at their own pace and on their own.

Netcoh and Bishop (2017) also witnessed the power and challenges of PLEs when they evaluated the effectiveness of a Middle School's PL program called E-Time. This initiative sought to provide students 55 minutes a day to pursue an independent project using any of the tools, resources, or technologies that were available to them. Each of the personalized project plans was vetted and reviewed by a teacher who served as an instructional coach and partner instead of an authority figure. Participants were all required to create a deliverable and instructors were available to support the students' learning process, provide check-ins, inquire about student progress, as well as offer suggestions, advice, and mentorship.

The findings of this experiment showed that students valued and embraced the autonomy associated with pursuing their own learning goals. On the other hand, tensions arose between teachers and students regarding the boundaries of autonomy. Since boundaries were not clearly defined or delineated early on, a few students expressed that teacher inquiry infringed on their independence. Teachers, on the other hand, mentioned concerns about the academic rigor of the student projects and were concerned about timelines for deliverables. Some students also struggled with the profusion of choice and indicated feeling lost or unmotivated without teacher guidance. In these instances, teachers had difficulty structuring new pathways to learning and knowing when to guide or inform student choices. Finally, teachers also struggled to know which times they should expose students to new ideas or embrace student choices.

Given this tension, future initiatives may benefit by setting expectations early on, emphasizing the student's choice as a commitment between the student and teacher towards a mutually agreed upon goal. It is also clear that training may be helpful to support teachers as they navigate the framing, norms and expectation-setting phase, set scaffolds for struggling students, and to navigate how to best facilitate the collaborative relationship between teachers and students.

Learner-Based Personalization in Higher Education Contexts

Similar themes of setting expectations early on reverberate in Higher Education settings as well. Utilizing the framework of the personal learning environment (PLE), Valtonen et al. (2012) studied the construction of PLEs created by 33 students from vocational and polytechnic schools based in Finland. As part of a one-credit course, students were encouraged to develop a PLE following introductory sessions that explored both the conceptual framework of PLEs and how to construct a PLE using technological tools. An analysis of the artifacts revealed that students perceived PLEs as environments for reflection, areas to showcase skills, and places to support collaboration and networking (p. 735). Challenges associated with PLEs included frustrations regarding the compulsory nature of PLE construction, issues with collaboration, and difficulties navigating new information communications technologies (ICT). Lack of time, unsurprisingly, was also cited as a common obstacle for learners. Valtonen et al. also found that students often did not explore past the technologies that were modeled by the instructor creating significant obstacles for the students to collaborate. Ultimately, this study suggested that future interventions that support the development of PLEs in higher education contexts include increased scaffolding, information communications technologies demonstrations, as well as increased instructor and technological support.

In another approach to learner-based PL, Perez-Garcia et al. (2022) explored flexible learning itineraries, or co-created collaborative curriculums developed by professors and students as an approach to PL with students in the Balearic Islands to evaluate if this approach supported students in the development of self-regulation skills while also offering a sense of autonomy. Despite reported difficulties, the researchers reported that students indicated a high level of engagement and satisfaction in the learning process with the argument that this approach also facilitated 21st-century skill development by developing learners' skills and interdisciplinary knowledge.

Dabbagh, Kitsantas, Al-Freih, and Fake (2015) conducted a qualitative case study on how learners construct personal learning environments (PLEs) to achieve their learning goals. In-depth semi-structured interviews revealed that students constructing PLEs engaged in self-regulated learning skills, including goal setting, task strategies, self-monitoring, and self-evaluation. Also, participants described feeling intrinsically and extrinsically motivated while creating their PLEs. The presence of self-regulated learning (SRL) skills suggests that learners were starting to take charge of their learning process supporting previous evidence that SRL processes can be enabled through social media technologies (Dabbagh & Kitsantas, 2012; Dabbagh & Kitsantas, 2013). Given these findings, the construction of PLEs as an approach to learner-based personalization could foster the development of lifelong learning skills. Ultimately, supporting students in the development of these skills could be critical in preparing workforce learners for the challenges of the 21st-century world.

Learner-Based Personalization in Workforce Training and Development Contexts

Student-driven approaches to PL in workplace training and development contexts have also seen encouraging empirical results. In 2014, 80 teachers from 45 Denver Public Schools (DPS) engaged in Project Cam Opener. As a part of the teachers' professional development, participating teachers worked with an online mentor to create a Personal Professional Learning Plan (PPLP) to improve their teaching. Participants were tasked to capture and post six recordings of their teaching and reflections before, during, and after the filmed classroom session over a six-month period on Google+. Instructional coaches and peers commented on the posts and offered feedback.

According to the Department of Education's case study of Raleigh's program, an end-of-year survey showed that 90% of teachers felt engaged in their professional learning (Raleigh, 2014). Teacher attrition rates also dropped below historic levels facilitating several development opportunities for the participating teachers while also increasing loyalty, engagement, and reducing employee turnover. Further exploration is necessary to understand if this program supported enhanced teaching practices or student outcomes. The evidence suggests, however, that PPLPs may increase engagement in training programs by fostering and incentivizing ownership over the learning process.

In yet another approach to learner-based PL, researchers explored and questioned how Personal Learning Environments (PLEs), or personal and social learning spaces that encourage self-directed learning enabled by Web 2.0 technologies could translate to corporate workplace learning environments (Caboul, Chleffer & Vaissiere, 2016). While Learning Management Systems (LMS) and eLearning programs are common within the workplace, the researchers pointed out that the adoption of PLEs is still limited. Citing potential organizational obstacles associated with privacy and security, Caboul et al. (2016) emphasized that PLEs may support increased self-directed training opportunities. On the other hand, the researchers argue that PLEs will also need to show a clear return on investment in order to be adopted within the workplace. Other obstacles to adopting PLEs in the workplace included gaining buy-in from key stakeholders, obtaining sufficient IT and infrastructure support, reconciling misalignment between individual and workplace goals, and transitioning from a didactic pedagogical model to one that is more collaborative in nature. Ultimately, the researchers felt the implementation of PLEs would be difficult to employ within the workplace due to these organizational challenges. Instead, they suggested the use of system-based personalization to support PL and development in the workplace.

Wunderlich (2016) argues that PLEs have been present organically in organizations and in training programs that support self-directed learning (SDL) as part of their training initiatives. Wunderlich points to multiple examples of Fortune 500 companies that support an SDL approach, including Disney, Aetna, Xerox, American Airlines, and Motorola. In her mixed methods exploratory research study, Wunderlich (2016) investigated how healthcare professionals constructed PLEs in a Leadership Academy to facilitate ongoing training and development for new supervisors and managers. She found that PLEs decreased the centralization of employee learning, created a higher demand for technology training, increased opportunities to challenge the institutional authority, required high levels of motivation and informational literacy, and benefited from clear company technology rules and regulations. For example, many employees were concerned that their internet searches were monitored and were unclear whether or not they could use social media or Web 2.0 technologies at work to build their PLEs. Wunderlich suggests that organizations should offer technical and informational literacy courses as well as increase operational awareness of existing technological regulations. Ultimately, she highlighted that the practice of learner-based personalization such as the creation of PLEs could help learners develop critical thinking skills, support a habit of continuous learning, and assist learners as they adapt to the ongoing changes facing professionals in the workforce.

In learner-based personalization, the focus is on student ownership, agency, and interests. The research here demonstrates how PLEs foster the development of self-regulated learning skills which support the continuous learning necessary for 21st-century contexts. Trailblazing the path to implementation, Raleigh reported on an example of how PL could be leveraged to decrease employee attrition rates while increasing loyalty and engagement in the teaching process. Her program not only leveraged a PL technique to encourage reflection and experimentation, but also facilitated new professional relationships and a culture of learning and experimentation amongst colleagues. Finally, Caboul (2016) and Wunderlich (2016) explored the potential opportunities, obstacles, and concerns associated with integrating PLEs, a learner-based PL approach, into the workforce context.

These studies support the argument that scaffolding or facilitating the development of PL environments will encourage the formation of lifelong learning skills and self-regulated learning in students and learners overall. The results suggest helpful recommendations for how to create PL for higher-order thinking skills and how to extend educational opportunities beyond the formal classroom. The application of PLEs in Higher Education and Workforce Training and Development Programs provides encouraging insights into the practice. It is clear, however, that alternative methods of assessment would be useful to promote this powerful construct and advance its use in Workforce Training and Development Programs. Continued experimentation with the application of PLEs, new mechanisms of assessment, and exploration into how to measure the effectiveness of PLEs offer great opportunities for future research. All in all, these studies indicate that learner-driven personalization offers a promising space (assuming student motivation) to increase employee ownership of the learning and development process.

Research on Blended Personalized Learning

Not all personalization systems are exclusively user or system-centric. Many PL initiatives mix aspects of systems-based and user-based personalization. Therefore, in this book, **Blended Personalized Learning** refers to implementations where both systems and learners are involved in personalizing the learning experience. This approach seeks to leverage systems to perform tasks that support the individual learner while also respecting learner ownership and agency in the learning process. Recognizing that learning occurs in a range of contexts, Blended Personalized Learning implementations tend to consider the comprehensive learning experience. Technology, therefore, is used to enhance an individual's holistic learning experience, rather than being used to make decisions for the learner based on a linear or pre-defined branched pathway of predetermined learning tasks.

An example of Blended Personalized Learning could include systems that recognize user locations and offer content relevant to the goals or tasks that learners have indicated an interest in or check-ins about learning goals with an instructor or coach following an experience with instructional technology (Freed et al., 2014).

Blended Personalized Learning in K-12 contexts

Blended PL initiatives have already shown positive results in the domain of K-12 education. According to the Bill and Melinda Gates' sponsored report conducted by the RAND Corporation, initial research into blended personalized programs learning shows statistically significant increases in math and language arts scores for students in 62 elementary and middle charter schools (Pane et al., 2015). Students who were exposed to blended PL strategies went from being below to above national averages in less than two years.

As an aspect of this study, the RAND corporation analyzed the school's implementation of the five PL strategies to include developing learner profiles, personal learning paths, competency-based progression, flexible learning environments, and initiatives to encourage college and career readiness. In these implementations, learners leveraged a variety of social, content, and technological touchpoints to achieve their learning goals. The researchers found that these elements were applied differently within each school system. Also, they stated that some of the initiatives, like competency-based learning, were more difficult for schools to implement than others. According to the report, three practices emerged as being particularly beneficial to the PL programs. These included grouping students based on their learning data with individuals who had similar needs, discussing data with students to help shape and refine their learning goals, and cultivating learning environments and spaces that supported PL practices.

Another success in K-12 comes from Leap Innovations, an organization that recognized that a more holistic and blended approach to PL was necessary for the success of PL programs in the school system. LEAP Innovations provided grants and funds to public schools in order to match schools with vetted educational technologies or learning platforms that supported literacy through PL. Following the selection of educational technology, LEAP Innovations worked with educators to implement the technology and later on to evaluate whether the educational technology intervention supported learner and program success (LEAP Innovations, 2016). Evaluating criteria used in the selection of learning technologies required that the technology or learning platform be: (1) learner connected – which was defined by the researchers as a means to offer a learner resources beyond the traditional confines of the traditional school system, (2) learner-focused to support tailored instruction that adjusts based on the learner's strengths, weaknesses, and interests, (3) learner demonstrated to present learners the ability to advance or review content and training based on individual performance, and (4) learner-led to give students the opportunity to take ownership over their personal development. Results of the LEAP program suggest that students who qualified for free or reduced-price lunch noticed a 45% reduction in the achievement gap after participating in LEAP's Personalized Learning Programs. An interesting facet of this is how blended learning techniques (e.g., those that encouraged social touchpoints) tended to perform better than those which were more focused on the technology. These findings suggest that a consideration of the technology, people, processes, and procedures are all important when considering integrating PL.

Another interesting finding of the LEAP Innovations (2016) study suggests that educational technology implementations that embraced one device per child or provided supplementary instruction performed better than instructors who pursued a rotation model which involved students practicing literacy tasks by visiting different stations. Therefore, in addition to implementing new technologies, considerations of instructional structure, environment, and approach can have a net positive outcome in cultivating a robust learning environment.

In yet another approach to blended personalizing learning, Massachusetts' 54 Innovation Schools implemented a flexible learning system to support students and their authentic and self-directed educational choices (U.S. Department of Education, 2017). In this approach, schools were encouraged to explore new strategies to improve learning outcomes and reduce the achievement gap. Led by Governor Patrick, this initiative sought to provide funding to schools that were interested in experimenting with introducing flexibility into the school's curriculum, budget, schedules and calendars, staffing, professional development, and school district policies. For example, Pentucket Regional School District's program implemented an approach that allowed students to choose learning opportunities beyond the normal school day to include online and blended coursework as well as off-campus learning opportunities, internships, and apprenticeships (U.S. Department of Education, 2017). The results of these initiatives are currently being gathered. However, it does demonstrate that school systems are embracing multiple strategies and resources to cultivate a more personalized approach toward learning.

Blended Personalized Learning in Higher Education

In Higher Education, Roberts, Howell, and Seaman (2017) explored the usage of personalized student dashboards and facilitated a co-design workshop with students to understand what might support their further growth and development within the existing data analytics system used in Australia. Five key themes emerged about the design of these big data analytics dashboard systems that would further support the students' learning. Themes from this research indicated that each student wanted to have access to the same learning opportunities regardless of their performance in the system, an ability to elect whether to compare their performance data to others or not, ensure that dashboards remained private, and if any comparison were enabled that it would be delivered as an anonymous aggregate, automate any alerts, and allow students to customize the metrics that are most important to them in their learning process.

An element of the existing dashboard that received mixed feedback was the use of a traffic light indicator (green, yellow, and red) regarding someone's performance in a learning experience. While some students valued the simplicity of the approach, others complained that these types of indicators are vague and can be somewhat discouraging. These findings suggest that students are demanding opportunities to customize learning dashboards to best suit their learning, motivational, and emotional needs.

Student responses indicated that they were interested in the system supporting their personal choices rather than alerting them about work they should be doing stating that these types of interactions might be pesky and decrease the desired usage within the system.

Ku, Hou, and Chen (2016) conducted a study with (N = 120) undergraduate and postgraduate students at a Northern Taiwanese university to evaluate two game-based learning implementations that **personalized the presentation of the learning materials based on the learner's identified cognitive style**. This study sought to explore the impact of Pask's holism and serialism cognitive styles on perceptions of two different game environments. Following a cognitive preferences assessment, students were assigned to either a customized or personalized game-based learning environment. In the customized condition, the students were able to alter the interface and enable or disable certain features and functionalities of the game. In the personalized condition, however, participants were offered a different experience based on the results of their cognitive styles assessment. To measure the two experimental conditions, game preferences, game behaviors, satisfaction levels, as well as pre and post-test scores, were documented. The results indicated there were no statistical differences in performance between customized or personalized game-based learning environments. However, players were more satisfied with games that supported a customized user interface and allowed for adjustments to the available features and functionalities. Beyond the discovery of increased satisfaction rates, researchers also found that holists were more likely to turn off the music while playing the game and use hints in order to guide and support their performance.

The findings imply interesting behavioral differences between holists and serialists. It is also interesting to note how customization and personalizing an interface impacted learner satisfaction. While both customized and personalized game-based learning supported learner performance, these findings may also indicate that encouraging learner ownership, embracing learner agency, and supporting customization by introducing personalized interfaces could increase user satisfaction and also potentially increase continued participation in learning and development programs.

Blended Personalized Learning in Workforce Training and Development

Recognizing the lack of personnel resources for onboarding, training, and mentoring new and existing employees, SRI International and Advanced Distributed Learning (ADL), collaborated to create the Pervasive Learning System (PERLS), a personal assistant learning mobile tool that adapts to the learner based on what learning tasks they would like to pursue as they transition to a new organization, organizational role, or in keeping pace with changes inherent in the modern age (Craig et al., 2022; Freed et al., 2014). PERLS promotes various learning actions by providing recommendations on general topics as well as parameters based on the learner's location, learning history, training requirements, content engagement, desired learning activities, available time, and interests. Conceptually, the system is designed to predict user patterns, behaviors, and preferences in order to suggest training content that may reflect the user's context. For instance, if a meeting is delayed and hosted in a new location, then the user may receive a prompt to explore resources through the learning app to fill the time and learn about their new location. The learner then has the choice of whether to engage in the content or browse an assortment of options based on their previous browsing or consumption patterns. In doing this, the technology identifies the opportunity for training, and the individual can then select from a series of options that align with their learning needs and interests.

The implementation of PERLs has resulted in significant reductions in attrition in Army Air Assault School and has even been advocated and advanced by NATO to address the training and development needs of DoD employees. Here the fusion of learner agency and data-informed contextual awareness support and prompt self-directed learning activities by identifying times and places where learning could occur. For example, PL for PERLS requires a consideration of the participant's location, user patterns, time of day, learning behaviors, preferences, and potentially espoused learning goals. As the tool continues to be developed, the various variables and dimensions associated with this interpretation of PL will become clearer.

In Workplace Training and Development, Advanced Distributed Learning, an organization focused on training programs for the Department of Defense, has identified PL as a strategy for optimizing learner outcomes and supports multiple projects that are further exploring its impact on learner outcomes (ADL website, n.d.). Research on the PERvasive Learning System and Personal eBook for Learning seeks to explore PL from learning assistants to adaptive resources. The continued investment in these domains suggests that the DoD continues to see the promise of PL.

Ultimately, this chapter reveals that there are still several gaps in the research with regard to understanding the impact personalization could have within online learning environments and what impact PL practices may have on making content more engaging, impactful, and relevant in online learning. Very few studies from this chapter for example have looked at how personalizing the channel (e.g., e-mail, text message, podcast, etc.), learning interface, functionality, or learning environment (e.g., classroom setting, community of practice, self-driven eLearning, study groups) could impact learning outcomes. As you will note, a majority of the studies focus solely on personalizing content. Combining different PL methods could yield interesting experiments and results.

Of the studies reviewed, PL was shown to increase engagement, loyalty, and retention in teacher development and even air assault schools. These initatives effectively connect workforce learners with learning resources. PL was also seen by the American Institute of Research as being a compelling strategy for overcoming the challenges of teaching adults lacking basic educational backgrounds and skills. Wunderlich (2016) demonstrated that PL happens organically, but may be stifled unless organizations are cognizant of how certain learning activities are perceived. Observing the PLEs of healthcare professionals, Wunderlich provided heuristics and insights into what policies and initiatives organizations could pursue to support ongoing and self-directed continuous education efforts. Finally, Fake and Dabbagh (2020) detailed current perceptions and ad hoc implementations of PL within corporate contexts and found that practitioners struggle to understand how to successfully implement PL into Workforce Training and Development Programs.

Beyond these studies, it is also important to note and recognize that there are a few platforms that currently "personalize" learning. These include powerful cloud-based software systems like Degreed, Codeacademy, and Skillsoft. These platforms tend to employ adaptive pathing which references information gathered in data mining, user behavior, user performance, and explicit feedback as the main instructional methods. Degreed and Skillsoft also are centralized learning management systems (LMSs) that utilize a wide spectrum of tools to personalize learning. While adaptive path technologies and forward-thinking LMSs may be powerful ways to engage workforce learners, it is important to explore broader and more flexible applications of how to empower individuals by using and embedding learning technologies and programs since these implementations may not be best suited for all learning outcomes.

It is also important to note that adaptive path technologies are an attractive way to scale PL as well as retrieve learner metrics. However, many of the available adaptive systems may be expensive and difficult to implement within a typical organizational environment. Also, a recent report by Ho, Jones, Cole, and Sanchez (2018) indicates that of the training and development leaders (N = 271) surveyed, only 13% believe their adaptive programs are currently effective. Adaptive path PL efforts may also be less effective at facilitating learning for ill-structured, emotionally driven, and complex high-order thinking tasks compared to other PL approaches.

Based on the existing review, there is strong evidence that PL is an effective strategy for improving learning outcomes in K-12, Higher Education, and even in the limited studies available for Workforce Training and Development. As such, implementing PL as a strategy appears to be a valuable means of supporting professionals as they learn and grow as 21st-century practitioners. The research suggests that PL may also be an effective means to help organizations become more competitive, flexibly respond to change and uncertainty within the business environment, and retain top talent. While PL is viewed favorably by the literature, Training Teams struggle to develop and implement PL (Fake & Dabbagh, 2018). As mentioned before, to implement PL workforce leaders may require additional frameworks, tools, technologies, and proven techniques for integrating PL into their existing curricula.

We continue in the next chapter describing the Personalized Learning Interaction Framework (PLiF) and how this approach can provide a flexible framework for supporting the development of personalized learning programs.

References

Amro, F. (2019). Scaffolding students problem solving skills in a computer-based adaptive learning program: An analysis of scaffolding types and strategies. Doctoral dissertation, George Mason University. Proquest.

Bersin, J. (2017, March 27). The disruption of digital learning: Ten things we have learned [web log post]. Retrieved from https://joshbersin.com/2017/03/the-disruption-of-digital-learning-ten-things-we-have-learned/.

Bimba, A. T., Idris, N., Al-Hunaiyyan, A., Mahmud, R. B., & Mohd Shuib, N. L. B. (2020). Adaptive feedback in computer-based learning environments: A review. *Adaptive Behavior*, 25(5). https://doi-org.mutex.gmu.edu/10.1177/1059712317727590.

Caboul, E., Chleffer, N., & Vaissiere, C. (2016). Adapting Personal Learning Environments to the workplace? [PDF file]. Retrieved from https://f.hypotheses.org/wp-content/blogs.dir/1236/files/2016/10/Article_AdaptingPLE.pdf.

Chookaew, S., Panjaburee, P., Wanichsan, D., & Laosinchai, P. (2014). A personalized e-learning environment to promote student's conceptual learning on basic computer programming. *Procedia – Social and Behavioral Sciences*, *116*, 815–819. 10.1016/j.sbspro.2014.01.303.

Craig, S. D., Siegle, R. F., Li, S., Cooper, N. R., Liu, Y., & Roscoe, R. (2022). An investigation of the PERvasive learning systems impact on soldiers' self-efficacy for self-regulation skills. *Proceedings of the Human Factors and Ergonomics Society Annual Meeting*, *66*(1), 742–746. DOI:10.1177/1071181322661491.

Crompton, H. (2013). A historical overview of mobile learning: Toward learner-centered education. In Z. L. Berge & L. Y. Muilenburg (Eds.), *A Historical Overview of Mobile Learning: Toward Learner-centered Education*. Routledge.

Dabbagh, N., & Castaneda, L. (2020). Beyond personalization: The PLE as a framework for lifelong learning. *Educational Technology Research and Development, Special Issue*, 68(6), 3041–3055.

Dabbagh, N., & Fake, H. (2016). Tech Select decision aide: A mobile application to facilitate just-in-time decision support for instructional designers. *TechTrends (2017)*, 61, 393–403. Available from https://link.springer.com/article/10.1007/s11528-016-0152-2.

Dabbagh, N., & Kitsantas, A. (2012). Personal learning environments, social media, and self- regulated learning: A natural formula for connecting formal and informal learning. *Internet and Higher Education*, 15. 10.1016/j.iheduc.2011.06.002

Dabbagh, N., & Kitsantas, A. (2013). Using learning management systems as meta-cognitive tools to support self-regulation in higher education contexts. In R. Azevedo and V. Aleven (Eds.), *International Handbook of Metacognition and Learning Technologies* (pp. 197–212). New York, NY: Springer Science.

Dabbagh, N., Kitsantas, A., Al-Freih, M., & Fake, H. (2015). Using social media to develop Personal Learning Environments (PLEs) and self-regulated learning skills: A case study. *International Journal of Social Media and Interactive Learning Environments*, 3(3), 163–183. 10.1504/IJSMILE.2015.072300

Dede, C., Richards, J., & Saxberg, B. (2019). *Learning Engineering For Online Education: Theoretical Contexts and Design-based Examples*. Routledge, Taylor & Francis Group.

Drexler, W. (2010). The networked student model for construction of personal learning environments: Balancing teacher control and student autonomy. *Australasian Journal of Educational Technology*, 26(3), 369–385.

Domenech, D., Sherman, M., & Brown, J. (2016). *Personalizing 21st Century Education: A Framework for Student Success*. Wiley.

Fake, H. (2018). *A Delphi Study on the Dimensions of Personalized Learning in Workforce Training and Development Programs*. [Doctoral dissertation, George Mason University]. Proquest.

Fake, H., & Dabbagh, N. (2019). *Dimensions and Applications of Personalized Learning in Workforce Training and Development Programs: A Delphi Study*. Proceedings of eLearn 2019. New Orleans, LA: Association for the Advancement of Computing in Education (AACE).

Fake, H. & Dabbagh, N. (2020). Personalized learning within online workforce learning environments: Exploring implementations, obstacles, opportunities, and perspectives of workforce leaders. *Technology, Knowledge and Learning*. Advance online publication. 10.1007/s10758-020-09441-x

Fake, H., & Dabbagh, N. (2021, October). The Personalized Learning Interaction Framework: Expert Perspectives on How to Apply Dimensions of Personalized Learning to Workforce Training and Development Programs. In *Ninth International Conference on Technological Ecosystems for Enhancing Multiculturality (TEEM '21)* (pp. 501–509).

Fan, H., & Poole, S. (2006). What is personalization? Perspectives on design and implementation of personalization information systems. *Journal of Organizational Computing and Electronic Commerce*, 16(3), 179–202. 10.1207/s15327744joce1 603&4_2

Folsom-Kovarik, J. T., Chen, D.-W., Mostafavi, B., & Brawner, K. (2019). Measuring the complexity of learning content to enable automated comparison, recommendation, and generation. *Adaptive Instructional Systems*, 188–203. 10.1007/978-3-030-22341-0_16

Freed, M., Yarnall, L., Dinger, J., Gervasio, M., Overholtzer, A., Roschelle, J., & Spaulding, A. (2014). *PERLS: An Approach to Pervasive Personal Assistance in Adult Learning* [Conference presentation]. Interservice/Industry Training, Simulation, and Education Conference (I/ITSEC), Menlo Park, California.

Gallagher, P. S., & Prestwich, S. (2013). *Developing a Personalization Strategy for Online Learning Environments*. Unpublished manuscript.

Graesser, A., & McNamara, D. (2010). Self-regulated learning in learning environments with pedagogical agents that interact in natural language. *Educational Psychologist*, 45(4), 234–244.

Griff, E. R., & Matter, S. F. (2013). Evaluation of an adaptive online learning system. *British Journal of Educational Technology*, 44(1), 170–176. 10.1111/j.1467-8535.2012.01300.x

Hannafin, M. H., Land, S., & Oliver, K. (1999). Open learning environments: Foundations, methods, and models. In C. Reigeluth (Ed.), *Instructional-design Theories and Models: Volume II* (pp. 115–140). Mahwah: Lawrence Erlbaum.

Ho, M., Jones, M., Cole, M., & Sanchez, I. (2018). Personalized and adaptive learning [white paper]. Retrieved from https://www.td.org/research-reports/personalized-and-adaptive-learning-shaping-employee-development-for-engagement-and-performance.

Hooshyar, D., Pedaste, M., Yang, Y., Malva, L., Gwo-Jen, H., Wang, M., Lim, H., Delev, D., (2021). From gaming to computational thinking: An adaptive educational computer game-based learning approach. *Journal of Educational Computing Research*, 59(3), 383–409. https://journals-sagepub-com.mutex.gmu.edu/doi/pdf/10.1177/0735633120965919.

Kitsantas, A., & Dabbagh, N. (2010). *Learning to Learn with Integrative Learning Technologies (Ilt): A Practical Guide for Academic Success*. Information Age Publishing. Available from http://infoagepub.com/products/Learning-to-Learn-with-Integrative-Learning-Technologies.

Ku, O., Hou, C. C., & Chen, S. Y. (2016). Incorporating customization and personalization into game-based learning: A cognitive style perspective. *Computers in Human Behavior*, 65, 359–368. 10.1016/j.chb.2016.08.040.

Kulkarni, P. V., Rai, S., & Kale, R. (2020). Recommender system in eLearning: A survey. In: S. Bhalla, P. Kwan, M. Bedekar, R. Phalnikar, and S. Sirsikar (Eds.), *Proceeding of International Conference on Computational Science and Applications. Algorithms for Intelligent Systems*. Springer. 10.1007/978-981-15-0790-8_13.

Kwon, K., Cho, J., & Park, Y. (2010). How to best characterize the personalization construct for e- services. *Expert Systems with Applications*, 37, 2232–2240. 10.1016/j.eswa.2009.07.050.

Kwon, K., & Kim, C. (2012). How to design personalization in a context of customer retention: Who personalizes what and to what extent? *Economic Commerce Research and Applications*, 11, 101–116. 10.1016/j.elerap.2011.05.002.

Lavie, T., Sela, M., Oppenheim, I., Inbar, O., & Meyer, J. (2010). User attitudes towards news content personalization. *Journal of Human-Computer Studies*, 68, 483–495. 10.1016/j.ijhcs.2009.09.011

LEAP Innovations (2016). *Finding what works: Results from the LEAP Innovations Pilot Network*. Retrieved from http://www.leapinnovations.org/images/PN_C1_Research_Brief_FINAL_red.pdf

Leone, S. (2013). *Characterisation of a Personal Learning Environment as a Lifelong learning tool*. New York, NY: Springer Science & Business Media. 10.1007/978-1-4614-6274-3.

McRae, P. (2015, June 17). *Myth: Blended Learning Is the next ed Tech Revolution - Hype, Harm and Hope*. National Education Policy Center. Retrieved November 29, 2022, from https://nepc.info/blog/myth-blended-learning.

Milicevic, A. K., Vesin, B., Ivanovic, M., & Budimac, Z. (2011). E-Learning personalization based on hybrid recommendation strategy and learning style identification. *Computers & Education*, 56. 10.1016/j.compedu.2010.11.001

Netcoh, S., & Bishop, P. A. (2017). Personalized learning in the middle grades: A case study of one team's successes and challenges. *Middle Grades Research Journal*, 11(2), 33–48. 10.1080/00940771.2017.1297665

Pane, John, Steiner, Elizabeth, Baird, Matthew, & Hamilton, Laura. (2015). *Continued Progress: Promising Evidence on Personalized Learning*. 10.7249/rr1365

Pelster, B., Johnson, D., Stempel, J., & van der Vyver, B. (2017, February). *Careers and learning: Real time, all the time* [Research Report]. Retrieved from Deloitte Insights: https://www2.deloitte.com/insights/us/en/focus/human-capital-trends/2017/learning-in-the-digital-age.html?id=us:2el:3dc:dup3818:awa:cons:hct17#endnote-4.

Perez-Garcia, A., Tur Ferrer, G., Villatoro Moral, S., & Darder-Mesquida, A. (2022). Itinerarios de aprendizaje flexibles en entornos digitales para un aprendizaje personalizado en la formación docente, RIED. *Revista Iberoamericana de Educación a Distancia*, 25(2), 173–193.

Puntambekar, Sadhana, & Kolodner, Janet L. (2005). Toward implementing distributed scaffolding: Helping students learn science from design. *Journal of Research in Science Teaching*, 42, 185–217. 10.1002/tea.20048.

Quintana, C., Reiser, B. J., Davis, E. A., Krajcik, J., Fretz, E., Duncan, R. G., Kyza, E., Edelson, D., & Soloway, E. (2004). A scaffolding design framework for software to support science inquiry. *Journal of the Learning Sciences*, 13(3), 337–386. 10.1207/s15327809jls1303_4.

Raleigh, J. (2014). *Project Cam Opener [Syllabus]*. Denver, CO: Denver Public Schools. Retrieved from https://canvas.instructure.com/courses/990019.

Roberts, L. D., Howell, J. A., Seaman, K. S., & Gibson, D. C. (2017). Student attitudes toward learning analytics in higher education: "The fitbit version of the learning world". *Frontiers in Psychology*, 7. 10.3389/fpsyg.2016.01959.

Romero, C., & Ventura, S. (2010). Educational data mining: A review of the state of the art. *IEEE*, 40(6), 601–618. 10.1109/TSMCC.2010.2053532.

Shemshack, A., & Spector, J. M. (2020). A systematic literature review of personalized learning terms. *Smart Learning Environments*, 7(1). 10.1186/s40561-020-00140-9.

Skillsoft (2014). *Skillsoft's Big Data Initiative Delivers Improved Learning and Engagement Outcomes*. Retrieved from http://www.skillsoft.com/about/press_room/press_releases/november_18_14_ibm.asp.

Skinner, B. F. (1958). Teaching machines. *Science*, 128(3330), 969–977. 10.1126/science.128.3330.969

U.S. Department of Education. (2017). Reimagining the role of technology in education: 2017 National education plan update. Retrieved from National Educational Technology Plan Website https://tech.ed.gov/files/2017/01/NETP17.pdf.

Valtonen, T., Hacklin, S., Dillon, P., Vesisenaho, M., Kukkonen, J., & Hietanen, A. (2012). Perspectives on personal learning environments held by vocational students. *Computers & Education*, *58*, 732–739. 10.1016/j.compedu.2011.09.025.

Verpoorten, D., Chatti, M., Westera, W., & Specht, M. (2010). Personal Learning Environment on a procrustean bed – Using PLEM in a secondary-school lesson. In C. A. Shoniregun, & G. A. Akmayeya (Eds.), Proceedings of the London International Conference on Education (LICE) (pp. 197–203). LICE.

Walkington, C., & Bernacki, M. (2021). Making classroom learning personalized. *APA Division 15 Policy Brief Series*, *1*(4), 1–6.

Wang, Y., & Liao, H. C. (2011). Data mining for adaptive learning in a TESL-based e-learning system. *Expert Systems with Applications*, *38*(6), 6480–6485. 10.1016/j.eswa.2010.11.098.

Watters, A. (2021). *Teaching Machines*. MIT Press.

Wunderlich, D. (2016). *Personal Learning Environments for Business Organizations* (Doctoral dissertation). Retrieved from Proquest (10105016).

Zhong, L. (2022). A systematic review of personalized learning in higher education: Learning content, structure, learning materials sequence, and learning readiness. *Interactive Learning Environments*. Advance online publication. 10.1080/10494820.2022.2061006

Zulfiani, Z., Suwarna, I. P., & Miranto, S. (2018). Science education adaptive learning system as a computer-based science learning with learning style variations. *Journal of Baltic Science Education*, *17*(4), 711–727.

Designing Personalized Learning Experiences Using the PL Interaction Framework (PLiF)

Using the Delphi Method to Establish A Framework for Personalized Learning

Linstone and Turoff (2002) argue that throughout history, humans have performed ceremonies, liturgies, and rituals to cultivate a better understanding of the future. Whether it was through sacrificing animals, interpreting the alignment of stars, or consulting the induced visions of Pythia, the priestess of Apollo, humans have consistently sought mechanisms to understand, interpret, and forecast future events and scenarios.

As time has progressed, the forecasting rituals of ancient civilizations have been debunked, demystified, and replaced with new practices which reflect the latest thinking on how to interpret the world. One such method that controls for social pressures and embraces the iterative refinement of expert opinions is the Delphi Method. The Delphi Method has been employed in multiple industries and areas of study to inform decision-making, forecast the future, or comprehensively explore a divisive issue (Brady, 2015; Iqbal & Pipon-Young, 2009; Mitroff & Turoff, 2002; Parente & Anderson-Parente, 2011; Zolingen & Klaasen, 2003).

Popularized by the RAND Corporation during the Cold War, and ultimately supporting a wide range of use cases and circumstances, the Delphi Method is firmly rooted in the branch of Pragmatism and the social-constructivist paradigm (Turoff, 2002). The method operates under the

DOI: 10.4324/9781003121008-3

assumption that knowledge and decisions are influenced by the collective expertise of stakeholders involved in an area of inquiry (McIntyre-Hite, 2016; Vygotsky, 1978). While the applications of Delphi may vary, the method assumes that expert opinions will accurately predict future outcomes, define priorities, develop decision-making models, or explicitly explain the differences between several divergent opinions. The method is most often used in circumstances wherein there is no precise way to observe the phenomena or topic at hand such as personalized learning (Franc, 2016; Linstone & Turoff, 2002).

As a research technique, the Delphi Method supports a variety of contexts and circumstances. These could include instances wherein:

- The research problem cannot be actively observed or analyzed, but would benefit from collective subjective assessment (Keeney, Hasson, & McKenna, 2011; Linstone & Turoff, 2002).
- When problems are ill-structured and broad. In these situations, the researcher sees the benefit of sampling multiple perspectives (Linstone & Turoff, 2002).
- When questions are politically divisive in nature and could be influenced by a majority opinion or dominant personalities (Bolger & Wright, 2011; Linstone & Turoff, 2002; Mitroff & Turoff, 2002).
- When logistical limitations restrict the experts' abilities to meet on a normal basis (Linstone & Turoff, 2002).

Each of these conditions is met in the challenge of better understanding conceptions and dimensions of personalized learning within higher education and workforce contexts. Here it is important to note that this work focuses on higher education and workforce training and development programs since the foundational research grounding the PLiF originates from these two aforementioned contexts. In the paragraph below, we explore how the study of personalized learning adheres to these research requirements.

To begin with, the nature of Higher Education and Workforce Training and Development is such that many of the individuals involved in developing personalized learning initiatives may not have ongoing contact with one another or venture across their respective domains. Organizational silos are common in both higher education and workforce development. Given these silos and lack of contact, personalized learning is not a strategy that can be actively observed or analyzed. This is not only because there are limited personalized learning initiatives within industry and higher education, but also because even within the existing initiatives, practitioners and researchers are using the same terms to mean vastly different personalized learning implementations (Betts, 2018; Fake, 2018). Since there is no clear consensus on what the term "personalized learning" means and since these characterizations of personalized learning vary, research studies on personalized learning as a practice are ill-structured and broad. Observing programs in Workforce Training and Development programs is also a challenge given the proprietary nature of the programs.

In addition to fostering a forum for exchange, anonymity is a key feature of Delphi designs. Anonymity seeks to control the social dynamics that may be present in focus groups. According to Hsu and Sandford (2007), the aspect of participant anonymity is key to mitigating any coercion, manipulation, or pressure to conform inherent in any group interaction. Therefore, a critical strength of the Delphi method may be to help preserve the opinions of experts while revealing any latent or unexplored assumptions, uncover differences of opinion, as well as identify areas of authentic consensus (Zolingen and Klaasen, 2003).

Using the Delphi method, we used multiple rounds of iterative survey research in order to chart consensus and disagreements about the conception of personalized learning, what dimensions are necessary to consider in personalized learning, as well as how these dimensions and components of these dimensions should be applied given different case studies.

Of the 224 experts initially recruited for this study, N = 79 expert researchers, practitioners, and workforce leaders participated in the first survey (35% of the originally identified expert group). Of the experts in the first round, n = 32 were researchers, n = 33 were practitioners, and n = 15 were workforce leaders. Responses to the 65 overall personalized learning variables and individual survey items had a high-reliability rate (α = .92).

Experts were each selected on carefully vetted criteria to include a consideration of their leadership roles and titles, education, years of experience in Learning and Development and Higher Education, conference presentations, involvement in professional associations, publications in the domain of personalized learning, awarded grant funding, and social presence in the Learning Development Community. In order to maintain the anonymity of the experts, demographic information was not disclosed throughout the iterative surveys.

The result of the Delphi Study, which included 32 researchers, 33 practitioners, and 15 workforce leaders, yielded a framework for personalized learning called Personalized Learning Interaction Framework (PLiF). We present the PLiF framework and its five types of interaction in the paragraphs below.

The Personalized Learning Interaction Framework (PLiF)

This research found that experts perceived personalized learning as a learner-driven exercise. Experts considered the following themes to be elemental to personalized learning to include embracing **flexible resources** (e.g., multimedia experiences or organizational interactions), **competency mapping and setting expectations, assessment** (e.g., self-assessment, needs assessments, assessment in general), **involving a community of practice or a network** (e.g., interacting with self-selected small groups or peers), **mentor or coach involvement** (in an individual or group capacity), as well as providing overall **implementation considerations.**

These larger themes in themselves suggest a series of interactions that are imperative to creating a personalized learning ecosystem for learners or a Personalized Learning Interaction Framework (PLiF). Already inherent in these themes are relationships between the **learner and the content** (Chapter 4), the **learner and other learners** (Chapter 5), the **learner and small groups** (Chapter 6), the **learner and the mentor or coach** (Chapter 7), and the **community of practice or social network** (Chapter 8). Therefore, the themes which emerged from this research suggest that effective personalized learning is built upon an ecosystem of interactions between the learner and the outside world, emphasizing learning as a social process.

The integration of different learning interactions is reminiscent and builds upon Moore's three-level interaction model. In this model, Moore proposes that distance education involves three types of interactions. This includes a **learner-content interaction**, a **learner-teacher instructor**, and a **learner-learner interaction** (Moore, 1989). Dabbagh and Bannan-Ritland expanded Moore's types of interaction and added learner-group interaction (Dabbagh & Bannan-Ritland, 2005). While Moore's three types of interaction (and Dabbagh and Bannan-Ritland's addition) were proposed for use in distance education, the application of Moore's theory has more recently been leveraged and extended to support blended learning environments (Best & Conceição, 2017; Dron, Seidel, & Litten, 2004; Murray, Perez, Geist, & Hedrick, 2013). Since the agreed upon personalized learning variables associated with learning in Higher Education and Workforce Training and Development Programs include both in-person and virtual components, Moore's framework serves as a foundation to ground a framework of personalized learning. Thus, this research yielded a framework of personalized learning adding to Moore's three-level interaction model. Figure 3.1 shows the types of interactions embedded in PLiF. Later in this chapter, we provide an example of how PLiF might be implemented in an applied scenario.

48 Using the PL Interaction Framework (PLiF)

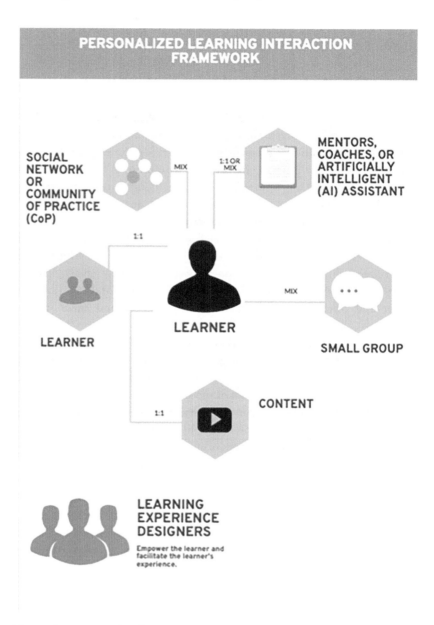

Figure 3.1 Personalized Learning Interaction Framework (PLiF).

As you can see in Figure 3.1, there are five types of interactions. These include (1) learner to content, (2) learner to learner, (3) learner to mentor, coach, or Artificial Intelligent (AI) Assistant, (4) learner to small group, and (5) learner to social network or community of practice. We will explore these interactions and potential design considerations for implementing these interactions in the paragraphs below.

Despite the acceptance of Learning Experience Designers (LED) or Instructional Systems Designers (ISD) as stakeholders in personalized learning, there was no reference to their role in expert responses. This suggests that the role of LEDs and ISDs may be more passive in nature and instead involved in setting up the systems, resources, and processes to support overall Workforce Training and Development Programs. Therefore, as you will notice in Figure 3.1, LEDs and ISDs have been included but are situated outside of the 5 types of interactions. Their positioning reflects comments about LEDs and ISDs embracing a resource model wherein they are responsible for managing the learning environment, curating and evaluating sources for cultivating different learner interactions, and overseeing certain program elements. In this model, LEDs and ISDs become curators to support personalized learning. While LEDs and ISDs are not central to the design of the PLiF, in this framework, their role transforms to support learners in continual facilitation of the learner's ongoing growth and development.

Please note the additional data in graph 3.1 that documents the type of engagement that is enabled in the PLiF. This represents further expert feedback In response to questions regarding how personalization should occur. Experts referenced in this study only agreed on two methods of engagement that constitute personalized learning. This included **1 to 1** and ***a mix of 1 to 1 and 1 to N (or Number of Overall Participants) engagements***.

The learner's ownership and agency over the learning process is further upheld with experts rejecting *Number of Participants (N) to Many or Total Number (M)* (e.g., personalizing based on observing the characteristics of a group of learners, categorizing them, and applying these defined categorizations to a larger population.), *M to N* (e.g., by using generalized data patterns of a large population and then applying those patterns to an individual) and *One to N* (e.g., by grouping individuals based on similar characteristics). Examples could include, but are not limited to, grouping individuals based on their performance on a task.

What is common in each of these rejected methods of personalization is that in each of these approaches (N to Many, Many to N, or One to N), a judgment is made upon the individual which defines their experience.

Instead, expert responses suggest that the learner should be empowered. The acceptance of a mix of 1 to 1 and 1 to N methods towards enabling engagements also acknowledges a social dimension to personalized learning, however, this may be more aligned with the idea that at some point a learner may require an external community of practice, social network or small group support. This lines up with the findings surrounding who should personalize learning since social relationships are inherent in the interactions mentioned here.

Learner to Content Interaction

Learner to content interaction was described throughout the expert responses in the Delphi study. In this, several design parameters emerged. To begin with, the availability of multimedia resources to support learning (e.g., text, video, audio, podcast) and flexible learning pathways were expressed as critical in the learner-to-content interaction. This flexibility extended not only to the types of content, but also the delivery type (e.g., web-based, text messages, email) and technology that delivers the content (e.g., LMS platforms, social media platforms), the instructional modality (e.g., synchronous, asynchronous, blended), and the learning activities.

Key design parameters included that content needed to be enabled to be referenced on the go, anytime, anywhere, and on any device. Also important to note is the availability or range of different types of resources, accessibility of resources, and the ability to self-select which resources are utilized. In Chapter 4, we further explore the design parameters associated with supporting this learner-to-content interaction. It can be anticipated that learners pursuing a content interaction may need additional support in identifying good resource materials. In this, learners will need to develop the skill sets to identify what makes a resource credible and useful in the digital age.

Learner-to-Learner Interaction

Learner-to-learner interactions (which may also be referred to as peers) were described as exchanges that enriched the learner's experience by offering ongoing dialogue and feedback about their training. Learners were described by experts as gaining proficiency not only through their coaches, but by gathering insights and resources from other learners or peers to complement their strengths, address weaknesses, and improve overall learner performance.

Experts espoused that learner-to-learner interactions would cultivate a more collaborative organizational environment. This, in turn, offers a collegial and collaborative discourse between learners which may further foster and cultivate continual and self-sustaining training and development opportunities for workforce learners. The literature supports these claims suggesting peer-to-peer learning experiences support learners in benchmarking their performance while also developing independent learning, relationship-building, and collaboration skills (Batty & Sinclair, 2014; Ma, Xing, & Du, 2018). An exploration of best practices to provide learner-to-learner or learner-to-peer interactions is provided in Chapter 5.

As noted in Figure 3.1, the learner-to-learner interaction is a 1:1 engagement but can be done with different partners which may facilitate several 1:1 engagements depending on the topic or way the interaction is facilitated.

Learner to Small Group Interaction

Small groups were also referenced as important interactions to support personalized learning. Experts described the purpose of small group interactions as a place to meet with others to address similar needs, questions, or challenges based on specific strengths or weaknesses.

According to experts, how the groups are formed, their purpose or topic, and how someone joins, are important aspects for consideration in personalizing the learning experience. Here self-selection is a key design consideration. This resounding expert response reflects themes of self-selection (e.g., selecting content or selecting social interactions) that resonate throughout the findings. It is also interesting to note that many of the expert responses seemed to imply that small groups would be internally organized as opposed to including individuals from outside the organization.

Small groups also enable a mix of 1:1 and 1:N engagements as learners may talk with other individuals or in the group as a whole. Design parameters for setting up successful small groups will be explored more thoroughly in Chapter 6.

Learner to Coach, Mentor, or Artificially Intelligent (AI) Assistant Interaction

Experts also mentioned coaches, mentors, and AI assistants and their role in the creation of personalized learning. Personalization facilitated by coaches can provide direction on the competencies required. Coaches may additionally point to resources and training materials that are relevant to the learner. In expert responses, coaches or mentors were described as resource providers, sounding boards, facilitators, and prompters that provided accountability checks. Coaches were also seen as a force that could personalize learning for an individual or a group suggesting a multifaceted interaction with not only the individual learner, but also within a group of learners.

Coaches, Mentors, and AI Assistants support 1:1 or a mix of 1:1 or 1:N modes of engagement according to experts. This indicates an acknowledgment that coaching, mentorship, or AI Assistants may support learners individually or within groups. A distinction, however, must be made as a small group also may support a mix of 1:1 or 1:N engagements. We will explore the distinctions between coaches, mentors, and AI assistants further in Chapter 7.

It is important to note that additional resources may be needed to train and develop coaches and mentors to be effective in embracing all the different roles that they will need to fulfill in this personalized learning framework (e.g., how to hold someone accountable, which resources might help learners, providing encouragement, reviewing company metrics, etc.) Therefore, in implementing personalized learning, organizations may need to invest time and resources to support coaches in gaining the necessary skill sets they need to serve Workforce Training and Development Programs.

Learner to Community of Practice

The Learner to Community of Practice interaction reflects the acceptance of "the network or community of peers" as a dimension of personalized learning. Communities of practice are "groups of people informally bound together by shared expertise and passion for a joint enterprise" (Wenger & Snyder, 2000, p. 139). The construct has become popular in the business community and in organizations that focus on knowledge as intellectual capital. Communities of practice are different from formal work groups or project teams in that they are defined by knowledge rather than task, and members are self-selecting rather than assigned by a higher authority (Allee, 2000). Interactions between the Learner and the Community of Practice are seen as involving peers outside of the organizational context. This offers learners the opportunity to leverage the insights of those who are dealing with similar challenges, but in different use cases. Exposure to ideas outside of the employee's organizational context may offer new perspectives and insights into how to approach internal problems.

Similar to small groups, communities of practice also enable a mix of 1:1 and 1:N engagements. Participants in a community of practice again may find themselves interacting in a multitude of ways given the multi-faceted nature of group interactions.

A Note on Other Roles Explored By Experts

Interestingly, experts did not perceive personalized learning as a strategy supported purely by technologies. A hypothesis of the researchers prior to the study was that experts would perceive personalized learning on a continuum with adaptive path or system-based personalization technologies as better suited for well-structured tasks. Conversely, ill-structured and wicked domains, such as learning leadership skills would be better suited for user-based or hybrid forms of personalized learning. The operating hypothesis was that the type of learning technology selected would be associated with the learning task. Expert responses, however, seemed to indicate that personalized learning was an approach that transcended task-based thinking, but rather was a strategy that could be leveraged on a curricular or programmatic level. Pre-programmed adaptive path systems, recommendation systems, and learning management systems were all rejected as technologies associated with personalizing learning. Rather, personalized learning entailed setting up systems of interactions to include a mix of social, technological, and technologically enabled interactions which theoretically facilitate a self-sustaining and ongoing ecosystem of resources and support.

The findings from this research suggest that experts perceive personalized learning as an overarching strategy to approach training programs. Experts described personalized learning as a larger instructional strategy. In this, experts suggest a personalized learning strategy is made up of a comprehensive ecosystem of resources for learners which may encompass a range of instructional approaches, activities, and interactions that are enabled by technology rather than driven by tools.

The PLiF presented here is a reflection of these expert opinions which iteratively evolved through the Delphi study. It represents a learner-centered framework for PL which does not necessarily require technology, however, is enhanced by leveraging the tools available in the market and given distributed workforces. An advantage of this approach is that despite any budgetary constraints, the PLiF can be integrated to support and enable a learner-centered training approach grounded in the principles of andragogy. We explore this alignment in the paragraphs below.

Alignment with Andragogy

Expert responses continually supported the role of the learner in driving and personalizing their learning experience. It follows that the findings from this research align well with the theories of andragogy, or the study of adult education. According to Knowles (1984), andragogy is founded on four principles. These include that:

1 Adults need to be involved in the planning and evaluation of their instruction.
2 Experience (including mistakes) provides the basis for learning activities.
3 Adults are most interested in learning subjects that have immediate relevance to their job or personal life.
4 Adult learning is problem-centered rather than content-oriented.

Based on this research, these principles of andragogy are well aligned with the PLiF.

Alignment of Knowles (1984) *Principles to Personalized Learning*

Knowles Principles	How PLiF Supports Principle
Principle 1: Adults need to be involved in the planning and evaluation of their instruction.	Learner selection of interaction and resources facilitates this principle within the framework. We will explore this more in Chapter 10.
Principle 2: Experience (including mistakes) provides the basis for learning activities.	PLiF supports the development of lifelong learning skills by offering a framework that can be leveraged throughout one's career.
Principle 3: Adults are most interested in learning subjects that have immediate relevance to their job or personal life.	Learner selection of interaction and resources facilitates this principle within the framework. PL encourages learning activities that are meaningful and relevant to learners, driven by their interests, and often self-initiated. PL incorporates the learner's voice and choice of how and what they learn. PL motivates learners by increasing the relevancy of their learning experience

(Continued)

Knowles Principles	How PLiF Supports Principle
Principle 4: Adult learning is problem-centered rather than content-oriented.	The PLiF supports learning beyond learning to content interactions, providing support to the learner in a multitude of ways as they seek to solve a problem. It also provides project-based, authentic learning activities.

As can be seen from this alignment, according to this research, experts perceive personalized learning as a strategy that addresses all of the principles of andragogy. The alignment of adult learning principles to personalized learning is a powerful way to engage learners by encouraging ownership and self-sustaining interactions that maintain the learning and development process.

The principles of andragogy also advocate that the learner should be involved in the process of defining expectations, determining how they will be assessed and evaluated, formulating their learning plan, and challenged to tackle projects and topics that are relevant to their personal life. The learner agency or ownership described in andragogy is interesting in light of the potential tensions which may arise in industry or higher education. It is clear that the struggle between efficiency, return on investment, behavior tracking, and the learner's agency may also be a tension inherent in training programs.

An Example Application

In Figure 3.2, one can see an example of the PLiF in action. Here the learner has identified public speaking or presentation skills as their area of focus. To begin, the learner conducted a self-assessment of their current skills to identify skills, gaps, and learning goals associated with public speaking. Then, following the PLiF framework, the learner selects resources and support from the corresponding interactions. We explore these in the following table (Table 3.1).

Ultimately, experts support that personalized learning strategies should encourage individual ownership over the learning process. The PLiF supports learners in aligning the dimensions of personalized learning to their ultimate learning goal or task. The guidelines presented here will support a multi-faceted self-sustaining framework for personalized learning that enhances the effectiveness and design of Higher Education and Workforce Training and Development Programs. It is anticipated that the success of the proposed

56 Using the PL Interaction Framework (PLiF)

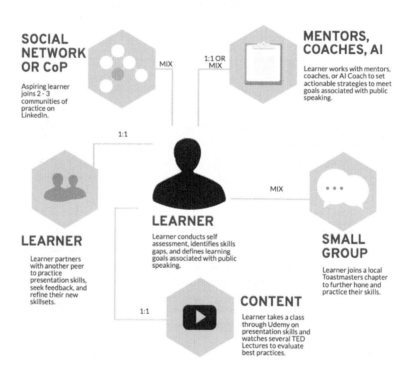

Figure 3.2 Application of PLIF for Presentation Skills.

Table 3.1 Example of Developing Public Speaking Skills Using the PLiF

Interaction	Learner Practice
Learner to Content	Learner takes a class through Udemy on presentation skills and watches TED lectures to evaluate best practices.
Learner to Learner	Learner partners with another learner to practice presentation skills, seek feedback, and refine skill sets.
Learner to Mentor, Coach, or AI Assistant	Learner works with mentors, coaches, or AI Assistant to set actionable strategies to meet goals associated with public speaking.
Learner to Small Group	Learner joins a local Toastmasters chapter to further hone and practice their skills.
Learner to Social Network or Community of Practice	The aspiring learner joins 2–3 communities of practice on LinkedIn.

personalized learning strategy will be reflected in decreased attrition rates, increased engagement in learning and development programs, and increased confidence for the individual learner.

This research suggests that enabling learner agency in training and development programs by encouraging learners to engage in the five learning interactions of the PLiF will translate to positive business outcomes by increasing productivity, meeting employee expectations, and supporting companies as they weather the ebbs and flows of an ever-changing operational context. We continue by exploring how the thoughtful design of each of these interactions in forming a personalized learning culture will enhance the development of personalized learning interventions to empower individuals and organizations to reskill, retool, and adapt to the demands and pace of the modern age. We will also provide use cases and pragmatic tools to exemplify how to implement this framework in your organization.

References

Allee, V. (2000). Knowledge networks and communities of practice. *OD Practitioner*, *32*(4). http://www.odnetwork.org/odponline/vol32n4/knowledgenets.html

Best, B., & Conceição, S. C. (2017). Transactional distance dialogic interactions and student satisfaction in a multi-institutional blended learning environment. *European Journal of Open Distance and E-Learning*, *20*(1), 138–152.

Betts, B. (2018). Demystifying personalized learning [Massively Open Online Course]. Retrieved from https://beta.curatr3.com/courses/demystifying-personalised-learning

Bolger, F., & Wright, G. (2011). Improving the Delphi process: Lessons from social psychological research. *Technological Forecasting & Social Change, 78*, 1500–1513. 10.1016/j.techfore.2011.07.007

Brady, S. R. (2015). Utilizing and adapting the Delphi Method for use in qualitative research. *International Journal of Qualitative Research Methods, 14*(5). 10.1177/1609406915621381

Batty, C., & Sinclair, J. (2014). Peer-to-peer learning in the higher degree by research context: A creative writing case study. *New Writing, 11*(3), 335–346. 10.1080/14790726.2014.932814

Dabbagh, D., & Bannan-Ritland, B. (2005). *Online learning: Concepts, strategies, and applications.* Pearson Education.

Dron, J., Seidel, C., & Litten, G. (2004). Transactional distance in a blended learning environment. *Research in Learning Technology, 12*(2), 163–174. 10.1080/0968776042000216219

Fake, H. (2018). *Personalized learning within online workforce environments.* Fairfax, Virginia, United States: Manuscript in preparation, College of Education and Human Development, George Mason University.

Fake, H., Dabbagh, N., & Zhang, Z. (2019). Student perspectives of technology use for learning in higher education. *RIED. Revista Iberoamericana de Educación a Distancia, 22*(1), 127–152.

Fake, H., & Dabbagh, N. (2020). Personalized learning within online workforce learning environments: Exploring implementations, obstacles, opportunities, and perspectives of workforce leaders. *Technology, Knowledge, and Learning, 25*(1), 789–809. DOI: 10.1007/s10758-020-09441-x

Franc, J.M. (2016, October 24). *Delphi technique: The do nots and why nots* [video file]. Retrieved from https://www.youtube.com/watch?v = GN6B8hgjQcw

Hsu. C.-C., & Sandford, B. A. (2007). Minimizing non-response in the Delphi process: How to respond to non-response. *Practical Assessment, Research, & Evaluation, 12*(17). https://pareonline.net/getvn.asp?v = 12&n = 17

Iqbal, S., & Pipon-Young, L. (2009). The Delphi method. *The Psychologist…, 22*, 598–601. Retrieved from https://thepsychologist.bps.org.uk/volume-22/edition-7/delphi-method

Keeney, S., Hasson, F., & McKenna, H. (2011). Consulting the oracle: Ten lessons from using the Delphi in nursing research. *Journal of Advanced Nursing, 53*(2), 205–212. 10.1111/j.1365-2648.2006.03716.x

Knowles, M. (1984). *The adult learner: A neglected species* (3rd ed.). Houston, TX: Gulf Publishing.

Linstone, H.A., & Turoff, M. (2002). Introduction. In H.A. Linstone and M. Turoff (Eds.), *The Delphi method: Techniques and applications* (pp. 3–12). Boston, MA: Addison-Wesley Publication Company.

Ma, N., Xing, S. X., & Du, J. Y. (2018). A peer coaching-based professional development approach to improving the learning participation and learning design skills of in-service teachers. *Educational Technology & Society, 21*(2), 291–304.

McIntyre-Hite, L. (2016). A Delphi study of effective practices for developing competency-based learning models in higher education. *The Journal of Competency-Based Education, 1*(4), 157–166. 10.1002/cbe2.1029

Mitroff, I. I., & Turoff, M. (2002). Philosophical and methodological foundations of Delphi. In H.A. Linstone and M. Turoff (Eds.), *The Delphi method: Techniques and applications* (pp. 35–67). Boston, MA: Addison-Wesley Publication Company.

Moore, M. G. (1989). Three types of interaction. *American Journal of Distance Education, 3*(2), 1–7. 10.1080/08923648909526659

Murray, M., Perez, J., Geist, D., & Hedrick, A. (2013). Student interaction with content in online and hybrid courses: Leading horses to the proverbial water. *Informing Science: The International Journal of an Emerging Transdiscipline, 16*, 99–115. 10.28945/1779

Parente, R., & Anderson-Parente, J. (2011). A case study of long-term Delphi accuracy. *Technological Forecasting & Social Change, 78*, 1705–1711. 10.1016/j.techfore.2011.07.005

Turoff, M. (2002). The design of a policy Delphi. *Technological Forecasting and Social Change, 2*(2), 149–171. 10.1016/0040-1625(70)90161-7

Vygotsky, L. (1978). Interaction between learning and development. In Guavain & Cole (Eds.) *Readings on the development of children* (pp. 34–40). New York, NY: Scientific American Books.

Wenger, E.C., & Snyder, W.M. (2000). Communities of practice: The organizational frontier. *Harvard Business Review, 78*(1), 139–146.

Zolingen, S. J., & Klaasen, C. A. (2003). Selection processes in a Delphi study about key qualifications in Senior Secondary Vocational Education. *Technological Forecasting and Social Change, 70*, 317–340. 10.1016/S0040-1625(02)00202-0

Designing for Learner–Content Interaction

4

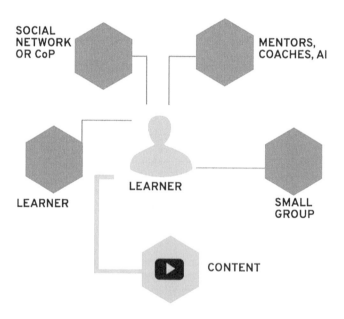

Figure 4.0 Learner-content interaction.

When designing for learner content interaction, one must take into consideration the multimedia modality of the content (e.g., text, video, audio), the communication or technology medium used to deliver the content (e.g., web-based, text messaging, email, social media), the instructional delivery modality of the content (e.g., synchronous, asynchronous,

DOI: 10.4324/9781003121008-4

blended, or bichronous), and the types of learning activities that will engage learners with the content (e.g., online discussions, writing a blog or a paper, creating a presentation, solving a problem). It is typical to have so many variables to consider when using technology to design learner-content interactions and it is also important that instructional designers be intentional with how they design these interactions (Fake, 2018; Hodges et al., 2020). So again, the variables under consideration for this dimension of the Personalized Learning Interaction Framework (PLIF) are:

- Multimedia modality of content
- ICT (Information Communication and Technology) medium
- Instructional delivery modality (also known as communication synchrony)
- Types of learning activities or tasks

We discuss each of these variables in this chapter and end with a case study example.

Multimedia Modality of Content

Multimedia learning is defined by Mayer (2001) as a form of computer-aided instruction that uses two modalities for delivering content concurrently such as visual learning (pictures, written text, animations, and videos) and verbal learning (spoken narration) (Swerdloff, 2016). In 2001, researcher Richard Mayer introduced the twelve principles of multimedia design in his book *Multimedia Learning*, where he discussed the best practices for using multimedia in eLearning products (Mayer, 2001). In 2011, Clark and Mayer discussed two specific relationships between multimedia and the learner's experience with either static graphics (i.e., photos or illustrations) or dynamic graphics (i.e., video or animations). More specifically, this multimedia principle attempts to answer the following questions: do graphics help learners learn more deeply than just words alone, and if they do, how can instructional designers best leverage graphics in developing eLearning?

To begin, we should define the major components of most eLearning products. Regardless of industry, most eLearning products consist of words in printed or spoken form and graphics in static (i.e., illustration, photo, charts, graphs, etc.) and dynamic (i.e., animation, video, etc.) forms. eLearning formats can be considered asynchronous web-based courses using Authoring software (i.e., Articulate Storyline, Adobe Captivate, or Lectora, etc.)

or web 2.0 authoring (i.e., Articulate Rise), or online synchronous/asynchronous courses using a Learning Management System (LMS) such as courses developed in Blackboard, Canvas, or Moodle. In addition, instructional videos, casual and serious games for learning, and personalized learning products that include a combination of learner-learner and learner-content interaction are popular formats of learning that are dominating the eLearning field as of late. However, it is important to keep in mind that in any eLearning format, words and graphics continue to serve as the primary delivery component, so it is imperative for us to spend a little time discussing some best practices in graphic use for eLearning products before diving into the discussion on content interaction for personalized learning.

Mayer's Multimedia Design Principle: Include Both Words and Graphics

People learn best when they are learning actively. Active learning is defined as "a method of learning in which students are actively or experientially involved in the learning process where there are different levels of active learning, depending on student involvement" (Bonwell & Eison, 1991). In a virtual or eLearning environment, learners need to engage in relevant cognitive processing through activities within the course or training module, mentally organize material in their minds into coherent cognitive representation, and integrate the new knowledge obtained from the material presented in their minds with their existing knowledge (Clark & Mayer, 2011). To help learners participate in an active learning process, instructional designers must ensure their designs within the eLearning environment guide and assist learners. One way to do so is through the use of graphics in addition to textual information. Here are some recommendations that were originally offered by Clark & Mayer (2011):

1 **Select graphics that support learning**: Use graphics with specific functions whenever possible. Functions of graphics may include:
   a Decorative graphics – for decoration only and should be minimized. If you are using decorative graphics, try using graphics that relate to the textual content to avoid any cognitive disconnect.
   b Representational graphics – graphics that portray a single element. This type of graphic is best used to demonstrate one physical item.
   c Relational graphics – graphics that show quantitative relationships, such as bar graphs or line graphs. This type of graphic is best used when discussing statistics.

- d Organizational graphics – graphics that show the relationship among elements. This type of graphic is best used when discussing processes and procedures.
- e Transformational graphics – graphics that show the change in an object over time. This might seem similar to organizational graphics, but this type of graphic should be used when you are demonstrating how certain things change over time, so this is best used when giving step-by-step instructions.
- f Interpretive graphics – graphics that demonstrate invisible relationships. This type of graphic should be used to show elements or situations that cannot be seen by the naked eye, such as the direction of the air.

2 **Use graphics to teach content types** – Clark and Mayer (2011) identified five different kinds of content (described below), and graphics can be used to enhance the teaching of each kind of content:
- a Facts – isolated information. Use representational (i.e., screenshots) and organizational (i.e., company org charts) graphics.
- b Concepts – categories of objects, events, or symbols represented by a single name. Use representational (i.e., pictures of mammals), organizational (i.e., how mammals are organized), or interpretive (i.e., cats and tigers with arrows between them to show relationship) graphics.
- c Process – description of how things work. Use transformational (i.e., images showing the different stages of water when boiling it), interpretive (i.e., process graphics), or relational (i.e., Venn diagrams) graphics.
- d Procedure – a series of task-related steps. Use transformational graphics (i.e., step-by-step screenshots of a software).
- e Principle – cause-and-effect relationship or the guidelines behind a task. Use interpretive (i.e., animation demonstrating the result of combining two chemicals) or transformational (i.e., instructional videos of a mathematical concept) graphics.

3 **Use graphics as topic organizers** – If you are designing your own learning environment using course authoring software such as Articulate Storyline or Adobe Captivate, you may wish to use graphics as your topic organizers to show the progress and relationships of each topic. In a web 2.0 course development environment such as Adobe Rise, you may be somewhat limited to using graphics as an overall course organizer, but you may still use it with smaller concepts through the creative use of various image tools.

4   **Use graphics to show relationships** – When discussing relationships and processes, it is often challenging for learners to comprehend through text descriptions alone. A recommendation would be to start the process explanation with a graphic to show the relationships and procedures, followed by a textual description so learners can actively connect the concepts cognitively.
5   **Use graphics as lesson interfaces** – You may also use a large image as an overview of the concepts discussed with interactive points as subtopics (i.e., using an image map) to give learners the freedom to discover knowledge themselves. Whether the concepts are more organizational (i.e., an org chart of a company) or a closer look at a concept (i.e., an open image of a single cell with different parts of a cell highlighted), graphic use can help learners connect the concepts together to allow learners to create their own cognitive connections.
6   Examples of these principles are shown in Figures 4.1 and 4.2.

As described earlier, learning is a process in which the learner is actively making sense of the information presented to them cognitively, and teaching or instruction is the process through which a series of appropriate activities are used to guide the learners in making such cognitive connections. One of the important parts of active processing of the content is for the learner to mentally construct representations of the material, whether the representation is pictorial or textual, and connect new information with their existing knowledge. Through the use of both text and graphic elements, instructional designers can assist learners in achieving this goal.

Another important consideration is the level of experience of the learners. According to Mayer and Gallini (1990), novice learners who have low knowledge of the domain require more assistance learning with graphics than experts who have high knowledge in the domain, and learn well with or without graphics since they can form mental images from their prior knowledge. However, some studies, such as ones led by Kalyuga et al. (Kalyuga, 2005; Kalyuga, Ayres, Chandler & Sweller, 2003), warned of the expertise reversal effect, where instructional support aimed at novices may not help or could even hurt experts. This is an important consideration when you are in the analysis phase of the instructional design process, working with subject-matter experts, where you need to spend time discussing the level of expertise of your target audience to make multimedia design decisions. Keep in mind that if you are creating training that applies to an enterprise audience (i.e., mandatory training that is aimed at the entire organization), you may need to apply additional strategies to cater to experts while keeping the learning content targeting novices to ensure training is delivered effectively.

Designing for Learner–Content Interaction 65

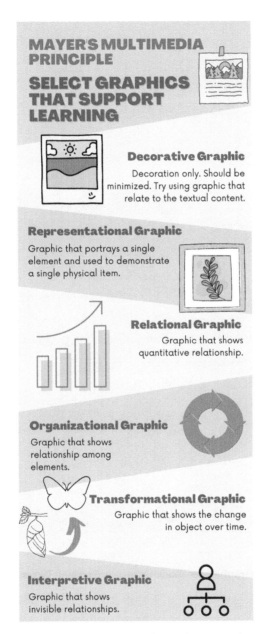

Figure 4.1 Mayer's Multimedia Principle: Select Graphics that Support Learning.

66 Designing for Learner–Content Interaction

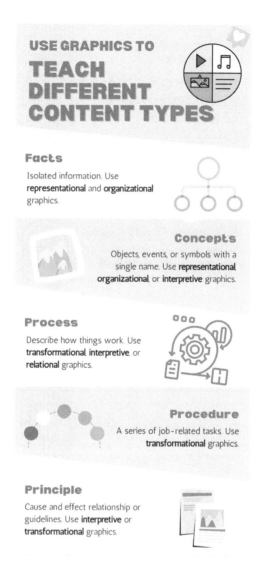

Figure 4.2 Use Graphics to Teach Different Content Types.

Special Consideration for Videos/Animations

With the relative ease of creating videos and animations currently, compared to the past, there is a growing demand for using videos and animations for visual learning. However, there are some reservations from researchers that you may wish to consider. The first is that videos and animations, sometimes termed "active medium", may foster passive learning behavior in learners since they do not need to form mental images as all information is presented to them. Another is that animations may cause cognitive overload with sensory distractions such as music, flashing graphics, or images that are too rich in detail. While the active medium has its place, it should be used as supportive material to text and graphics, or "passive medium", since texts and graphics allow learners to create images and animations cognitively using the new information with the learner's existing knowledge. So when should videos or animations be used rather than texts and images?

One recommendation is when the instructional objective requires performing motor or complicated manual skills, which asks the learners to do what the instruction is telling them without any conceptual knowledge. An example of using videos rather than texts and images would be the active shooter training that is now mandated in many state and governmental agencies. As the learners are required to act in a high-stressed situation, learners should react instinctively which is considered low in cognitive processing. Therefore, the instructions should be clear, succinct, and demonstrative when using videos so that learners can act and react accordingly. In other words, the passive medium (text and graphics) may be most effective for understanding concepts and processes, while the active medium (videos and animations) may be more effective for hands-on procedures or actions (Clark & Mayer, 2011).

Technologies for Content Delivery

When designing learner-content interactions, considering the type of technology used to deliver the content to the learner is critical. In other words, how (through what medium) the content is communicated to the learner is paramount. And why is that? Because technology is not just a delivery tool or medium, rather, different technologies have different potentials or educational benefits. Therefore understanding the "affordances" (action potentials) of technology will help us make discerning decisions about which tools are the most appropriate for a given learning context (Bower, 2017). As Marshall McLuhan, a Canadian philosopher whose work is among the cornerstones of the study of media theory purports: *the medium is the message*. In other words, one cannot separate the medium from the message because the medium impacts or shapes the message. McLuhan went further to say that communication technology is the primary cause of social change underscoring the power technology has in shaping our sociocultural interactions. Gibson (1979) proposed that objects (e.g., technologies) have certain affordances (capabilities) that lead organisms (e.g., people) to act based on their perceptions of these affordances. The theory of affordances and McLuhan's Media Theory have direct implications on how we understand the potential of learning technologies and the impact technology has on the delivery of instructional content and the design of learner-content interactions (Dabbagh, 2004; Dabbagh & Reo, 2011).

For example, the new activities that grew out of Web 2.0 technologies (e.g., blogging, wikis, creating and posting videos) moved web-based learning towards a more learner-centered approach. Why? First, Web 2.0 technologies made it possible for learners to engage in high levels of dialogue, interaction, collaboration, and social negotiation through the use of social networks and provided learners with the ability to generate and share knowledge across learning networks. Second, Web 2.0 technologies deflected control of learning away from a single instructor or expert by distributing learning among all participants in the learning community, promoting agency in the learning process and an appreciation of diversity, multiple perspectives, and epistemic issues. And third, Web 2.0 technologies enabled learners to personalize their learning environment by selecting the technologies they wish to use (e.g., on mobile devices), accessing and organizing information sources, customizing the user interface of technology, and building personalized learning and professional networks (Dabbagh & Fake, 2017). These reasons are a testimony to McLuhan and Gibson's principle that technology has the potential to shape our teaching and learning practices. Rather than treating media as a delivery vehicle or a transmissive educational technology (Jonassen, 2002), media should be considered as a key component in the overall design process.

In order to better understand the affordances of learning technologies and the role they play in the delivery of instructional content, we provide a classification (Figure 4.3) that separates the affordances of different classes or types of technology based on their instructional potential (Dabbagh et al., 2019).

Figure 4.3 shows 6 classes of learning technologies as follows:

1   Technologies for Content Creation and Delivery
2   Technologies for Collaboration and Communication
3   Technologies for Information Search and Resource Management
4   Technologies for Knowledge Representation
5   Technologies for Assessment and Analytics
6   Technologies for Immersive Learning

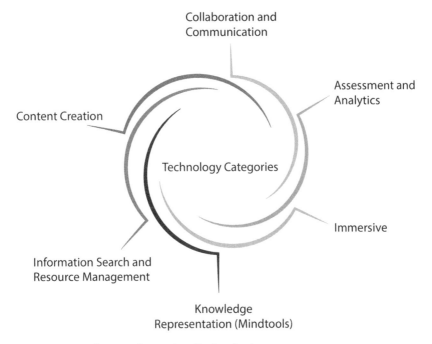

Figure 4.3 6 Classes of Learning Technologies.

Below we discuss the classes of technologies that are most relevant to designing learner-content interaction and focus on the primary affordances of these technologies. We also provide examples of use.

Technologies for Content Creation and Delivery

Content creation technologies are primarily used by instructional designers or instructors to create and manage digital content but they can also be used by learners to contribute content such as assignments, journals, and resources. Examples of content creation technologies include tools embedded in Learning Management Systems (LMS) such as course templates for setting up the course syllabus and content modules; a repository for content sharing, tagging, and reuse (e.g., a digital portfolio, wiki spaces); and instructional design tools for creating flexible learning sequences and designs (e.g., Articulate Storyline, Articulate Rise) among others. Figure 4.4 below provides a snapshot of these technologies.

When used by learners, content creation and delivery tools can serve as powerful learning strategies. They enable learners to demonstrate their

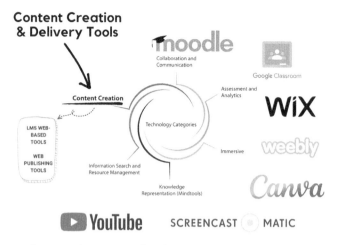

Figure 4.4 Content Creation and Delivery Tools.

understanding of discipline-specific principles by developing content that synthesizes their knowledge and engages them in complex individual and collaborative projects that include interactive multimedia elements such as audio and video. For example, learners can use Web 2.0 publishing tools and media-sharing tools that support the creation and sharing of learning content in a variety of formats such as podcasts and vodcasts.

When used by instructors or instructional designers, content creation and delivery tools have particular significance for designing learner-content interactions:

- Content creation and delivery tools have features or affordances that enable content organization, clarity, and completeness. For example, content creation and delivery tools have features that support the grouping of content into pages or modules.
- Content creation and delivery tools support version control for both instructors and students so that users can review the presentation and organization of content to improve its delivery.
- Content creation and delivery tools have features that support providing feedback to learners.
- Content creation and delivery tools have intuitive navigation controls and a clear dashboard interface.

Although LMSs – e.g., Canvas, Moodle, and Blackboard – are perhaps most frequently used to create and deliver digital content in higher education and workplace learning contexts, content can also be created and delivered via web publishing tools and resource-sharing tools. Table 4.1 shows examples of

Designing for Learner–Content Interaction 71

Table 4.1 Content Creation Tools

LMS-Based Tools	Web Publishing and Resource-Sharing Tools
Course module creation and display	HTML editors
Course documents to display	Website creation engines/content management systems (e.g., Weebly, Wix, WordPress)
Announcements	Social bookmarking tools (e.g., Pearltrees, Diigo, Delicious)
Assignment creation and management	Cloud-based document sharing (e.g., Google Drive)
Shared content areas where students as well as designers and instructors may upload content (e.g., course wikis or digital dropbox)	Audio and video creation and editing tools (e.g., ScreenFlow, Camtasia)
Course navigation tools (e.g., menu structures)	Video and photo sharing (e.g., YouTube, Vimeo, Flickr)
Mashups that allow insertion of web-based materials (e.g., videos) external to the LMS to be presented	e-Learning content creation tools (e.g., Captivate, Articulate Storyline, Articulate Rise)

content creation tools categorized as either LMS-based or web publishing and resources sharing tools.

While Table 4.1 presents LMS and web publishing tools separately as they do represent two distinct types of tools but are not necessarily exclusive of one another. LMS developers have recognized that the direct integration of web-based content into LMS-created content is important for keeping content current and for making navigation easier for the end user. Figure 4.5

Figure 4.5 Example of Embedded Video in Canvas Course Site.

shows an example of how the LMS Canvas allows designers to include direct access (with a thumbnail image) to a relevant video.

Technologies for Immersive Learning

Another class of technologies that facilitates learner-content interaction is immersive technologies (see Figure 4.6). Immersive technologies refer to technologies used to create a digital environment that allows participants to be totally "immersed" in the context that the environment represents. Immersive technologies create virtual experiences or digital spaces that strive to look and feel like a real-world setting, allowing participants to be "in" or "immersed in" the experience to the extent possible (Pagano, 2013). Figure 4.6 below shows examples of immersive learning tools.

Immersive learning environments can be created as either a "classic" immersive reality where the participant may wear goggles or a headset, and interact with the environment using a joystick or other input device or controller. The other type of immersive learning is created using flat-screen technologies. Participants "watch" the flat screen device (e.g., computer, handheld, television) and interact with the environment via a keyboard, joystick, mouse, or other input devices. Either type of immersive environment may allow the participant to create an avatar to represent themselves.

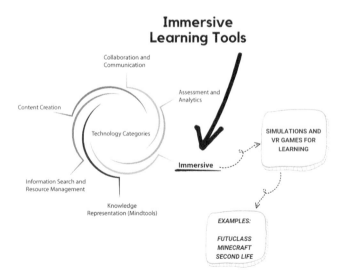

Figure 4.6 Immersive Learning Tools.

Designing for Learner–Content Interaction   73

Simulations, educational games, virtual (3D) reality (VR), augmented reality (AR), and mixed reality (XR) environments are all examples of immersive learning environments created using immersive technologies. The immersive environment would include a 3-dimensional visual experience, audio, and potentially olfactory stimuli.

As an example, Second Life by Linden Lab, one of the most popular virtual world environments launched in 2003, continues to be one of the most utilized 3D learning environments among educators (Reisoğlu et al., 2017). This open-ended 3D environment allows educators to build learning environments and house different resources, such as images, videos, and interactive assets to simulate real-life experiences. Players create avatars within the Second Life environment and can interact with other players or the non-playable characters (NPCs) using text or audio. Educators have used Second Life to encourage students to practice second language acquisition skills through authentic interactions with native speakers or go on virtual field trips to different museums in the world (see Figure 4.7).

The number of these immersive learning environments has grown greatly over the past decade as immersive technologies have become numerous, easier to use, and predominantly cloud-based, hence not requiring anything more than a standard keyboard. This means that immersive technologies are

The Museum of Computing History in Dalton, across from the historic Linden Village, is a creative and educational space to learn about the history of computing. They currently have a number of exhibits including Pre-PC Early Computers, Computers and Telecommunications, and Personal Computing.

Figure 4.7 The Museum of Computing History in Dalton, Created in Second Life.

appropriate for designing learning experiences that facilitate multiple types of learner-content interaction. Immersive technologies offer a way to provide "virtual practice" and to interact in meaningful ways with the content and help develop different aspects of a problem or skill set. As DeAngelis (2012) suggests, the "virtual practice" of skills can be as effective, or even more effective, than real-life practice. Hence, immersive technologies are most suited for developing learning experiences that focus on demonstrating performance and skills.

Here are the *affordances* of immersive learning technologies that make them both attractive and effective for designing learner-content interaction:

- Immersive learning technologies can be used to design learner-content interactions that target the most common or the most difficult situations that learners encounter on the job. This may be impossible using real-world settings for training due to safety, ethical, or resource concerns (e.g., think about virtual surgical training versus training on limited availability cadavers or patients).
- Immersive learning technologies allow for learning-by-doing experiences, as opposed to learners being passive recipients of knowledge transmission-type learning. Put another way, immersive learning technologies enable the design of learning activities that center on learners actually performing the skills, or solving a problem, rather than simply learning "about" a skill, or "about" problem-solving.
- Immersive learning technologies can be used to create content at varying levels of authenticity so as to focus learner attention on the characteristics that are most important to a learning domain. For example, just as a well-done line drawing of a human heart can focus attention on the primary parts of the heart (e.g., aorta, left and right ventricle, etc.), an immersive environment for developing surgical skills can create animated digital images that, in the early stages of learning, might simplify the surgical field a bit to focus learners attention on – for instance – identifying the location for the first incision, and then identifying how to find the heart within the chest cavity.
- Immersive learning technologies can be used to provide learners with immediate feedback. For instance, a virtual frog dissection environment can immediately communicate to the learner if they have created the incision in the correct location or not. And of course, said participant can simply "reset" their frog and try again!

Simulations and Virtual Reality as Immersive Learning Environments

Simulations are a type of immersive environment that create imitations of some real thing, state of affairs, or processes. Simulations imitate phenomena by allowing learners to manipulate key characteristics or variables within a physical or abstract system. Clearly, the computational capabilities of computers make these possible. The simulation designer builds a model of the phenomena or processes that enable learners to see how the system works. By changing variables, learners make predictions about the behavior of the system.

Simulations are used in a broad range of teaching and training operations. They vary tremendously in detail and complexity. For instance, flight simulators that include a physical 3-D mock-up of a cockpit and controls are an important part of pilot and astronaut training. These simulators can present complex and dramatic situations that the pilots must deal with. Simulators that create 2D and even 3D representations are now available to learners and educators via 3D VR goggles that provide a visual 3D experience to the wearer, or simply via the powerful graphics available in commonly available 2D displays.

There are hundreds of commercially available educational simulations. Many exist for medical and nursing applications where practice and the possibility of mistakes in a real setting are unacceptable or costly (either in terms of life and death or simply the monetary cost of expensive equipment, such as an airplane). As mentioned before, one of the advantages of these types of environments is that tasks where a mistake may be critical, such as medical procedures, or learning to fly an airplane through emergencies – can be done virtually without the risk of causing harm.

Games as Immersive Learning Environments

A game is another example of another type of immersive technology-based learning environment. Just as in a simulation, an immersive game puts the player into a digitally created world where the player may interact with the elements of the world (which may include other players). In a game, however, the interactions are designed to accomplish the goals or objectives of the game, with the ultimate goal of achieving a winning state. The popularity of gaming – referring to the playing of digital games that may be cloud-based or hosted on a personal computer, game console, or mobile device – has grown tremendously in the last decade and those who regularly play digital games span many generations. A recent survey conducted by the Pew Research Center in 2017 found that 43% of adults in the United States often or sometimes play video games on a computer, TV, game console, or mobile device (Perrin, 2018). Further, the gender split is nearly even with 50% of men compared to 48% of women reporting ever having played a digital game (Duggan, 2015).

The use of games for learning has also become significant. Research indicates that Game-Based Learning (GBL) supports statistically significant improvements in problem-solving (Akcaoglu & Koehler, 2014), feelings of self-efficacy (Ke, 2014), and higher levels of motivation, critical thinking, achievement, and engagement (Robertson & Howells, 2008; Yang & Chang, 2013). Additionally, data from a 2018 poll shows that nearly 80% of teachers use games and other digital resources for teaching (Games & Learning, 2019). Game usage is not limited to school settings either, as more than 100 Fortune 500 companies are using games for some sort of training activities. The core reasons that games are attractive as learning tools build upon the reasons for using immersive environments and include the following:

- Games can be engaging and intrinsically motivating.
- Games can increase learner engagement.
- Games offer a format that is familiar to many learners.
- Games can engage players in higher-order cognitive learning outcomes such as problem-solving, analysis, and decision-making.
- Games can also help develop "soft" skills such as teamwork, planning, and communication.

Countless "educational" games are being developed for necessary but lower-level learning outcomes, such as recall/recognition or application skills (e.g., Duolingo, for developing new language skills through various recall games). However, games can also be designed to support more complex learning. We will provide examples of such games in the last section of this chapter.

Instructional Delivery Modality

Another variable that impacts the design of learner-content interaction is the modality or synchrony of the instructional delivery which can be described as synchronous, asynchronous, or bichronous (blended). Synchronous instructional delivery requires all learners (and the instructor) to be present online at the same time in a scheduled timeframe. Methods or strategies that support synchronous communication include instant messaging, live chats, video conferencing, and live broadcasting. Zoom, Microsoft teams, and Skype are among the technologies that can be used to facilitate synchronous delivery of instructional content. Figure 4.8 below shows a snapshot of the methods, strategies, and technologies used to design learner-content interactions for synchronous instructional delivery.

The primary educational benefit of this modality is the ability to engage learners in live discussions and real-time interactions with the content. Also, synchronous learning is more impactful in the immediate sense due to the high social presence and sense of community it can foster. However, there are also some disadvantages to synchronous learning such as not having access to high-speed internet and challenges of keeping learners engaged for the entire duration of the synchronous session.

Asynchronous instructional delivery is when the learners and the teacher or instructor do not meet online at the same time, rather, the learner interacts with the content and completes the learning tasks at their own pace and time, or following a specific timeframe. Asynchronous methods or tools used to design learner-content interactions using this modality include audio/video recorded lectures, discussion forums, interactive video lessons, and collaborative wiki spaces where learners can work on projects as teams, games, and simulations among others. Several technologies can be used to support the asynchronous learning format, including LMSs such as Moodle or Canvas as well as the web publishing tools described earlier in this chapter.

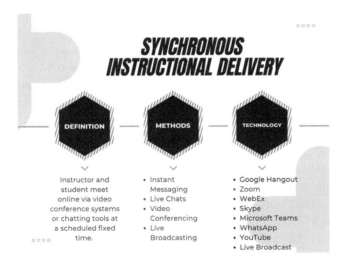

Figure 4.8 Synchronous Instructional Delivery.

Figure 4.9 Asynchronous Instructional Delivery.

Figure 4.9 shows a snapshot of the methods, strategies, and technologies used to design learner-to-content interactions for asynchronous instructional delivery.

Asynchronous learning offers more flexibility, focus (as measured by time on task), more opportunities to reflect on one's learning, and is more self-directed and self-paced. On the other hand, bichronous learning or bichronous instructional delivery is defined as the blending of both asynchronous and synchronous online learning. In this approach, students can participate in anytime, anywhere learning during the asynchronous parts of the course or the training, but can also participate in real-time synchronous activities that support immediacy, community, and real-time audiovisual communication. Martin, Polly, and Ritzhaupt (2020) contend that the blend of synchronous and asynchronous online learning potentially reduces some of the challenges of all synchronous or all asynchronous learning environments and maximizes the benefits of both of these instructional delivery modalities. Figure 4.10 shows a snapshot of the methods, strategies, and technologies used to design learner-to-content interactions for bichronous instructional delivery.

Additionally, traditional instructor-led training formats and materials can limit access to educational opportunities. Approaches to teaching and learning that require students or learners to be in a specific place, at a specific time, and for a fixed duration, necessarily bound opportunities for interaction. Those

Designing for Learner–Content Interaction

Figure 4.10 Bichronous Instructional Delivery.

boundaries can limit the ways in which learners work with both instructors and peers to solve problems, seek help, or engage deeply with content in and out of the physical classroom. Similarly, familiar educational resources, such as textbooks and readings, limit how content can be presented to learners and how they can process that content. Therefore, it is highly recommended that institutions of higher education and workplace learning organizations leverage technology to help learners learn more productively by varying, blending, or accelerating instructional delivery formats. Packaging course content this way helps to minimize cost, maximize accessibility, and accommodate different learning preferences (Dabbagh et al., 2019).

Specifically, administrators can encourage instructors and instructional designers to use technology to create blended or flipped courses, in which some lecture material and other course content are delivered in a synchronous, asynchronous, or bichronous format. These formats or instructional delivery modalities may preserve more in-person class time for hands-on and other experiential activities, group assignments, and individualized instruction, rather than for lectures. Such formats can also be used to accelerate instruction by allowing learners to go at their own pace. This, in turn, may accelerate their completion of a course of study or professional development training.

Technology can also be used to package content in multiple ways that help learners access and study course or training materials. This is especially true when the interface is interactive, flexible, and offers multiple ways and times for learners to access the content. Learners' understanding of course or training content can be deepened by providing them with digital representations of that content that help them visualize complex processes. Course interfaces can also include digital review and study tools, such as podcasts, that provide multiple ways for learners to access and study course material (Mayer, 2001).

Learning Activities

Traditionally, an instructional designer follows a linear process to design instruction beginning with some given set of criteria such as the lesson's purpose and subject matter, the learners' general characteristics, and likely some logistical constraints. From these, designers extrapolate the type (e.g., psychomotor, cognitive, affective) and level of learning outcomes (e.g., remembering and understanding, applying and understanding), objectives of the associated assessments (e.g., formative, summative), and other delivery factors (e.g., course schedule, perhaps). They break the goals into objectives, the objectives into tasks, and then select some set of instructional strategies to help learners achieve the learning outcomes. They continue working in this linear fashion—breaking down the plans into smaller and smaller parts, and carefully considering the content, delivery, and learner activities for each. This is known as "backwards design" (Bannan, Dabbagh, & Walcutt, 2019). See Figure 4.11.

Instructional strategies are what instructors, instructional designers, or instructional systems do to facilitate student learning (Dabbagh et al., 2019). They are described as "the plans and techniques that the instructor or instructional designer uses to engage the learner and facilitate learning" (Jonassen, Grabinger, & Harris, 1991, p. 34).

For example, if the instructional strategy is lecture, learning activities would include active listening, taking notes, asking questions, reviewing the lecture after class, and using one's understanding of the lecture content to complete an assignment or take a test. Alternatively, if the instructional strategy is problem-solving, associated learning activities would include generating and testing a

Figure 4.11 Backwards Design Process.

hypothesis, identifying learning needs to better understand the problem at hand, and determining an action plan to seek appropriate information and resources that would help formulate a solution to the problem. Learning activities are the fourth variable that impacts the design of learner-content interaction. We discuss learning activities in this last section of the chapter and provide examples of how technology can be used to support the design of learning activities that engage learners with the content.

Let's discuss learning activities that engage learners with the content at low and high levels of Bloom's taxonomy. Specifically, the instructional strategy of providing practice to facilitate recall, long-term retention, and skill building, which aligns with the lower levels of Bloom's taxonomy (recall, understanding, and application) can be implemented through the use of casual games. Casual games are a learning technology that support the design of structured activities with simple rules and goals (Gee, 2007). Examples of casual games include puzzles, word games, hidden object games, and strategy games. Casual games are an appropriate digital technology for providing practice. Research shows that casual games allow players to achieve mastery through repeated trial and error attempts (Gee, 2007), try new skills without fear of failure (Gredler, 1996), and support the development of key learning skills such as cognitive processing, logical thinking, and independent decision making (Prensky, 2001). Casual games can be played on a computer, in a browser, or on a smartphone as mobile apps.

Lumosity is an example of a casual game designed to improve brain health and performance through rehearsal and practice. Providing practice can also be supported through embedded questions in a self-paced PPT presentation or an e-learning module prompting learners to practice their knowledge and understanding through knowledge checks. Digital audio and video playback simulations that model accurate performance and provide personalized feedback can also be used as a technology for providing practice (Arias & Herbert, 2015). Duolingo is an example of an instructional system that uses audio and video playback to provide practice for language learning.

Alternatively, the instructional strategy of problem-solving, which aligns with the higher levels of Bloom's taxonomy (analysis, evaluation, creation), can be implemented using 3D virtual worlds which is a technology that provides an immersive space for learners to explore, experiment, collaborate, communicate, and create (Downes, 2010; Good, Howland, & Thackray, 2008; Hew & Cheung, 2010). Problem-solving activities can also be facilitated through Learning Management Systems (LMS), specifically through the use of discussion, resources, and synchronous and asynchronous collaborative features (Livingstone, Kemp, & Edgar, 2008).

Use Case Example of Learner-Content Interaction Using Immersive Technologies

As an example, iCivics, founded by Justice Sandra Day O'Connor in 2009, is a series of topic-specific serious games that provides learners with knowledge and practices of government and civic duty as a citizen of the United States. Serious games are defined as games designed for the primary reason of training and education beyond the context of entertainment (Allbeck, 2010; Djaouti et al., 2016; Lugmayr et al., 2016). The iCivics website contains over 16 serious games that cover a variety of topics, such as Argument Wars, where players assume the role of the lawyer of influential cases decided in the Supreme Court, or Do I Have a Right? (Figure 4.12), where the player assumes the role of a lawyer who needs to decide if potential clients may or may not have their constitutional rights violated, just to name a few.

The immersive learning environment includes animations, audio, and decision-driven responses from non-playable characters. In the environment, learners work on higher-order thinking skills and build their knowledge on the topic at hand, whether it is case laws or constitutional rights. Additionally, key vocabulary terms are bolded throughout the game's texts. When the player selects the vocabulary, its definition is displayed to help learners focus on the simulation while providing necessary information to aid players' learning.

Figure 4.12 iCivics Argument Wars Screenshot.

Use Case Example of Learner-Content Interaction Using an LMS and GBL

In 2013, the Center for Distance and Online Learning (CDOL) at the Los Angeles County Office of Education (LACOE), as part of the California K-12 Student Mental Health Initiative grant provided by the Substance Abuse and Mental Health Services Administration (SAMHSA), developed a series of self-paced online courses to provide educators with evidence-based suicide prevention and other related students mental well-being program. For suicide prevention, three 4-hour online courses were developed, one each for teachers, administrators, and school mental health professionals, respectively.

The original target audience was pre-service teachers, administrators, and school mental health professionals, which include nurses, counselors, and school psychologists, and were aimed to provide foundational knowledge of warning signs and risk factors that educators should be aware of and best practices in speaking with students in order to refer them to the correct professionals to intervene with any suicidal ideations. At its inception, the course was designed for both standalone and blended use in a teacher-preparation university classroom. The course was developed using Moodle as its initial Learning Management System (LMS) and included text, decorative, relational, and organizational graphics, and videos. The text was written in a conversational tone, with sections of brief pauses to allow learners to reflect on the content. As a collaboration between Los Angeles and Placer County, an added feature of a serious game was included. The Placer County Office of Education provided the use of the Kognito Suicide Prevention for High School Educators (now renamed as Emotional & Mental Wellness for Educators & Staff) serious game to be integrated as a final assessment within LACOE's suicide prevention online courses.

To broaden its reach, LACOE collaborated with California State University, Los Angeles (CSULA), one of the largest educator training universities in Los Angeles County, and provided the suicide prevention course modules to the faculty of CSULA to be integrated into existing university courses that were part of the credential training programs for teachers, administrators, and school mental health professionals. To assist faculty in using the online courses, an additional user guide was developed to include usage models, samples (asynchronous as self-study for students or blended use both online and offline,) technical assistance, and discussion prompts that faculty can use in class.

Within one year of its pilot, over 2000 CSULA teachers, administrators, and student mental health professional students have completed the suicide prevention online courses. In a focus group, students expressed that the combination of traditional online course delivery methods (text, graphics, videos, etc.) and the Kognito serious game reinforced the learning of the content. They also stated that the practicality of the content delivery method prepared them to work with students and be cognizant of potential suicide risk factors and warning signs. Over 60% of the pre-service teachers interviewed expressed that they feel more confident knowing what to do (referring students to administrators and school mental professionals) should they observe warning signs in students.

References

Akcaoglu, M., & Koehler, M. J. (2014). Cognitive outcomes from the game-design and learning (GDL) after-school program. *Computers & Education, 75*, 72–81. 10.1016/j.compedu.2014.02.003.

Allbeck, J. (2010). Serious games. Games and Intelligent Animation. Retrieved October 31, 2022, from https://cs.gmu.edu/~gaia/SeriousGames/index.html.

Arias, B., & Herbert, P. (2015, June 12). *Case study: Audio and video feedback.* University of Bristol - Digital Education Office. Retrieved November 3, 2022, from http://www.bristol.ac.uk/digital-education/case-studies/pre-2018/audio-and-video-feedback-using-mdr/.

Bannan, B., Dabbagh, N., & Walcutt, J. J. (2019). Instructional strategies for the future. In J. J. Walcutt and S. Schatz (Eds.), *Modernizing learning: Building the future learning ecosystem* (pp. 223–242). Washington, DC: Government Publishing Office. License: Creative Commons Attribution CC BY 4.0 IGO.

Bonwell, C. C., & Eison, J. A. (1991). *Active learning: Creating excitement in the classroom.* School of Education and Human Development, George Washington University.

Bower, M. (2017). *Design of technology-enhanced learning: Integrating research and practice.* Emerald Publishing Limited.

Clark, R. C., & Mayer, R. E. (2011). *E-learning and the science of instruction: Proven guidelines for consumers and designers of multimedia learning.* Pfeiffer.

Dabbagh, N. (2004). Distance learning: Emerging pedagogical issues and learning designs. *Quarterly Review of Distance Education, 5*(1), 37.

Dabbagh, N., Bass, R., Bishop, M., Costelloe, S., Cummings, K., Freeman, B., Frye, M., Picciano, A. G., Porowski, A., Sparrow, J., & Wilson, S. J. (2019). *Using technology to support postsecondary student learning: A practice guide for college and university administrators, advisors, and faculty.* Washington, DC: Institute of Education Sciences, What Works Clearinghouse. (WWC 20090001) Washington, DC: National Center for Education Evaluation and Regional Assistance (NCEE), Institute of Education Sciences, U.S. Department of Education. https://ies.ed.gov/ncee/wwc/PracticeGuide/25.

Dabbagh, N., & Fake, H. (2017). College students' perceptions of Personal Learning Environments (PLEs) through the lens of digital tools, processes, and spaces. *Journal of New Approaches in Educational Research, 6*(1), 28–36. 10.7821/naer.2017.1.215.

Dabbagh, N., Howland, J., & Marra, R. (2019). *Meaningful online learning: Integrating strategies, activities, and learning technologies for effective designs.* New York, N.Y.: Routledge.

Dabbagh, N., & Reo, R. (2011). Impact of Web 2.0 on higher education. In *Technology integration in higher education: Social and organizational aspects* (pp. 174–187). IGI Global.

DeAngelis, C. (2012). *The Integration of Technology in the Twenty-First Century Composition Classroom* (Doctoral dissertation, Kent State University).

Djaouti, D., Alvarez, J., & Jessel, J.-P. (2016). Classifying serious games. Advances in Game-Based Learning, 118–136. 10.4018/978-1-60960-495-0.ch006.

Downes, S. (2010). Learning Networks and Connective Knowledge. In H. Hao Yang and S. Chi-Yin Yuen (eds.), *Collective Intelligence and E-Learning 2.0: Implications of Web-Based Communities and Networking.* IGI Global.

Duggan, M. (2015, May 30). *Gaming and gamers*. Pew Research Center: Internet, Science & Tech. Retrieved November 3, 2022, from https://www.pewresearch.org/internet/2015/12/15/gaming-and-gamers/.

Fake, H. (2018). *A delphi study on the dimensions of personalized learning in workforce training and development programs*. [Doctoral dissertation, George Mason University]. Proquest.

Games and Learning. (2019). *Digital games, tools move towards core of classroom*. Retrieved November 3, 2022, from https://www.gamesandlearning.org/2019/06/16/digital-games-tools-move-towards-core-of-classroom/.

Gee, J. P. (2007). *Good video games + good learning: Collected essays on video games, learning, and literacy*. Peter Lang.

Gibson, J. J. (1979). The theory of affordances. In *The people, place, and space reader* (pp. 90–94). Routledge.

Good, J., Howland, K., & Thackray, L. (2008). Problem-based learning spanning real and virtual words: A case study in second life. *Research in Learning Technology*, *16*(3). 10.3402/rlt.v16i3.10895.

Gredler, M. E. (1996). Educational games and simulations: A technology in search of a (research) paradigm. *Technology*, *39*, 521–540.

Hew, K. F., & Cheung, W. S. (2010). Use of three-dimensional (3-D) immersive virtual worlds in K-12 and higher education settings: A review of the research. *British Journal of Educational Technology*, *41*(1), 33–55. 10.1111/j.1467-8535.2008.00900.x.

Hodges, C., Moore, S., Lockee, B., Trust, T., & Bond, A. (2020, March 27). *The difference between emergency remote teaching and online learning*. EDUCAUSE. Retrieved October 29, 2022, from https://er.educause.edu/articles/2020/3/the-difference-between-emergency-remote-teaching-and-online-learning.

Jonassen, D. H. (2002) Learning to solve problems online. In C. Vrasidas and G. Glass (Eds.), *Distance education and distance learning* (pp. 75–98). Greenwich, CT: Information Age Publishing.

Jonassen, D. H., Grabinger, R. S., & Harris, N. D. (1991). Analyzing and selecting instructional strategies and tactics. *Performance Improvement Quarterly*, *4*(2), 77–97. 10.1111/j.1937-8327.1997.tb00029.x.

Kalyuga, S. (2005). Prior knowledge principle in multimedia learning. In R. E. Mayer (Ed.), *The Cambridge handbook of multimedia learning* (pp. 325–337). New York: Cambridge University Press.

Kalyuga, S., Ayres, P., Chandler, P., & Sweller, J. (2003). Expertise reversal effect. *Educational Psychologist*, *38*, 23–31.

Ke, F. (2014). An implementation of design-based learning through creating educational computer games: A case study on mathematics learning during design and computing. *Computers & Education*, *73*, 26–39. 10.1016/j.compedu.2013.12.010.

Livingstone, D., Kemp, J., & Edgar, E. (2008). From multi-user virtual environment to 3D virtual learning environment. *Research in Learning Technology*, *16*(3). 10.3402/rlt.v16i3.10893.

Lugmayr, A., Suhonen, J., Hlavacs, H., Montero, C., Suutinen, E., & Sedano, C. (2016). Serious storytelling - a first definition and review. *Multimedia Tools and Applications*, *76*(14), 15707–15733. doi:10.1007/s11042-016-3865-5.

Martin, F., Polly, D., & Ritzhaupt, A. (2020, September 8). *Bichronous online learning: Blending asynchronous and synchronous online learning*. EDUCAUSE. Retrieved October 29, 2022, from https://er.educause.edu/articles/2020/9/bichronous-online-learning-blending-asynchronous-and-synchronous-online-learning.

Mayer, R. E. (2001). *Multimedia learning*. Cambridge Univ. Press.

Mayer, R. E., & Gallini, J. K. (1990). When is an illustration worth ten thousand words? *Journal of Educational Psychology*, *88*, 64–73.

Pagano, K. O. (2013). *Immersive learning*. Association for Talent Development.

Perrin, A. (2018, September 17). *5 facts about Americans and video games*. Pew Research Center. Retrieved October 29, 2022, from https://www.pewresearch.org/fact-tank/2018/09/17/5-facts-about-americans-and-video-games/.

Prensky, M. (2001). The games generations; how learners have changed. *Digital Game-based Learning*, *1*(1), 1–26.

Reisoğlu, I., Topu, B., Yılmaz, R., Karakuş Yılmaz, T., & Göktaş, Y. (2017). 3D virtual learning environments in education: A Meta-Review. *Asia Pacific Education Review*, *18*(1), 81–100. 10.1007/s12564-016-9467-0.

Robertson, J., & Howells, C. (2008). Computer game design: Opportunities for successful learning. *Computers & Education*, *50*(2), 559–578. 10.1016/j.compedu.2007.09.020.

Swerdloff, M. (2016). Online learning, multimedia, and emotions. In S. Y. Tettegah and M. P. McCreery (Eds.), *Emotions, technology, and learning* (pp. 155–175). essay, Academic Press.

Yang, Y.-T. C., & Chang, C.-H. (2013). Empowering students through digital game authorship: Enhancing concentration, critical thinking, and academic achievement. *Computers & Education*, *68*, 334–344. 10.1016/j.compedu.2013.05.023.

Designing for Learner–Learner Interaction

5

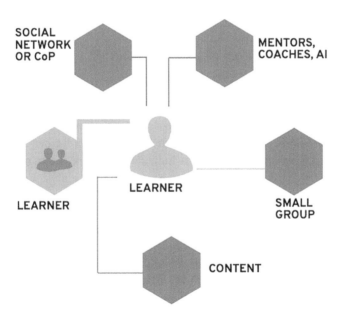

Figure 5.0 Learner-Learner Interaction.

Whether you call it "peer mentoring", "peer tutoring", "peer learning", peer-to-peer learning, or learner-to-learner interaction, research suggests that designing opportunities for individuals to learn from other individual learners can empower the development of metacognition, collaborative learning, interpersonal skills, communication, as well as a multitude of other

DOI: 10.4324/9781003121008-5

21st-century skills (Andrews & Manning, 2016; Carvalho & Santos, 2022; Sampson, Boud, Cohen, Gaynor, 1999; Zamberlan & Wilson, 2015). As defined by The Pennsylvania State University (2022), "Peer learning is a form of active, cooperative learning … . built off of the role of social interaction (discussion or dialogue) … [Peer learning] takes it one step further and places the student in the role of being a peer teacher, either formally or informally". Boud, Cohen, and Sampson (2001) focus on the reciprocal nature of the learning activity which involves the, "[shared] knowledge, ideas, and experiences between the participants" (p. 3). The shift towards learners as creators and constructors of knowledge rather than passive recipients also makes the development of peer programs an important scaffolding construct as learners gain a sense of proficiency and confidence in a safer individualized space with other individual learners (Duus & Cooray, 2022). It should be noted that we will use peer-to-peer and learner-to-learner interaction interchangeably in this chapter.

Differences Between Learner to Learner and Other PLiF Interaction Types

Before we go much further, we must make a distinction between the learner-to-learner interaction and learner-to-coach and/or mentorship interaction. While the learner-to-learner interaction is similar to a learner-to-coach or mentorship interaction in that it is individualized or a 1:1 engagement as mentioned in Chapter 3, the differences emerge when we consider the interaction between learners as involving equals or learners at the same level of proficiency (Boud et al., 2001; Zamberlan & Wilson, 2015). This interaction differs from learner-coach and learner-mentor interaction since coaches and mentors are not equals to the learner, but rather experts that support the learner from a position of authority and often one of power. In a learner-to-learner interaction, however, the individuals involved lack any influence, position, or power over one another. The lack of a power dynamic allows the learners to explore ideas, make mistakes, and confide in each other. The operating assumption within this interaction is that the learner will be more likely to relate and trust someone who is in the same situation compared to others who may come from a different perspective, level of expertise, or rank (Rabinowitz, 2022). A benefit of learner-learner or peer-peer interaction is that learners may be more likely to ask questions of a peer they view as an equal as opposed to others they perceive as having more expertise or authority.

It is also important to note there may be considerable overlap with the learner-to-small group interaction dimension of the PLiF. The difference between these two dimensions, as defined in this book, is that in a learner-to-learner interaction, participants learn from one another. The learner-to-small group interaction, however, may be better suited to tasks wherein groups pursue new learning alongside each other. We explore the advantages and disadvantages of each approach in the paragraphs below.

In a learner-to-learner interaction, the influence of group dynamics is less pronounced compared to the learner to small group interaction (Marjolaine et al., 2020). Without having to form, storm, norm, and perform, the dyad is allowed to develop an interpersonal relationship that is not privy to the same forces that may be at play within a larger cooperative learning setting (Tuckman, 1965). The individualized nature of the relationship allows students to share their ideas in a safer space without the considerations of power dynamics or judgment associated with exploring new topics or ideas. This, in turn, supports learners in speaking more freely while testing out ideas prior to sharing with a larger audience.

Learner-to-small group interactions, however, may be useful in supporting the learners' socialization skills. Much of being successful in the workforce entails knowledge of how to effectively operate and function in small groups or teams (Fisher & Phillips, 2021; Haas & Mortensen, 2016). Therefore, facilitating and enabling exposure to this type of interaction will encourage the development of relational skill sets that are critical to accomplishing important project-based tasks.

Group dynamics present in a learner-to-small group interaction may also contribute to conformity and groupthink. Influential German sociologist Georg Simmel, wrote extensively on the effects group size had on attitude and behavior noting that a group of three represented more threat to the loss of independence, isolation, and segmentation compared to a dyad (Simmel, 1950). Therefore, intentional thought around how to organize and structure group work is necessary to support productive interactions between learners.

Ultimately, the learner-to-learner interaction taps into the experiences and expertise of the participants. As Knowles (1984) emphasized, adult learners contain a depth of expertise and knowledge. From an organizational standpoint, employee experiences and knowledge are a tremendous asset to the classroom and to their organizations. In business, workers may benefit from speaking with employees in other departments, breaking down organizational silos with others who have an in-depth knowledge of their operational context (Palmer & Blake, 2018). Knowledge of the organization's goals, opportunities, limitations, constraints, technologies, people, and processes is a tremendous asset in collaboratively investigating solutions to identified organizational problems. Students in academic situations involved in a learner to learner interaction may also have more opportunities to explore ideas before presenting them to a larger group or test out and experiment with ideas prior to being in more formal environments (Centre for Teaching and Learning, 2021).

Designing for Learner-to-Learner Interaction

Sampson et al. (1999) advocated that defining the context clearly is important when considering the implementation of peer learning or the learner-to-learner interaction. Where the learner-to-learner interaction takes place, the nature of the implementation, and the ways in which teaching and learning are practiced all emerged as important factors for consideration. In the remainder of this chapter, we will consider each of the best practices in spaces wherein one can set up the learner-to-learner interaction, first by identifying the learning needs and objectives, defining where the learner-to-learner interaction might happen, how to facilitate the learner to learner selection process, categorical types of learner-to-learner interaction, potential learner to learner activities, technologies that enable learner-to-learner interaction, as well as potential considerations of when learner to learner interaction might be an effective mode of instruction.

It is important to note that many organizational and cultural elements are necessary to set the preconditions of any training and development program given the vulnerability needed to share stories, admit mistakes, and brainstorm new solutions. Creating an effective organizational learning culture where vulnerability and learning are encouraged is a well-trodden path and goes outside the scope of this book. For those looking for resources about creating a learning culture, please reference the additional reading section of this chapter.

Defining Learning Needs and Instructional Objectives

As with any interaction, the intentional consideration of a learner-to-learner interaction's design will be important to the effectiveness of its use within the classroom or organizational environment. Therefore, to begin, we must consider why we are leveraging this interaction in the first place.

The learner-to-learner interaction is best used when exploring conceptual problems or case studies, or in learning situations wherein individuals need to apply and discuss the key concepts, principles, or theories associated with a new domain (Centre for Teaching & Learning, 2021). For example, in an academic setting, a learner-to-learner interaction could involve two statistics students meeting to go over a homework assignment and complete a problem set. In Workforce Training and Development, learner-to-learner interaction might involve programmers reviewing each other's code before deploying the changes to the website they work on or even two coworkers using a "working session" to investigate a new software solution to see if the available options serve their needs. The different types of work represented here flavor how one might design these interactions. For example, within higher education, the academic setting is potentially more formalized based on curricular and academic requirements. Therefore, the types of objectives may be more structured. In Workforce Education, however, the learning objectives may need to focus more so on projects or business objectives which may constantly evolve and change. These experiences therefore may be less structured and tangentially translate to skill development.

Providing opportunities for peer feedback is yet another facet of the learner-to-learner interaction that offers workers and students opportunities to enhance their skill sets while practicing interpersonal communication and critical thinking skills (Zamberlan & Wilson, 2015). Leveraging feedback from students or workers may even help scale limited professorial or training resources within massive open online communities (MOOCs) and create a sense of belonging in online learning environments to address complaints wherein students may feel alone in their learning process (Kulkarni, Kotturi, Bernstein, & Klemmer, 2016).

Where Learner to Learner Interaction Occurs

According to experts in this work's foundational study, personalized learning can occur almost anywhere. The formal classroom was rejected as a space for personalized learning, but this might be a reflection of the current passive pedagogical practices inherent in the traditional classroom. This transferability and flexibility of location can also be said about the learner-to-learner interaction. The learner-to-learner interaction may happen in person, in blended work or learning situations, and even in fully remote contexts. Operationally, the current work or classroom set-up may dictate what works best for students and workers. For example, an on-campus student body or workers situated in the same location may be able to leverage in person or hybrid approaches to the learner-to-learner interaction (e.g., with hybrid approaches incorporating both in person and virtual touchpoints for the learner-to-learner interaction). Geographically distributed student bodies of workforces, however, may need to focus primarily on virtual interaction with occasional in-person touchpoints if economically feasible.

Asynchronous and synchronous modalities are yet another set of variables to consider in the development of learner-to-learner interaction. Kulkarni et al. (2016) investigated the impact that asynchronous and synchronous learner-to-learner interaction had on student essays and learning outcomes using two peer learning software tools PeerStudio and Talkabout. PeerStudio was an asynchronous rapid essay assessment platform and Talkabout, prompted synchronous student conversations in Google Hangouts on course materials. In Talkabout, learners could meet with a peer to discuss important course topics and reflect on assigned content. The other software, PeerStudio, asked users to asynchronously "grade" peer essays based on a provided rubric with a few open-ended comments fields. The researchers found that rapid iterative feedback to students who submitted essays through the PeerStudio interface improved the final grades significantly, increased the speed of feedback, and supported teachers in scaling their courses to larger numbers of students, particularly in MOOCs.

The researchers leveraging PeerStudio and Talkabout for the learner-to-learner interaction found that the instructors' prompting was particularly important to encourage the use of these learner-to-learner interaction technologies. These findings suggest that setting expectations regarding the use of available tools, therefore, will be an important aspect of any learner-to-learner interaction. Another challenge cited in this study associated with remote learner-to-learner interaction was the lack of ambient student engagement and energy often found in a face-to-face classroom. Designers, thus, may consider incentivizing or making opportunities for learners to interact, collaborate, and celebrate their interdependence, set positive community norms, and structure ongoing interactions between peers. A large number of participants also made it difficult for instructors to observe the interactions between peers within the peer learning systems. Professors shared that the rich contextual data provided by students was hard to parse through, and little visibility beyond engagement was available for instructors to understand areas wherein students were struggling in the PeerStudio and Talkabout platforms. It was difficult for faculty to ascertain where students were struggling with the learning content. Future iterations to the existing platforms may consider leveraging existing engagement metrics (e.g., number of average conversations over time, natural language processing sentiment analysis, time to task completion, etc.) as well as student interviews, course feedback, and other research methodologies to bring these areas to light.

Facilitating the Learner to Learner Interaction Selection Process

The learner-to-learner interaction may be set up in a variety of ways, including self-selected, topic or project-based, rotated, or computer automated. Each approach may be better suited for different learning environments than others. We explore the design implications of each approach in the paragraphs below.

Self-selection has been shown to have advantages and disadvantages in the learning and development process (Centre for Teaching and Learning, 2021). One potentially obvious advantage of self-selection stems from the ownership the learner has in their selection of a partner. Conversely, students or learners may be attracted to pair with someone of the same ethnic group or with another individual wherein they perceive a sense of comfort and familiarity. As a consequence learners may avoid anyone that seems different (Centre for Teaching and Learning, 2021). Therefore, building inclusivity is an important design consideration when developing peer-to-peer programs. Essentially, it is important to design learner-to-learner programs that are diverse across several dimensions to include inherent diversity (e.g., age, gender, ethnicity, sexual diversity, etc.) and acquired diversity (e.g., different skill sets, roles, life experiences, etc.) (Hewlitt, Marshall & Sherbin, 2013). One way to support self-selective pairing may be asking students to select a few different peers they think might be good to work with and encouraging learners to consider the value of pairing with someone who may have a different perspective.

A self-selection approach may work best when students have direct contact with and can get to know one another over time. Setting up opportunities to meet one another may support facilitating this self-selection process.

While much of project-based learning tends to be in small groups of 3–7, the dyad may be useful in instances of peer review (Pozzi et al., 2016). In an analysis of interactions between dyads and groups conducting peer reviews in a Moodle course, Pozzi et al. (2016) found that dyads as well as course tutors helping dyads tended to be more actively engaged. In peer review sessions, dyads sent 139 messages on average compared to 42 messages between students in groups. Overall, this research suggests the dyads supported higher levels of cognition, individual knowledge building, and frequency of dialogue. There were even higher observed rates of cohesion and affection between analyzed comments in dyads compared to groups. **Topic or project-based peer selection, therefore,** may be best suited for instances wherein a pair will work together based on a shared interest, project, or peer review. In this situation, the project or topic should dictate the pairing more so than any preconceived notions of affinity between peers. In this model of peer selection, learners must be able to either share or post a project idea and solicit connections based on the ideas.

This approach to peer selection seeks to minimize the learners' preconceived notions of affinity and encourage the learner to take ownership of the problem space. At the same time, this type of selection process may also be susceptible to the disadvantages of the self-selection process if learners select tasks based on the other learners as opposed to the task. Anonymity of the learner proposing the task may be one tactic to control this behavior.

Rotated selection is yet another way to enable learner-to-learner interaction. In this model, learners are paired up for a defined amount of time and then later rotated to a new peer upon completion of a learning task, learning unit, or defined deliverable. This may give the learner exposure to a multitude of viewpoints. The tradeoff, however, is that learners may not be able to sustain or form longer-term peer-to-peer relationships this way.

Computer-automated learner-to-learner interaction may introduce learners to one another based on defined parameters. These parameters may be defined based on a multitude of variables explicit (defined by the user), implicit (defined by the user's interaction with the system), or a mix of both explicit and implicit data sources. Examples of data sources could include **learner-defined data** (e.g., learner preferences, personalized learning plans, learner goals, desired learning activities, learner profiles, espoused interests), **behaviorally defined data** (implicitly defined interests, information consumption behaviors, learner patterns, navigation preferences, behavioral logs, or perceived motivational level), **contextually defined data** (e.g., location, time, organizational role, type of task, language, instructor input), **relationship-driven data** (e.g., content relationships or community relationships), or even **performance data** (e.g., learner performance, existing expertise/prior mastery, completions, academic outcomes, self-report metrics, levels of proficiency) (Fake, 2018). Other parameters that previous researchers have considered include espoused media preference, learner cognitive styles, biometrics or neurological data, satisfaction, length of training activity, or promotion or position changes, however, experts previously have not acknowledged these data sources as supporting personalized learning. Therefore, if using computer automated systems to facilitate the learner to learner interaction, considering the aforementioned types of data sources may support connecting two students or workers depending on a variety of metadata surrounding their interests, behaviors, contexts, attributes, connections, or performance, potentially identify peer matches that may have not have formed otherwise.

This approach may make the most sense when needing to pair learners in a larger ecosystem. Leveraging the explicit and implicit data may support pairing users at scale given the big data and analytics capabilities that may be required to form pairs. Therefore, this approach might be best suited to learning ecosystems that need to prioritize scale like MOOCs or large organizations.

With the design considerations associated with pairing outlined, we continue with a discussion regarding the five different types of peer-to-peer or learner-to-learner interaction.

Categories of Peer Learning in Learner-to-Learner Interaction

The Centre for Learning Excellence (2021) and Gilbert, Hunsaker, and Schmidt (2007) identified five different categorical types of learner-to-learner and learner-to-small group interaction. According to the paper, these include **Peer Interaction** (which is a categorical type of learner-to-learn interaction as defined in the paper and not to be confused with the overarching interaction we are speaking about in this book), **Peer Response**, **Peer Collaboration**, **Peer Feedback**, and **Peer Facilitation**. Since this chapter focuses on the learner to learner interaction, we will explore the two categorical types that are more aligned with an individualized interaction approach, including **Peer Interaction** and **Peer Feedback**. The other types of learner engagements will be revisited (e.g., Peer Response, Peer Collaboration, and Peer Facilitation) in Chapter 6 where we will explore the design considerations of the learner-to-small group interaction.

According to the categorical types outlined in the research, **Peer Interaction** involves students brainstorming and discussing course topics with one another without the assistance of faculty or ISDs. These interactions are great for helping the students assess their understanding prior to introducing new content, providing opportunities for reflection, and offering opportunities to socialize.

The other type of peer learning, **Peer Feedback** gains an important role throughout the learner-to-learner interaction, so it is no surprise that many groups have sought to understand best practices in how to structure peer feedback (Gielen & De Wever, 2015; Klassen, 2004; Lopez-Pellisa, Rotger, Rodriguez–Gallego, 2021; Oosta & Hoatlin, 2015). When feedback is used, how it is structured, the number of reviewers, and whether or not the reviewers are anonymous are all items of consideration when designing peer feedback activities (Centre for Teaching and Learning, 2022). Please note, peer feedback may also be used in small group interactions and we note where the different activities could be leveraged in both use cases.

Instructing learners on mechanisms of providing constructive feedback may be critical to enabling impactful learner-to-learner interaction. In interviews and analysis of over 300 learner-to-learner feedback letters, Oosta & Hoatlin (2015) note that peer feedback can often be reactionary, negative, or vague which suggests that instructors must dedicate time and resources to encourage the development of effective feedback skills which underpin this approach. For example, the researchers found that rubrics can be helpful in strengthening feedback conversations. Having a set benchmark helps focus the conversation and provides learners the opportunity to understand the aims of the assignment and how the worked example achieves (or doesn't achieve) that aim. In evaluating the impact of structured versus unstructured peer feedback, Gielen and De Wever (2015) discovered structure translated into higher quality peer feedback which increased deliverable alignment with defined criteria. This research suggests that the more forethought we place into conceiving the goals and roles of peer feedback or work to create systems and rubrics to support these types of sessions, the more likely we can guide the learner to the learning moments we hope to cultivate through our instructional experiences.

Klassen (2004) helps further differentiate between types of feedback that may be useful to writers with classifications to include **the red pen** or editing, correcting, or fixing someone's work, **the back pat** or praise of the writer's efforts, **analysis**, or an interpretation of the deeper meaning suggested by the work, **seed gathering** or sharing what works well from the reader's perspective, and **power notes** or indications of the personal impact the writing has had on one's experiences. Defining these types of feedback may be helpful to learners as they consider the best ways to structure their reactions and comments on others' work.

Earlier in this chapter, we spoke of the considerable overlap between a learner-to-learner and learner-to-small group interaction. Therefore, many of the activities shown below may be adjusted to support the learner in small group interaction. To support the development of the PLIF, however, both interactions (e.g., learner-to-learner and learner-to-small group) must be present in order to create the self-sustaining learning framework proposed in this book.

The activities below represent different ways to structure the learner-to-learner interaction types in asynchronous, synchronous, or bichronous learning environments. It is important to note that each approach may influence what technologies are used to facilitate these interactions. In parenthesis, we've included what type of peer learning is supported in each activity (Table 5.1).

Designing for Learner–Learner Interaction 97

Table 5.1 Designing the Peer-to-Peer Interaction by Type of Peer Learning

Category of Peer Learning	Type of Learning Activity	Description	When to Use	Also Supported in Learner to Small Group Interaction?
Peer Interaction	Paired Discussion	A dyad is encouraged to talk about a topic based on a prompt.	When learners would benefit from solidifying and applying the understanding of old content before introducing newer content. To encourage relationships between learners.	Yes, as Group Discussions
Peer Interaction	Think-Pair-Share	A question is posed to the learners. The learners may then discuss their thoughts amongst themselves in a more private conversation. Typically pairs are asked to share later in the larger group.	This is good for introducing multiple viewpoints to a topic area while also controlling for group dynamics.	Yes, this combines learner-to-learner and learner-to-group interactions. Pairs could also support a group discussion format.
Peer Interaction	Debates	Two learners take opposing views on a	Debates help develop argumentation,	Yes when structured for groups

(Continued)

Table 5.1 (Continued)

Category of Peer Learning	Type of Learning Activity	Description	When to Use	Also Supported in Learner to Small Group Interaction?
		topic that they choose or is provided to them	presentation, and critical thinking skills.	
Peer Feedback	Peer Assessment	One learner evaluates the work of another learner to provide constructive feedback about their performance on a task.	This approach supports the development of critical thinking, analysis, and interpersonal communication skills.	Yes
Peer Feedback	Peer Tutoring	One learner evaluates the work of another learner to provide feedback. This can be useful when one learner may be a bit more proficient in the domain than the other.	This approach can be useful when you have a wide spectrum of skills and abilities within the classroom. Here the more proficient learner can offer support and still learn through their process of teaching the domain.	No, would likely become Peer Facilitation – another type of peer learning

Technologies that Enable Learner-to-Learner Interaction

The technological classifications described in Chapter 4, map well to the learner-to-learner interaction. The most common technologies that support learner-to-learner interaction include collaboration and communication tools, content creation tools, and assessment tools (Dabbagh et al., 2019) (Figure 5.1).

The table below represents the technologies used to teach a Business Analytics course to a midsize company in the Mid-Atlantic as well as tools an institute of higher education might leverage to enable similar interactions (Table 5.2).

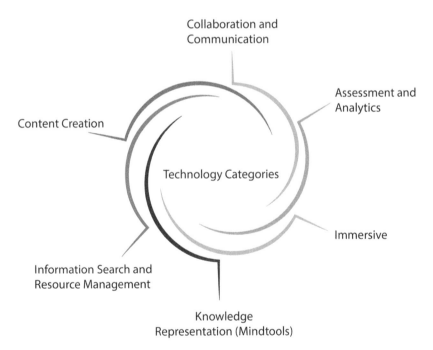

Figure 5.1 Technology Categories.

Table 5.2 Examples of Technologies Used to Support Peer-to-Peer Learning for a Business Analytics Class

Category of Peer Learning	Type of Digital Task	Higher Education Digital Platforms and Tools	Workforce Training and Development Tools	Technological Classification
Peer Interaction	Learner to Learner Paired Discussion/ Think-Pair-Share	Discussion Boards and wikis (e.g., Blackboard, Canvas, etc.)	Messaging platforms (Slack, Google Chat, Microsoft Teams, Cisco WebEx, Zoom, Google Docs, etc.)	Collaboration and Communication Tools
Peer Interaction	Debates/Video-Based Communication & Presentation	Kaltura through Blackboard Collaborate, Youtube, Screencastify, Google Slides, PowerPoint	Loom Camtasia Jing	Content creation tools
Peer Feedback	Peer Tutoring	Blackboard Collaborate, Google Chat, Texting, Phone Calls	Messaging platforms (Slack, Google Chat, Microsoft Teams, Zoom, Google Docs, etc.)	Collaboration and Communication Tools
Peer Feedback	Peer Assessment	ComPAIR, PeerStudio, Peerceptiv, Visual Classrooms, Microsoft 365, Google Docs	360 Reviews through Employee Performance Software (e.g., Happeo, WorkHuman, CultureAmp, Workday, Cornerstone)	Assessment and Analytics Tools

When to Implement Learner-to-Learner Interaction

When designing the learner-to-learner interaction, it may also be appropriate to consider when might be best to prioritize providing these opportunities. In the following paragraphs, we will explore different points in the learner journey including during student or employee onboarding, during performance evaluations, and even design implications for providing learner-to-learner interaction throughout their experiences with their respective organization.

During Onboarding or Orientation

A common complaint during onboarding is the sense of vulnerability that stems from being new and needing to ask one's supervisor questions about the operational or academic environment (Baker, 2020). Struggling to connect with other workers when starting at a new organization has been further complicated by COVID, the mass resignation, and the move towards a more remote workforce (Naji, 2022). In a virtual space, "watercooler moments" have to be carefully constructed and may be limited by our current technologies that have less flexibility in cultivating the range of interactions between peers that may happen in a face-to-face context.

According to Nichols (2020), 600 surveyed employees indicated that while 26% would be interested in learning from their manager the most, there were 22% who were interested in learning from their fellow peers. Therefore, new employee onboarding or student orientations can be a critical time to consider prompting the learner-to-learner interaction. Depending on the scope and scale of the institution or organization leveraging the learner-to-learner interaction could be facilitated either using an existing platform or through pairing up learners leveraging one of the techniques introduced earlier in this chapter.

An example of peer onboarding programs stems from the University of California's Office of Information Technology (OIT). Given the challenges of COVID, the remote nature of work, and the diverse nature of the organization, the Peer Onboarding Program sought to support employees in connecting with each other (2021). Participation in this program required that workers pair with individuals outside their teams at a similar professional level and that the dyads meet for a minimum of 3–6 months. Employees with a "buddy" reported 36% increases in satisfaction along with higher perceived rates of organizational connection and engagement.

During Evaluations

Performance evaluations are yet another space where learner-to-learner interaction may prove helpful. We will delve further into the formative and summative modes of evaluation in Chapter 9, but a few spaces to consider incorporating the learner-to-learner interaction include reflective peer conversations, during 360 reviews wherein peer feedback is solicited across organizational silos and in continuous peer training engagements.

Constantly

The benefits of learner-to-learner interaction extend beyond specific times. Other spaces to consider incorporating learner-to-learner individualized lunch and learns, pair sharing, buddy systems, co-working sessions, pair-coding, "flipped learning" pair workshops, coffee chats, or even peer learning programs based on a class.

One example of class-based peer learning programs includes the Digital Peer Learning Hubs for undergraduate, postgraduate, MBA, and executive programs at the University of London, ETH Zurich, and Hult-Ashridge (Duus & Cooray, 2022). The Digital Peer Learning Hubs has been designed to support both short and long-term courses to capture students' submissions, enabling peer-to-peer feedback, and offering transparency into how different learners approached a problem or set of tasks.

The faculty developing The Digital Peer Learning Hubs leveraged a three-staged framework of Action, Reflection, and Growth as the theoretical basis of their platform. Each stage was supported by different activities and peer interaction. For instance, in the Action stage, learners completed tasks in advance and received structured peer feedback on their work. In the reflection stage, the students reflected on this feedback and incorporated a set of action responses based on the inputs from their peers. In the growth stage, the learners were tasked with reviewing others' solutions to see how others approached similar challenges. Throughout the application of this framework, learners were offered templates and materials to support peer feedback and reflection. Instructors also reported increases in student performance, high acquisition of digital skills, and a larger sense of class cohesion.

Case Study/Use Case: Donut

Donut is a peer-to-peer learning application that integrates with Slack, an internal organizational messaging and communication solution, to randomly assign and facilitate connections between peers. Once the Donut App has been installed, users are able to self-select into the program and indicate their desired level of involvement, which is adjustable and may even be prompted for adjustment by the app if low levels of involvement are detected. Once a user has self-selected into the program, the app automatically prompts participating users to connect on an ongoing basis (e.g., weekly, bi-weekly, monthly) and suggests that two (or more) individuals set aside time for coffee. In addition to arranging and prompting peer-to-peer introductions, the app suggests times based on openings in one's calendaring application of choice. Since the Donut App prompts the users to meet, the app can reduce any anxiety a newer employee may feel when asking to meet with others either remotely or in person.

When peers meet for 30 minutes, they can select the topics of the conversation, however, the app may also offer topics, ask questions, or offer suggestions on what might be good to discuss during the sessions. Ultimately, the two participants can decide how they wish to engage with one another.

Prompts following the meeting also can be configured for peers to share feedback on what was most useful in the session, ask additional questions, or leave a compliment for the other participant. Donut also extends its functionality by creating pairings for job shadowing, knowledge sharing, or automatically assigning peers to conduct quality assurance work or code reviews.

At the time of this writing, Donut has helped 15,000 teams including Okta, Betterment, Gitlab, Zapier, and Invision make over 6+ million connections across departments, office locations, and continents. Enabling in-person, hybrid, and virtual meetings, Donut offers a flexible framework for connecting learners to one another.

Additional Reading

A New Culture of Learning: Cultivating Imagination for a World of Constant Change, https://www.amazon.com/New-Culture-Learning-Cultivating-Imagination/dp/1456458884

Building a Culture of Learning: The Foundation of a Successful Organization, https://ctdo360.td.org/pdf?src=00000159-6b7a-d69f-a5fd-7b7bf27f0000

References

Andrews, M., & Manning, N. (2016). A guide to peer-to-peer learning: How to make peer-to-peer support and learning effective in the public sector. *Effective Institutions Platform*. https://www.effectiveinstitutions.org/files/The_EIP_P_to_P_Learning_Guide.pdf

Baker, G. (2020). *The Energy Equation: Unlocking the hidden power of energy in business*. John Wiley & Sons, Inc.

Boud, D., Cohen, R., & Sampson, J. (2001). *Peer learning in higher education: Learning from & with each other*. Psychology Press.

Carvalho, A. R., & Santos, C. (2022). Developing peer mentors' collaborative and metacognitive skills with a technology-enhanced peer learning program. *Computers and Education Open*, *3*, 10.1016/j.caeo.2021.100070

Dabbagh, N., Howland, J., & Marra, R. (2019). *Meaningful online learning: Integrating strategies, activities, and learning technologies for effective designs*. New York, N.Y.: Routledge.

Duus, R., & Cooray, M. (2022, August 2022). Empowering students to learn from each other: How digital tools can enhance peer learning across student teams. *Harvard Business Publishing Education*. https://hbsp.harvard.edu/inspiring-minds/empowering-students-to-learn-from-each-other

Fake, H. (2018). *A delphi study on the dimensions of personalized learning in workforce training and development programs*. [Doctoral dissertation, George Mason University]. Proquest.

Fisher, J., & Phillips, A. (2021). *Work better together: How to cultivate strong relationships to maximize well-being and boost bottom lines*. McGraw Hill-Ascent Audio.

Gielen, M., & De Wever, B. (2015). Structuring peer assessment: Comparing the impact of the degree of structure on peer feedback content. *Computers in Human Behavior*, *52*, 315–325. Doi: 10.1016/j.chb.2015.06.019

Gilbert, C. G., Hunsaker, S., & Schmidt, B. (2007). Peer instruction: Faculty as architects of peer learning environments. BYU-Idaho *Perspective*, 98–115.

Haas, M., & Mortensen, M. (2016, June). *The secrets of great teamwork*. Harvard Business Review. Retrieved November 30, 2022, from https://hbr.org/2016/06/the-secrets-of-great-teamwork

Hewlett, S. A., Marshall, M., & Sherbin, L. (2013). How diversity can drive innovation. *Harvard Business Review*, *91*(12), 30–30.

Indian Institute of Management Bangalore Centre for Teaching & Learning. (2021). *Peer Learning: Designing Better Learning Environments*. PDF. Bengaluru, India.

Klassen, J. (2004). *Tools for Transformation: Write your way to new worlds of possibility in just five minutes*. Infinity Publishing.

Knowles, M. (1984). *The adult learner: A neglected species* (3rd ed.). Gulf Publishing.

Kulkarni, C., Kotturi, Y., Bernstein, M. S., & Klemmer, S. (2016). Designing scalable and sustainable peer interactions online. In *Design Thinking Research* (pp. 237–273). Cham: Springer.

López-Pellisa, T., Rotger, N., & Rodríguez-Gallego, F. (2021). Collaborative writing at work: Peer feedback in a blended learning environment. *Education and Information Technologies*, *26*(1), 1293–1310.

Marjolaine, M. D., Lavoie, S., & Gallagher, F. (2020). Elements of group dynamics that influence learning in small groups in undergraduate students: A scoping review. *Nurse Education Today*, *87*, 104362. 10.1016/j.nedt.2020.104362.

Naji, H. (2022). Long-Term Effects of COVID-19: A Systemic Review. *European Journal of Medical and Health Sciences*, *4*(4), 8–12. 10.24018/ejmed.2022.4.4.1378

Nichols, M. (2020). *Transforming Universities with Digital Distance Education: The future of formal learning*. Routledge Taylor & Francis Group.

Oosta, A., & Hoatlin R.-L. (2015). Developing Stronger Peer-to-Peer Feedback in the Undergraduate Creative Writing Workshop. *Young Scholars in Writing*, *9*, 64–76. Retrieved from https://youngscholarsinwriting.org/index.php/ysiw/article/view/129

Palmer, K., & Blake, D. (2018, November 18). *How to help your employees learn from each other*. Harvard Business Review. Retrieved November 30, 2022, from https://hbr.org/2018/11/how-to-help-your-employees-learn-from-each-other

Pedagogical Approaches with Canvas. (2022). *Peer Learning*. Retrieved November 30, 2022, from https://sites.psu.edu/pedagogicalpractices/peer-learning/

Pozzi, F., Ceregini, A., Ferlino, L., & Persico, D. (2016). Dyads versus groups: Using different social structures in peer review to enhance online collaborative learning processes. *International Review of Research in Open and Distributed Learning*, *17*(2), 85–107.

Rabinowitz, P. (2022). *Section 8. Establishing a peer education program*. Chapter 24. Improving Services | Section 8. Establishing a Peer Education Program. Retrieved November 30, 2022, from https://ctb.ku.edu/en/table-of-contents/implement/improving-services/peer-education/main

Sampson, J., Boud, D., Cohen, R., & Gaynor, F. (1999). Designing peer learning. In *HERDSA Annual International Conference* (pp. 1–12). Melbourne: HERDSA Annual International Conference.

Simmel, G. (1950). *The Sociology of Georg Simmel*. Free Press.

Tuckman, B. W. (1965). Developmental sequence in small groups. *Psychological Bulletin*, *63*(6), 384.

University of California Office of the President. (2021). *UCOP Human Resources*. Retrieved November 30, 2022, from https://www.ucop.edu/local-human-resources/manager-resources/hiring-process/on-boarding.html

Zamberlan, L., & Wilson, S. (2015). Developing an embedded peer tutor program in design studio to support first year design students. *Journal of Peer Learning*, *8*(2015), 5–17.

Designing for Learner–Small Group Interaction

6

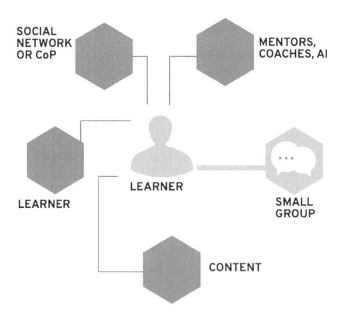

Figure 6.0 Learner-Small Group Interaction.

Learner-Small Group Interaction

In Chapter 3, we described learner-small group interaction as an important interaction for supporting personalized learning. Experts who participated in

DOI: 10.4324/9781003121008-6

the Delphi study described the purpose of small group interactions as a place to meet with others to address similar needs, questions, or challenges based on specific strengths or weaknesses. Experts also noted that how groups are formed, their purpose or topic, and how someone joins a group, are important aspects for consideration in personalizing the learning experience. Small group learning is defined as "a method that can supplement case discussions, lectures and other class formats" where "students work together in groups of typically 3–6 members, helping each other think critically, master course concepts, and apply them to real-world situations" and where "students are motivated toward a common goal and work together to support each other's learning" (*Teaching a Course*, n.d.). It is important to note that small group learning is different from working in teams. Working in teams or teamwork typically involves longer periods of time than small group learning, and team members are usually consistent across time, and there is more interdependence in completing the task. Whereas small group learning tends to be more informal and brief and can happen multiple times in one class or training session.

In higher education contexts, learning science research has shown that small-group learning (when compared to competitive and individualistic learning) improves academic achievement, relationships with classmates and faculty, and promotes psychological well-being (*Teaching a Course*, n.d.). Johnson et. al. (2014) conducted a meta-analysis of small group learning in higher education and summarized the benefits as follows:

- Small group learning enables students to develop a deeper understanding of the content regardless of the subject matter and helps students become better at problem-solving.
- Small group learning improves attendance, efficiency, and persistence.
- Small group learning helps students develop social and leadership skills.
- Students who engage in small group learning are more likely to integrate across different ethnic, cultural, language, class, ability, and gender groups.
- Small-group learning encourages people who normally would not participate in front of the whole class to participate.
- Small group learning promotes self-esteem when compared to competitive or individualistic learning.

Learner-small group interaction has also been effective in supporting workplace or professional learning. For example, in health professional education, small group learning has been implemented using strategies or teaching approaches such as Problem-Based Learning (PBL) and Case-Based Learning (CBL).

Research has shown that small group methods remain the preferred approach when compared to lecture-based teaching, instructor-led training, or self-paced individualized learning (Burgess, van Diggele, Roberts, et al., 2020). Burgess et al. argue that small group learning in the workplace encourages active participation in the learning process and enhances the learning experience by promoting self-directed learning (an adult learning principle), supporting a range of perspectives from peers, providing opportunities to give and receive feedback from peers, allowing the testing of ideas and attitudes with peers, and developing critical thinking and problem-solving skills. Small group learning or learner-small group interaction is sometimes referred to as collaborative or cooperative learning.

In Valamis' Develop and Maintain Learning Culture Workbook (2022), cooperative learning is defined as either formal, informal, or small group based. Additionally, five fundamental elements that distinguish cooperative learning from other forms of group learning are provided. These include (1) positive interdependence, (2) individual and group accountability, (3) interpersonal and small group skills, (4) face-to-face interaction, and (5) group processing (Siikanen et al., 2020).

Collaborative learning on the other hand, or collaboration, is the act of fostering interaction, conversation, and joining of resources by two or more learners to complete any number of learning activities (Dabbagh et al., 2019). The goal of collaborative learning is to require learners to solve problems and to reflect on, articulate, and explore knowledge with peers and instructors (Laal & Ghodsi, 2011). Collaborative learning can look quite different depending on the instructional environment in which it is implemented. It is most easily understood as pairs or groups of students interacting with one another to maximize their own and one another's learning (Oliveira, Tinoca, & Pereira, 2011). Learners control the learning in collaborative activities and the role of the instructor, facilitator, coach, or mentor is to help learners negotiate through the learning activity (Dabbagh, Marra, & Howland, 2019).

Types of Learner-Small Group Interaction

As mentioned in Chapter 5, The Centre for Learning Excellence in Bangalore India (2021) identified five different types of learner-learner and learner-small group interactions: (1) Peer Interaction, (2) Peer Feedback, (3) Peer Collaboration, (4) Peer Response, and (5) Peer Facilitation. The first two types, Peer Interaction and Peer Feedback, were discussed in Chapter 5,

Designing for Learner To Learner Interaction. In this chapter we focus on Peer Collaboration, Peer Response, and Peer Facilitation, and how these types of interaction work in small group contexts. It is important to note that Peer Interaction and Peer Feedback may also be adjusted to fit learner-small group interaction.

Peer Collaboration

Peer collaboration involves working in groups or teams to solve problems, gain proficiency in a concept space, or deepen understanding after a topic has been introduced. In this type of learner-small group interaction, instructors function more as facilitators. The role of the instructor is to monitor the progress of learners, facilitate dialogue, and ensure teams are formed that support diverse perspectives. The inevitable debates that may arise between learners in this type of interaction help develop social, argumentation, and reasoning skills, as is the case in Problem-Based Learning (PBL). In PBL, students, in small groups of 5–7, deliberate on a complex problem using what they collectively understand by applying their knowledge to the problem. Through the group's interaction, learners elaborate on their understanding while realizing that they lack some of the knowledge that is necessary to solve the problem. Students summarize what they know about the problem and what they need to learn to fully understand the problem (Blumberg, 2019).

An example of peer collaboration could be found in many "tiger teams" in a corporate work environment. For instance, at an organization in the Mid-Atlantic region, a group of workers had identified the problem that there was no central repository for locating customer testimonials and feedback despite the fact that the organization had collected a range of data about the customer voice to include surveys, interviews, member services calls, social media feedback, product reviews, and more. In this situation, a small group of workers sought manager project approval given the challenges they saw. Upon obtaining approval, the workers met on a weekly basis to conduct an internal "listening tour" with stakeholders, capture requirements, identify potential feedback repository solutions, centralize resources using the appropriate technology, and distribute access to the resulting repository. Throughout, the manager offered touchpoints with the team to ensure that the project was on track, that all viewpoints were taken into consideration, and offered suggestions on how to best position the project for success. This process made it easier for the organization to find resources and videos wherein members communicate their experiences. The end result was that problems were quickly identified in the source materials enabling the organization to address the feedback more effectively and efficiently.

Peer Response

Peer response leverages the Socratic method of instruction wherein faculty or instructors facilitate or moderate student discussions. In this type of learner-small group interaction, the instructor or trainer plays an active role in guiding the conversation toward learning outcomes by asking questions, redirecting focus, or even posing scenarios for the small groups to consider. Peer response interaction deepens learner understanding and engagement with the training content and may be helpful following the presentation of introductory content (Zakrajsek, 2018). instructional approaches where peer response interactions take place include case studies, concept tests, role plays, student panels, and class demonstrations. For example, in a Chief Learning Officer (CLO) professional development program at a large mid-Atlantic university, participants were asked to read a case study and respond to the following prompts in an online discussion forum:

- What are the organizational issues that Craig (the actor in the case study) is facing and what should he do next to move forward?
- What issues need to be discussed and made part of the consultant/client contract at the beginning of an instructional design project and how might you as a CLO implement an organizational strategy that would support such contracts?

After the CLO program participants responded to these prompts online, they were able to see peer responses and they were asked to respond to at least two peer posts. This created learner-small group interactions within the larger group through the discussion. When the online discussion ended, the instructor provided a debrief on the case, summarized participants online responses to the initial prompts, and engaged the participants in an in-person discussion to compare their responses with the case study debrief, creating a deeper understanding of, and engagement in the learning content.

Peer Facilitation (Peer Facilitated Instruction)

Peer facilitation can be described as a type of learner-small group interaction where students (not instructors) facilitate peer learning activities

(Centre for Teaching & Learning, 2021). The role of peer facilitation may fall to one single student (or learner) earmarked by the instructor or may rotate among learners. This type of learner-small group interaction requires that the instructor supports students or workers as they develop the skills to tutor other students in peer led facilitation, student-led curriculum development, mutual peer tutoring, or rotated instruction. The benefits of these instructional models or approaches are associated with extending the scale of faculty or instructors by offering students the chance to instruct their fellow peers. This gives facilitating learners an opportunity to more deeply learn about the topic, gain a sense of responsibility, and refine their communication skills. The non-facilitating students benefit by having increased levels of interaction with one another as well as increased access to a facilitator. While this type of learner-small group interaction may extend the scale at which an instructor can reach students, one must be cautious and careful to ensure that peer facilitators are trained and prepared for their engagements with clear outcomes and expectations. The facilitators may require ongoing feedback to ensure they are meeting the overarching objectives of the instruction or training.

Designing Learner-Small Group Interaction

Designing learner-small group interactions involves aligning the type of interaction with appropriate instructional strategies and learning activities to ensure effective implementation. Instructional strategies are what instructors, instructional designers, or instructional systems implement to facilitate student learning. Jonassen, Grabinger, and Harris (1991) described instructional strategies as "the plans and techniques that the instructor or instructional designer uses to engage the learner and facilitate learning" (p. 34). Instructional strategies are also referred to as teaching strategies or approaches. In the instructional design process, instructional strategies are selected after identifying the learning outcomes and assessment criteria for an instructional module, course, or curriculum. Additionally, instructional strategies break down into learning activities or tasks aimed at helping the learner achieve a specific learning outcome. Learner-to-small group interactions can be implemented in an in-person learning context (e.g., classroom) as well as an online learning context. Table 6.1 provides a snapshot of how the three types of learner-to-small group interaction provided in this chapter, i.e., peer collaboration, peer response, and peer facilitation, can be implemented using learning technologies. The categories of learning technologies that best support

Table 6.1 Designing Learner-Small Group Interactions

Types of Learner-Small Group Interaction	Supporting Instructional Strategies and Learning Activities	Supporting Learning Technologies
Peer collaboration More than two learners are paired to think through a problem or learning activity and come to solutions.	Collaborative Learning Cooperative Learning Problem Based Learning Project Based Learning Design Thinking/Design Problems Collaborative Brainstorming Authentic Problems/Scenarios Collaborative Argumentation Collaborative Presentations Fishbowl discussion or activities Think Pair Share Jigsaw Method	Collaboration and Communication Tools group workspaces such as wikis, google sites, dropbox; discussion forums, or audiovisual discussion tools such as Voice Thread or Flipgrid; communication tools such as Slack, text messaging, google chat, zoom) Knowledge Representation Tools concept mapping tools such as Coggle, Popplet, or Bubbl; whiteboarding and brainstorming tools such as Mural, Miro, Google Jam Boards; Knowledge sharing tools such as mentimeter, poll everywhere Content Creation Tools web publishing tools such as Wix, Weebly; Audiovisual presentation tools such as Loom, Canva, Slidesgo; Infographics, flowcharts & social media tools such as Genially, LucidChart, Piktochart, Canva, Visua.ly;
Peer Response Instructors facilitate this type	Socratic Questioning Case Study Method	Collaboration and Communication Tools (e.g., group workspaces such as wikis, google sites,

of interaction among learners. Instructors may define a scenario, pose questions, and redirect the flow of conversation during the learning activity.	Class Demonstrations Online Discussions Blogging/Journaling Role Plays Debates/Panels	dropbox; discussion forums, or audiovisual discussion tools such as Voice Thread or Flipgrid)
Peer Facilitation Students (not instructors) facilitate peer learning activities. The role of facilitation may fall to one single student learner earmarked by the instructor, or may rotate among the students.	Reciprocal Teaching Problem Based Learning (PBL) Rotated student-led instruction Online Discussions Lunch & Learn with PBL	Collaboration and Communication Tools (e.g., group workspaces such as wikis, google sites, dropbox; discussion forums, or audiovisual discussion tools such as Voice Thread or Flipgrid) Content Creation Tools (e.g., web publishing tools, presentation tools)

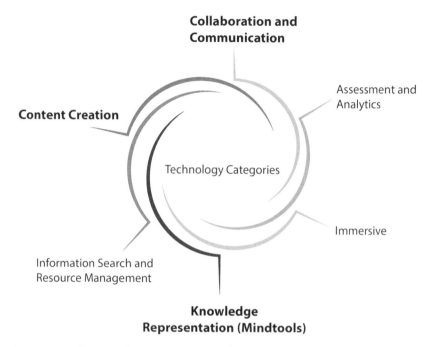

Figure 6.1 Classes of Learning Technologies.

the implementation of learner-to-small group interaction are Collaboration and Communication Tools, Knowledge Representation Tools, and Content Creation Tools (see Figure 6.1).

Below we select a few instructional strategies and corresponding learning activities from each type of learner-to-small group interaction listed in Table 6.1 and provide examples of how this can be implemented using appropriate learning technologies.

Peer Collaboration Using Design Thinking/ Collaborative Brainstorming

Design thinking is a human-centered approach to problem-solving and innovation that has gained momentum in the business world and higher education settings in recent decades (Brown, 2009; Gardner, 2017). Design thinking (or DT) is a collaborative process that engages participants in out-of-the-box thinking through empathy, invention, and iteration. The goal of design thinking is to effectuate positive change that responds to the needs of consumers and evolves the organization's culture blending both continuity and change (Vogel, 2009). Collaborative brainstorming is an excellent activity that supports design thinking.

More specifically, collaborative brainstorming or "brainstorming" is a cognitive activity or method that engages group members in creative problem-solving by encouraging them to share ideas while withholding criticism or judgment (Rudy, 2017). Brainstorming has become a standard tool for ideation (development of new ideas) that leads to innovation. The concept of brainstorming can be traced to Alex Osborn who believed that creativity is fundamental to business success and that everyone has the potential to be creative and learn creative skills (Osborn, 1952). Collaborative brainstorming is widely used in organizations and has taken on a variety of methods beginning with what Osborn called Creative Problem Solving or CPS which includes four steps (clarify, ideate, develop, and implement) to the more recent design thinking approach which is based on the principles of empathy, creativity, efficiency, and efficacy.

Collaborative brainstorming and design thinking exercises can be implemented with collaborative and communication technologies that support virtual chat and whiteboarding sessions such as Zoom, Skype, MS Teams, Blackboard Collaborate, and MURAL, as well as knowledge representation tools such as Coggle, Bubble, iBrainstorm, and Popplet. In order to support practitioners interested in integrating design thinking within their organizations, MURAL, a visual collaboration workspace and Hanno, a team of digital product designers, teamed up to create a two-and-a-half-hour virtual design thinking workshop (Kalbach, 2015). DT workshops are typically held face-to-face using lots of sticky notes and flipcharts because of their ease of use, versatility, and ability to foster communication. However, facilitating face-to-face DT workshops is no longer effective or even feasible in some cases given the modern-day workplace and remote work culture where organizational teams can be spread across multiple locations. MURAL and Hanno's goal was to facilitate a DT workshop virtually and they selected the following three technologies that belong to the category of Collaboration and Communication Tools and Knowledge Representation Tools for this exercise: (1) Zoom, a video conferencing tool, (2) Slack, a platform that facilitates group chat, and (3) MURAL, for mimicking a DT workspace and capturing and organizing ideas that emerged from the virtual session. Figure 6.2 demonstrates how the three technologies used for this workshop (Zoom, Slack, and MURAL) functioned simultaneously on a user's computer screen.

The DT workshop, which included 24 participants spread across different locations, sought to solve the problem of increasing employee trust and

116 Designing for Learner–Small Group Interaction

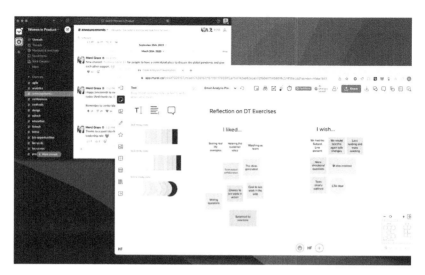

Figure 6.2 Design Thinking Workshop Facilitated Through Zoom, Slack, and MURAL.

collaboration in remote and virtual spaces using design thinking techniques. The virtual design thinking workshop began with a warm-up exercise (ice breaker activity) to get participants acquainted with the three different platforms (Zoom, Slack, and MURAL). Zoom was used to introduce participants to each other through real-time audio and video and to familiarize participants with its screen-sharing feature. After the warm-up exercise, the entire group reconvened in Zoom to reflect on the collaborative experience. Then, participants were divided into six breakout groups and each group (N = 4) was given a four-step design thinking challenge which engaged them in collaborative brainstorming. The workshop ultimately supported participants in learning a new behavior to bring back to their organizations as well as developing solutions and strategies for dealing with resistance to virtual work practice.

Collaborative brainstorming can also be facilitated using knowledge representation tools such as concept mapping tools. In a higher education class, students were asked to contribute concepts to a collaborative concept mapping software known as Popplet. Students were grouped into small teams and asked to share concepts in the form of a cognitive map using Popplet, provide definitions of these concepts, and articulate relations between and across these concepts. The goal was to develop a scale based on these concepts to be used in evaluating the learning design effectiveness of a

Designing for Learner–Small Group Interaction 117

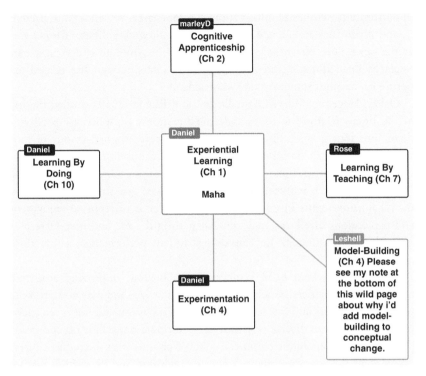

Figure 6.3 An Example of Using Popplet for Collaborative Brainstorming.

technology-supported learning environment. Figure 6.3 shows the concept map created by a group of four students in this class.

Peer Collaboration Using The Jigsaw Method

The Jigsaw method, or teaching technique, is a cooperative learning strategy that enables each student/learner of a small group to specialize in one aspect of a topic, learn about this topic, and present the topic to the group, enabling feedback from each member of the group using a set of guidelines or a rubric that has been set forth by the instructor. The group can then reconcile or synthesize their specialized research into a final report or presentation or use the feedback to improve their understanding of the topic. The final presentations provide all group members with an understanding of their own material, as well as the findings that have emerged from topic-specific group discussions. The jigsaw method is impactful because it gives learners the opportunity to synthesize information in a topic area well enough to present it, and it provides an efficient way to learn an altogether different topic area at the same time. Essentially, each individual becomes an expert in a particular defined domain and then pairs with someone who has related expertise on another topic to share knowledge.

Oakes, Hegedus, Ollerenshaw, Drury, and Richie (2019) studied the use of the Jigsaw Method to teach abdominal anatomy by splitting up 53 students into four groups. Fifty-three volunteers were assigned to one of four stations of the axial computerized topography of the abdominal cavity. Later, students were redistributed into their jigsaw groups to include at least one "expert" from each workstation. Pre and post-test assessments showed statistical improvements in quiz scores and high levels of reported enjoyment and perceptions of educational value suggesting the method may serve as a great short-term strategy for improving student performance, satisfaction, and motivation.

Nalls and Wickerd (2022) propose that beyond improving academic outcomes, the practices associated with the Jigsaw Method may also promote prosocial behaviors and increase perceptions of inclusion and improved social interaction between diverse populations. Additional research is needed to see if these theories manifest empirically, however, the work introduces interesting ideas for how one might design for inclusion and diversity in higher education and workforce training and development programs.

Yet another example of the Jigsaw method was observed in a motorcycle safety education course. The two police officers instructing the class asked different class members to read, review, and summarize the content in the provided book. Following the individualized study, students were asked to share their key takeaways in groups.

Peer Response Using Online Discussions

Online discussions (also known as "threaded discussions" because discussion boards break down into forums to accommodate multiple topics and forums are organized by threads to reflect subtopics or areas of interest) support articulation by engaging learners in dialogue or discourse about a specific topic. Online discussions provide learners with opportunities for explanation, reasoning, critique, justification, argumentation, and exposure to multiple perspectives all of which lead to meaningful learning (Dabbagh et al., 2019). Online discussions can be synchronous or asynchronous, structured or open-ended, and formal or non-formal. Structured or formal online discussions are designed to engage learners in discourse on a specific topic for a finite period of time, whereas open-ended or non-formal online discussions are designed to promote continuous or spontaneous dialogue surrounding multiple topics or topics selected by learners. Online discussions can be text-based or audio or video-driven depending on the technology used, the topic and nature of the discussion, the size of the learner group, and the goal of the discussion.

Asynchronous online discussions can be supported using Learning Management Systems (LMS) or other collaboration and communication tools such as VoiceThread, Google Groups, and Padlet. Formal online discussions require facilitators (moderators) to moderate the discussion. Moderating an online discussion involves posting engaging questions, prompting meaningful responses from participants, keeping the discussion focused on the topic, and providing a summary or synthesis at the end of the discussion that demonstrates collective knowledge construction and enables reflection. Although instructors typically assume the role of moderating an online discussion, learners can also be assigned as facilitators or moderators, particularly in large classes (an example of this was provided earlier in this chapter). Protocols and rubrics for participating in, moderating, and evaluating online discussions should be provided to learners before the discussion begins to establish goals and expectations.

Overall, the research highlights the benefits of asynchronous online discussions as providing opportunities for reflective learning and meaningful processing of subject matter content because of the "delayed" or asynchronous nature of the discourse or dialogue (Hara, Bonk, & Angeli, 2000). Asynchronous online discussions also allow students to participate at their own pace giving them time to read peer posts, think about the points made by their peers, and develop their own responses. Additionally, the collaborative and conversational nature of asynchronous online discussions allows learners to share their 'developing' understandings.

Peer Response Using The Case Study Method

As mentioned earlier in this chapter, the case study method (the use of cases for teaching) is an appropriate method to elicit peer response in learner-small group interaction. The Center for Teaching and Learning defines the case study method as follows: "This method is learner-centered with *intense interaction between participants* as they build their knowledge and work together as a group to examine the case" (Centre for Teaching and Learning, 2022). Using a case-based approach engages students in discussion of specific scenarios that resemble or typically are real-world examples. The instructor's role is that of a facilitator while the students collaboratively analyze and address problems and resolve questions that have no single right answer. As described by Savery (2019, p. 89, in Wiley PBL Handbook) "A case study is usually designed by an expert in the content domain with the intended purpose of telling a story that presents critical pieces of information needed to solve the case".

Harvard University's Law School and School of Business use the case study method as their instructional approach. Through the Case Development Initiative, this case study method of instruction uses real-world examples and video summaries of strategic and organizational issues to increase the fidelity and complexity of the cases. Learners must consider each situation from multiple perspectives, identify key challenges in the case, reconcile the interests of different stakeholders presented in the case, and develop appropriate strategies to resolve each case. For example, the learner may need to analyze both the stakeholders' interests and motivations and the underlying incentives and mission of the organization depicted in the case before arriving at a solution. These enhanced case studies use technology to bring real-life situations to classroom settings, helping students prepare for their professional careers (Harvard Kennedy School, n.d.). An extensive library of case studies organized by subject and implementation type (role play, workshop, or discussion) has been developed using this more authentic approach to the case study method.

Peer Facilitation Using Online Discussions

In this example of peer-facilitated instruction, the instructor of a doctoral class in a higher education institution created small student groups, five students per group, and assigned a peer facilitator for each group. Group members were selected based on their common research interests but members of each group were reassigned to different groups so that they can also learn from peers that have different research interests. There were four consecutive online discussions and two groups in each discussion. Peer facilitators were assigned for each group and new peer facilitators were assigned each time the group members were rotated. This gave each student the opportunity to be a peer facilitator. Table 6.2 provides an example of criteria that peer facilitators must follow or be held accountable for when facilitating online discussions, a type of peer-facilitated instruction.

Table 6.2 Criteria for Facilitating Online Discussions

Criteria for Facilitating Online Discussions

Facilitator or discussant will demonstrate an observable understanding of the topic being discussed. The understanding will be at the critical thinking and synthesis level.

Facilitator or discussant will demonstrate an ability to engage peers in a discussion that is relevant to the topic concepts. This can be done in a variety of ways including but not limited to: posing engaging and probing questions; eliciting responses; and building on responses.

Facilitator or discussant will demonstrate the ability to effectively organize the discussion. This includes: keeping the discussion focused on the topic; providing structure; staying within the timeframe allotted for discussion; and ensuring all participants are engaging and receiving commentary on their contributions.

Facilitator or discussant will demonstrate the ability to help participants relate the concepts discussed to personal and professional experience by using examples from everyday practices.

Peer Facilitation Using PBL "Lunch and Learn" in Workforce Contexts

An example of peer facilitation stems from a Mid-Atlantic financial management company that leverages peer facilitation using the format of a "lunch and learn" program and the Problem-Based Learning (PBL) teaching approach. Instruction in PBL begins with a problem to solve thereby engaging learners in complex problem-solving activities. Learners are placed in small groups of four to six and introduced to a real-world problem that is complex and has multiple solutions and solution paths, and are provided with an iterative heuristic problem-solving model (a reasoning process) that supports reasoning, problem-solving, and critical thinking skills. Tutors or teachers are assigned to each group and act as facilitators prompting the problem-solving process and providing appropriate resources. The major goals of PBL are to help students develop collaborative learning skills, reasoning skills, interpersonal and communication skills, and self-directed learning strategies (Barrows, 1985).

In the format of the lunch and learn session, the peer facilitator introduces a problem statement to the group and encourages a range of potential conversations they could select from to encourage inter-team conversations within defined breakout rooms. In one example, the User Research Team provided seven different rooms with seven separate peer facilitators. Each room represented seven different parts of the website that users could be exploring (e.g., new member onboarding, popular web pages, order page experience, etc.). Each peer facilitator met with the User Research Team prior to the live lunch and learn session, was offered a facilitator guide regarding the format of the session, was given access to curated user videos to be used in the session, and was offered conversation starters through a facilitator script. These scripts were drafted to encourage group dialogue about what participants were witnessing in the videos. Facilitators also had an online whiteboard they could use to capture the ongoing dialogue between group participants. After the session, participants were brought back to discuss their key findings and defined next steps.

Given that the lunch and learns involved participants from multiple departments, the practice sought to break down organizational silos, encourage cross-team idea sharing, and support collaborative and ongoing relationships that lead to increased understanding of the website and actionable insights. The process also brought more awareness to the challenges faced by users navigating and leveraging the resources of the site.

Use Case Integrating the three Types of Learner To Small Group Interaction

Harvard University's Collaborative on Academic Careers in Higher Education (COACHE) survey is an effort to help higher education institutions improve faculty recruitment, development, and retention. Using COACHE data, more than 300 colleges, universities, and state systems have strengthened their capacity to identify the drivers of faculty success and implement informed changes (Harvard Graduate School, 2022). George Mason University (GMU), a mid-Atlantic university in the U.S., is among the 300 colleges/universities that have benefited from COACHE data. One outcome of this research-driven initiative is the design and implementation of Faculty Mentoring Communities (FMC). We provide evidence in this last section of the chapter that FMC is an effective use case example of learner-small group interaction that exemplifies peer collaboration, peer response, and peer facilitation.

The COACHE survey revealed that new faculty members (NFM) need a system to help them integrate into the academic culture of the university and plan for academic success. It is no longer sufficient for NFM to attend formal workshops to understand how to navigate the tenure and promotion system nor to have the department chair be solely responsible for providing related advice, mentoring, or coaching. Given this data, GMU established the Faculty Mentoring Communities (FMC) program and began reaching out to incoming tenure-track faculty and assistant professors to participate in these communities.

So what exactly is an FMC? The Faculty Mentoring Communities program is a university-wide, interdisciplinary program that provides new tenure-track faculty with resources to enhance learning, conduct significant research, and develop strategies to boost engagement and well-being (see Faculty Resources, 2022). It is based on the concept of learning communities that facilitate a sense of community, relationships with colleagues across campus, and an environment to encourage interdisciplinary collaborations and ideas. More specifically, learning communities are groups of people who support each other in their learning agendas, working together on projects, learning from one another as well as from their environment and engaging in a collective sociocultural experience where participation is transformed into a new experience or new learning (Rogoff, 1994; Wilson & Ryder, 1998). Learning communities are considered informal learning environments that represent an intentional restructuring of participants' time and learning experiences around an interdisciplinary theme to foster more explicit intellectual and emotional connections between peers and between disciplines (MacGregor, Smith, Tinto, & Levine, 1999). They act as academic and social support structures that allow people to learn in more authentic and challenging ways.

Learning communities are also called knowledge-building communities (Dabbagh & Bannan-Ritland, 2005). Knowledge-building communities are learning communities in which communication is perceived as transformative (resulting in a new experience or learning) through knowledge sharing and generation. Participants in a knowledge-building community "share a common goal of building meaningful knowledge representations through activities, projects and discussion" and the instructor or tutor "is an active, learning participant in the community" (Selinger & Pearson, 1999, p. 41) (i.e., a peer). It is important to note that while the terms learning communities and communities of practice (COP) are synonymous constructs, the term learning communities is perceived as a broader or more loosely defined term that encompasses any social network or infrastructure that brings people together to share and pursue knowledge. In Chapter 8, we will look at COPs in depth and how they differ from learning communities when we discuss designing for learner-social network interaction.

As mentioned earlier in this chapter, learner-small group interaction is an important interaction for supporting personalized learning. Experts who participated in the Delphi study described the purpose of small group interactions as a place to meet with others to address similar needs, questions, or challenges based on specific strengths or weaknesses. Additionally, experts also noted that how groups are formed, their purpose or topic, and how someone joins a group, are important aspects for consideration in personalizing the learning experience. The FMC program aligns well with these experts' descriptions of learner-small group interaction. For example, selecting Distinguished Faculty Mentors (DFM) to facilitate FMC is based on the following criteria: DFMs must be tenured faculty who are established and respected scholars and researchers, recognized mentors of students or faculty in their discipline, highly regarded teachers, willing to learn and share, and who can speak to the University's" values and mission. Additionally, DFMs should represent the diversity of incoming faculty and be comfortable facilitating and working with individuals across disciplines.

The FMC program at GMU uses the core curriculum of the National Center for Faculty Development and Diversity (NCFDD) and focuses on the following six themes recognized as key to faculty success: (1) establishing a professional identity; (2) creating a successful research agenda; (3) strengthening teaching and learning effectiveness; (4) approaching mentoring; (5) successfully navigating the academy; and (6) developing strategies for work-life integration. Participants in the FMC program are mentored in small groups by teams of DFMs from across the university. Over two semesters, participants will create concrete goals, plans, and benchmarks to guide their paths toward the three-year review that leads to achieving tenure. As a DFM, I planned and facilitated six 1.5-hour FMC sessions with my peer DFM, during the fall semester of 2022. The sessions took place online, synchronously, and over Zoom. Our FMC had 6 NFMs who actively participated in these sessions.

Here is how the three types of learner-small group interaction: Peer Collaboration, Peer Response, and Peer Facilitation were exemplified in these FMC sessions:

- **Peer Collaboration** - NFMs worked in small groups to create a strategic plan, which is the first core skill of the NCFDD curriculum. In each session, two breakout rooms were created in Zoom for two groups of 3 NFMs each. The facilitators (DFMs) ensured the groups were formed in such a way as to support diverse perspectives given the interdisciplinary nature of the FMC. The groups worked on their strategic plan for teaching, research, and service. Each participant was provided a tab in a Google doc to document their strategic plan using a SMART

Goals template. The participants then shared their strategic plans verbally across groups and the DFMs facilitated the dialogue, monitored progress, and provided feedback.
- **Peer Response** - NFMs were asked to provide comments on each others' strategic plans directly in the google document using the commenting feature. During the second FMC session, participants were divided into small groups again using breakout rooms and were asked to address peer comments orally, whether they agreed with these comments (why or why not), and how they plan to address them. This was a round-robin or jigsaw method type of exercise. The DFMs guided the conversation within each breakout room toward learning outcomes by asking questions, redirecting focus, or even posing scenarios for the small groups to consider.
- **Peer Facilitation** - for the remaining three FMC sessions of the semester, three NFM participants were each assigned an NCFDD core skill that was not discussed in the first two FMC sessions and asked to watch the associated video on the NCFDD platform, summarize their understanding of that skill using PPT slides, and explain it to the group. This was peer facilitation using a rotated student-led instruction activity.

References

Barrows, H. S. (1985). *How to design a problem-based curriculum for the preclinical years*. New York: Springer Publishing Co.

Blumberg, P. (2019). Designing for Effective Group Process in *PBL* Using a Learner-Centered Teaching Approach. In M. Moallem, W. Hung, and N. Dabbagh (Eds.), *The Wiley Handbook of PBL* (pp. 343–365). Wiley & Sons Inc.

Brown, T. (2009). *Change by design: How design thinking transforms organizations and inspires innovation*. New York, NY: HarperCollins Publishers.

Burgess, A., van Diggele, C., Roberts, C., & Mellis, C. (2020). Feedback in the clinical setting. *BMC Medical Education*, *20*(460), 1–6.

Centre for Teaching and Learning. (2022). *Case-based learning*. Retrieved December 1, 2022, from https://www.queensu.ca/ctl/resources/instructional-strategies/case-based-learning

Dabbagh, N. & Bannan-Ritland, B. (2005). *Online learning: Concepts, strategies, and application*. Prentice Hall: Pearson Education.

Dabbagh, N., Howland, J., & Marra, R. (2019). *Meaningful online learning: Integrating strategies, activities, and learning technologies for effective designs*. Routledge.

Faculty Resources. (2022). *Faculty mentoring communities*. Retrieved December 1, 2022, from https://faculty.gmu.edu/professional-development/faculty-mentoring-communities

Gardner, L. (2017, September 10). Can design thinking redesign higher ed? *Chronicle of Higher Education*. Retrieved from http://www.chronicle.com/article/Can-Design-Thinking-Redesign/241126

Hara, N., Bonk, C. J., & Angeli, C. (2000). Content analysis of online discussion in an applied educational psychology course. *Instructional Science, 28*(2), 115–152.

Harvard Graduate School of Education. (2022, September 28). *Collaborative on academic careers in Higher Education.* COACHE. Retrieved December 1, 2022, from https://coache.gse.harvard.edu/

Harvard Kennedy School. (2022). *Teaching a course.* Retrieved December 1, 2022, from https://www.hks.harvard.edu/more/about/leadership-administration/academic-deans-office/slate/teaching-resources/teaching-course

Harvard Kennedy School (n.d.) *Teaching a course.* Retrieved November 4, 2022 from https://www.hks.harvard.edu/more/about/leadership-administration/academic-deans-office/slate/teaching-resources/teaching-course

Indian Institute of Management Bangalore Centre for Teaching & Learning. (2021). *Peer Learning: Designing Better Learning Environments.* PDF. Bengaluru, India.

Johnson, D. W., Johnson, R. T., & Smith, K. A. (2014). Cooperative learning: Improving university instruction by basing practice on validated theory. *Journal on Excellence in College Teaching, 25*(3&4), 85–118.

Jonassen, D. H., Grabinger, R. S., & Harris, N. D. C. (1991). Instructional strategies and tactics. *Performance Improvement Quarterly, 3*(2), 29–47.x.

Kalbach, J. (2015, March 10). Recap: MURAL + Hanno co-host a remote design thinking workshop. [Web log comment]. Retrieved from http://blog.mural.co/2017/03/11/recap-mural-hanno-co-host-a-remote-design-thinking-workshop

Laal, M., & Ghodsi, S. (2011). Benefits of collaborative learning. *Procedia Social and Behavioral Sciences, 31*, 486–490. https://blogs.ubc.ca/eoassei/two-stage-exams/

MacGregor, J., Smith, B. L., Tinto, V., & Levine, J. H. (1999). Learning about learning communities: Taking student learning seriously. Materials prepared for the National Resource Center for the First-Year Experience and Students in Transition Teleconference, Columbia, South Carolina, April 19, 1999.

Nalls, A. J., & Wickerd, G. (2022). The jigsaw method: Reviving a powerful positive intervention. *Journal of Applied School Psychology*, DOI: 10.1080/15377903.2022.2124570.

Oakes, D., Hegedus, E., Ollerenshaw, S. L., Drury, H., & Richie, H. (2019). Using the jigsaw method to teach abdominal anatomy. *Anatomical Sciences Education, 12*(3), DOI:10.1002/ase.1802.

Oliveira, I., Tinoca, L., & Pereira, A. (2011). Online group work patterns: How to promote a successful collaboration. *Computers & Education, 57*(1), 1348–1357. doi: 10.1016/j.compedu.2011.01.017.

Oosta, A., & Hoatlin, R. L. (2015). Developing Stronger Peer-to-Peer Feedback in the Undergraduate Creative Writing Workshop. *Young Scholars in Writing, 9*, 64–76. Retrieved from https://youngscholarsinwriting.org/index.php/ysiw/article/view/129

Osborn, A. F. (1942). *How to think up.* McGraw-Hill.

Osborn, A. (1952) *Wake up your mind: 101 ways to develop creativeness.* New York, NY: Scribner's.

Rogoff, B. (1994). Developing understanding of the idea of communities of learners. *Mind, Culture, and Activity, 4*, 209–229.

Rudy, L. J. (2017, January 16). What is the definition of brainstorming? (For groups and individuals) [web log post]. Retrieved from https://business.tutsplus.com/tutorials/what-is-the-definition-of-brainstorming–cms-27997

Savery, J. (2019). Comparative Pedagogical Models of Problem-Based Learning. In M. Moallem, W. Hung, and N. Dabbagh (Eds.), *The Wiley Handbook of PBL* (pp. 343–365). Wiley & Sons Inc.

Selinger, M., & Pearson, J. (Eds.). (1999). *Telematics in Education: Trends and Issues*. Kidlington, Oxford, UK: Pergamon, An Imprint of Elsevier Science.

Siikanen, R., Härkin, J., Lemmetyinen, J., & Vieira, D. (2020, August 11). Cooperative learning: Benefits, strategies, and activities. Valamis. Retrieved November 18, 2022, from https://www.valamis.com/hub/cooperative-learning#what-is-cooperative-learning

Siikanen, R., Härkin, J., Lemmetyinen, J., & Vieira, D. (2022, September). Develop and Maintain Strategy-Driven Learning Culture. Valamis. Retrieved November 18, 2022, from https://www.valamis.com/wp-content/uploads/2022/09/learning-culture-workbook.pdf

Vogel, C. M. (2009). Notes on the evolution of design thinking: A work in progress. *Design Management Review, 20*(2), 16–27.

Wilson, B., & Ryder, M. (1998). Distributed learning communities: An alternative to designed instructional systems. Available: http://www.cudenver.edu/~bwilson/dlc.html [2000].

Zakrajsek, T. (2018). Reframing the lecturer versus active learning debate: Suggestions for a new way forward, *1*(1), 1–3. DOI: 10.4103/EHP.EHP_14_18

Designing for Learner–Mentor, Coach, or AI Interaction

7

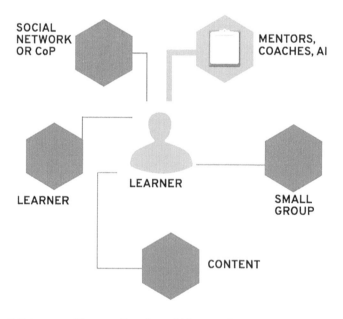

Figure 7.0 Learner-Mentor, Coaches, AI Interaction.

Defining the Terms

For the purposes of this chapter, it is first necessary to define our terms and differentiate between mentors, coaches, and AI coaches. As Marcdante and

DOI: 10.4324/9781003121008-7

Simpson (2018) promote, defining the distinctions within the relationships is necessary to ensure stakeholder expectations are in alignment (e.g., learner to trainer, coach, faculty member, etc.). In their definition, advising, coaching, and mentoring encompass three distinct approaches to providing guidance which is characterized by a spectrum of the intensity and duration of the engagement.

On the lower end of intensity and duration **advising** relates to a point in time event wherein the advisor is asked a specific question or opinion on a topic of focus wherein the learner may or may not follow the advice of an advisor. **Coaching** concentrates on the learners' short and longer-term goals referencing a specific performance target over time. As the International Coaching Federation (https://coachingfederation.org/about) defines, coaching involves, "partnering with clients in a thought-provoking and creative process that inspires them to maximize their personal and professional potential". Finally, towards the higher intensity and longer lasting portion of the spectrum, **mentoring** involves offering the learner guidance about long-term career growth. As defined by the Association for Talent Development, "Mentoring is a reciprocal and collaborative at will relationship that most often occurs between a senior and junior employee for the purpose of the mentee's growth, learning and career development". The practice of mentoring offers the learner an experience with a focus on enculturation and values, character development, socialization into the field, stories, and networking. Bersin (2021) further makes the distinction between coaching and mentoring by acknowledging that coaches serve more as teachers, guides, and helpful psychologists rather than an advocate, which is a role more often found in a mentor. Unlike coaches, mentors also tend to gain an advantage from their ongoing relationship with their mentee, creating a mutually beneficial relationship for long-term career development and professional movement (Reitman & Benatti, 2021).

As we move forward in these chapters, and given the overlap between coaching and mentoring – we will focus more on setting up coaching which can be further intensified by a longer duration and intensity of engagement like mentorship.

Types of Coaches

AI Coaches. A specific type of coaching we explore in this work based on the PLiF research is Artificially Intelligent (AI) coaches. AI coaches leverage deep learning algorithms, machine learning data, and cognitive speech analytics to provide feedback to learners about ways they might improve job skills providing, "a smartwatch for business relationships" (Bersin, 2021). Recognizing the challenge of scale, artificially intelligent coaches aim to provide coaching resources for more employees without requiring intensive personnel resources. While research suggests there may be times when human coaches may be better suited to navigating longer-term career goals, aspirations, as well as cultural challenges, researchers argue that AI coaches may be better positioned to provide data-backed and consistent feedback. This can be driven by the AI's ongoing observations of users in digital environments and based on the data-rich analytics enabled by these daily digital interactions (Bersin, 2021; Luo, Qin, Fang, and Qu, 2021). AI coaching may also be better positioned in large organizations wherein human coaching resources are limited to the C-Suite or in instances where larger-scale coaching programs may be cost-prohibitive. Scale, ongoing data-driven touchpoints with learners, and the democratization of coaching resources all serve as potential advantages of implementing AI coaches (Bersin, 2021).

E-coaching. E-coaching is yet another approach towards structuring the learner-coach, mentor, or AI interaction. Ribbers and Waringa (2015) argue that e-coaching is defined by where the coaching takes place. These researchers describe e-coaching as synonymous with "online coaching, remote coaching, web coaching, cyber coaching, i-coaching, distance coaching, and virtual coaching" (p. 5). They continue with an exploration of the software used to conduct the coaching session (e.g., chat program, webcam-based, text-based, and virtual communications or Voice over the Internet applications). Examples of educational communication technologies which may enable coaching include Microsoft Teams, Zoom, SMS texts, chatbots, and more. Ribbers and Waringa (2015) ultimately define e-Coaching as, "… a non-hierarchical development partnership between two parties separated by a geographical distance, in which the learning and reflection process is conducted via both analogue and virtual means" (p. 7). In this approach and unlike the types of guiding relationships listed above, the distinction for e-coaching stems from the modality of the environment where the coaching is conducted rather than the nature of the relationship between coach and learner.

We continue with an exploration of the theoretical frameworks commonly used in Workforce and adult coaching programs.

Theoretical Grounding in the Design of Coaching Programs

Coaching programs tend to be grounded in different models and frameworks. In the next few paragraphs, we will introduce a few of the different approaches to coaching programs that one may consider when designing a learner-coach, mentor, or AI-coach interaction. It should be noted that this overview is by no means a comprehensive review of existing coaching models and frameworks, however, it may give readers a starting point when theoretically grounding the design of coaching programs for their organizations.

Developed by Graham Alexander and popularized by Sir John Whitmore (1988) and his colleagues, the GROW coaching model first appeared in the book *Coaching for Performance* and continues to be one of the most widely used models for coach training and teaching programs (Grant et al., 2010; Panchal & Riddell, 2020; Seabrook, 2017; van Nieuwerburgh, 2014). The GROW model includes the following elements: **Goal** setting (aspirations), **Reality** checking (current situation, internal and external obstacles), **Options** and alternative strategies or courses of action (possibilities, strengths, resources), and what is to be done, when, by whom, and the **Will** to do it (actions and accountability) (Whitmore, 2010). We will explore the GROW framework in action in the section on AI coaching later in this chapter (Terblanche, Molyn, Hann, & Nilssons, 2022).

In the GROW model, goal setting is critical. Once a specific goal has been set, the learner is asked questions by the coach to explore their current reality and what motivates the changes they are aiming to achieve. Through this line of guided inquiry, coaches also seek to facilitate an awareness surrounding the internal and external blockers that may impede the changes needed to reach the learner's goal. Seabrook (2017) makes the distinction here regarding the non-directive approach espoused by the GROW model and the directive approach often applied in instructional coaching with results that suggest that the non-directive means of inquiry may be more impactful in the long term. This enables the participating learner the opportunity to explore the problem space in their own way, facilitating the learner's internalization of the problem space.

In the options stage, learners are asked to brainstorm or envision alternative behaviors they may "try on" or self-experiments they would like to pursue. They are also encouraged to consider internal or external support that they can use to achieve their espoused goals. After acknowledging the abundance of these support resources, the coach can assess what the learner is actually looking to achieve based on their actions and the corresponding level of accountability associated with those actions. At this point, the role of the coach evolves to support and track future progress (Miller, 2020).

The impact of the GROW model is well documented and supports the claims that it encourages higher work satisfaction, productivity, and performance (Whitmore, 2010). For example, an implementation of a coaching program theoretically grounded in the GROW framework has successfully increased assessments of perceived well-being and decreased reports of negative mental health symptoms for 109 school administrators in Southeast Nigeria (Okorie et al., 2022). GROW has also been shown to support positive learning experiences that support intentional teaching, personalized support, and continuous improvement processes in professional development for teachers (Seabrook, 2017).

While GROW is a popular coaching framework, critics espouse that it is too rudimentary and lacks details on goal setting, concept internalization, and the continued maintenance stages of coaching (Ribbers & Waringa, 2015). Another coaching framework that sought to enhance the GROW coaching model was developed in 2002 by Whittleworth and Gilbert called OSCAR (2002). This coaching model provides an acronym that stands for **Outcome** or what the learner is hoping to journey towards, **Situation** or the current starting point, **Choices** and consequences or the potential route options, **Actions** or a detailed plan, as well as **Review** or progress tracking. Focused on employee growth, this coaching model sought to arm managers with the questions to keep the coaching process "focused, structured, and time effective" (p. 39). The additional letter surrounding action being brought forth in this model supports an adjusted focus on an action plan that is more tangibly defined. Arguably, the action is assumed in the GROW model as the final step. OSCAR, however, seeks to build upon the popular GROW framework by further detailing the explicit steps that will be taken to achieve the intended outcome. Others have argued that OSCAR offers a more flexible approach to coaching which focuses on solutions rather than analyzing problems (Institute of Leadership and Management, n.d.)

Another popular coaching model comes from the acronym WOOP or Wish, Outcome, Obstacle, and Plan. Proposed by German psychologist Gabriele Oettingen (2014), WOOP sought to integrate motivational theory with coaching by leveraging a practice called mental contrasting. Leveraging this practice, Oettingen promotes considering the goal, anticipating a positive outcome, as well as considering the obstacles that could get in the way. After considering these factors, a plan can be formulated in response. Results from applying WOOP include lowering stress in health care providers, improving time management for students in vocational business school programs, and improvements in student outcomes (e.g., grades, time on task, and homework completion) for school children (Duckworth, Kirby, Oettingen, 2013; Oettingen, Kappes, Gutenberg, Gollwitzer, 2015; Saddawi-Konefka et al., 2017).

These coaching frameworks continue to evolve with more recent approaches focused on the application of appreciative, solutions-based, and cognitive behavioral coaching grounded in positive psychology (Ribbers & Waringa, 2015). What seems consistent in each of these models is that a goal, objective, or result is explicitly defined. Then strengths, tools, resources, support as well as obstacles are identified. Next, action plans are developed, monitored, evaluated, and periodically revisited to ensure that learners are still on the right track. The monitoring, evaluation, and adjustment phases are also important steps in self-reflection. Ultimately engagement with this type of framework may support self-regulation which in turn prepares the learner with the skills needed to internalize learnings and apply this framework to their future goals (Barrato & Moneo, 2021; Mann et al, 2022; Ribbers & Waringa, 2015).

Armed with the knowledge of different theoretical frameworks grounding the design of popular coaching programs, we will continue with an exploration of design considerations for online and e-Coaching programs, AI coaching, and further consider the overarching role of technology in the learner-coach, mentor, or AI interaction.

Designing for Online and e-Coaching Programs

When it comes to the design of online and e-coaching programs, Ribbers and Waringa (2015) outline different modalities of e-coaching, including coaching via video link (video coaching), coaching by phone (telephone coaching), coaching via chat program (chat coaching), and coaching via email (email coaching). It is important to note that text (text coaching) is yet another medium that might be employed.

As educational communication technologies evolve, other modalities may also emerge in virtual reality and augmented reality. In these environments, visual coaching alerts may be employed to support the development of new habits, behaviors, mentalities, or practices. For instance, an AR app may anticipate a lull in a learner's schedule and serve up an article corresponding to the content associated with a learner or employee's upcoming meeting. Another possibility is that AI could prompt the learner to take on newly defined or desired behaviors within the user's eyeglasses.

Ribbers and Waringa (2015) further differentiate e-Coaching from traditional face-to-face coaching by considering the following factors: **visibility** or whether or not the coach and learner can see one another, **proximity** or physical closeness, **time** (or whether the interaction is asynchronous, synchronous, or diachronous), and **means of expression** or how the communication happens (e.g., written, spoken, etc.). It is also important to note that a mix of coaching modalities may be used to capitalize on the advantages and address the disadvantages of the different approaches. One such program leveraging multiple coaching modalities is explored in the next few paragraphs.

In an attempt to address resident burnout in medical education programs, Mann et al. (2022) conducted a follow-up qualitative study to investigate the impact of their online group coaching program called Better Together. A coaching program founded based on the Circumstances, Thoughts, Feelings, Action, and Results (CTFAR) model, the program sought to provide residents a framework to enhance their resilience in the face of program attrition and burnout. The program offered twice weekly live coaching calls over Zoom (video coaching), unlimited written coaching via an anonymous forum (chat coaching), and self-study modalities (e.g., videos and worksheets). The six-month voluntary online coaching program was piloted with 101 women residents and had shown statistically significant improvements in perceptions surrounding emotional exhaustion, imposter syndrome, and self-compassion compared to a control group.

The success of these results indicates the potential value of multiple modalities in coaching approaches. For instance, the video coaching allowed participants to synchronously speak and view one another from a remote location. This provided learners with a flexible means of engaging with other learners as well as their coach without leaving their houses. Challenges associated with video coaching, however, include the necessity for fast, stable, and reliable internet connections. The visibility of the learner may also be restricted by the current camera set-up wherein important body language cues may be less observable. Finally, in group scenarios, it is also difficult to continue certain side conversations. For instance, a video-based coaching engagement requires that individuals take turns while speaking. The configuration of the call is less conducive to facilitating multiple conversations compared to face-to-face coaching sessions.

This study also supported chat conversations wherein learners could synchronously interact with remote coaches instantaneously using written communications. Writing out the conversation has the added benefit of allowing learners the chance to reflect and support cognitive and emotional processing that can be saved and documented for future reflection compared to the spoken word. Disadvantages of the approach include not being able to see the other participant, potential misinterpretations, and the length of time it takes to chat compared to a face-to-face or video-based coaching conversation. The flow of conversation may also be disruptive due to distractions. Finally, the e-coaching will also be dependent on the language and writing skills of the coach and learner.

Leveraging both video and chat coaching, the Better Together researchers sought to understand participant impressions and perceptions of the coaching resources following the completion of the program. Themes that emerged from 17 interviews included evidence of healthy coping strategies based on the learner's application of the CTFAR model, a perceived positive and ongoing impact on the learner's sense of being part of a larger community, and an appreciation for the accessible and customizable program design. The group-based coaching design, ability to solicit anonymous coaching feedback, an application of a theoretical framework guided by videos, resources, and discussion all supported the success of this program by providing flexible resources and frameworks, spaces to reflect, and the ability to connect with other women medical residents facing similar challenges at times and places that were convenient to the learners.

By integrating several e-Coaching modalities, Better together was able to offer flexible spaces for facilitating the learner-coach, mentor, or AI interaction. Their approach capitalized on the advantages and disadvantages of each modality by providing multiple avenues to obtain coaching feedback for the learners.

Considerations for the Design of AI Coaches

As Bersin (2021) indicates there is a range of software applications that are emerging in the sphere of AI coaching. One example is Cultivate, an AI-driven digital coaching application that highlights and reflects back a learners' existing behaviors based on email and chat interactions. These interactions provide and reflect back leadership or managerial insights that can be used to help the learner keep track of how they are (or are not) engaging with their teams. For example, with the move to remote work in 2020, Price WaterHouse Cooper leveraged an AI coaching program through Cultivate to foster better working relationships between their employees (Bersin, 2021). Cultivate bubbled up insights on the frequency in which managers praised their fellow teammates and employees or the number of times they acknowledged or interacted with individual team members. The insights can also reflect back when workers seem to be the most productive, encouraging wellness and enhanced productivity. The outputs also acknowledge when a worker or learner needs a psychological break. This tool, complemented by other data to include 360-feedback, engagement surveys, and email content can help learners become more aware of how they are treating others and get a sense of how they might refocus their efforts to create more inclusive work environments, improve relationships, or coach struggling employees to better outcomes.

Other examples of artificially intelligent coaches analyze language patterns through natural language processing to help determine the best ways to connect with other learners, employees, referrals, customers, or potential clients. One such example, Cyrano.ai, is included in the use case section of this chapter.

One area of exploration for AI coaches is in what spaces this technology may be most impactful compared to human coaches. To investigate this, Luo, Qin, Fang, and Qu (2021) researched the impact of human and AI coaches in a series of randomized field experiments in an organization with 429 sales representatives at two Fintech companies. The researchers were interested in how the artificially intelligent coaches impacted the experience of low, middle, and high performers and questioned whether or not the AI coaches were helpful to all participants.

AI and human coaches were asked to review 100–125 sales calls for sales feedback. In this initial analysis, the AI coach was able to detect more mistakes and solutions compared to its human counterpart.

Leveraging purchase rate and survey data as baseline metrics, the researchers found an inverted U-shaped pattern in performance gains, with both the lower and higher-performing agents achieving significant increases with the AI coach. Middle-of-the-road performers benefited the most from the AI coach showing the highest increases in sales and satisfaction with the coaching experience. These findings suggest that mid-level performers benefited the most and were able to enhance their performance by applying the lessons learned from the AI coaches to their work practice. While all workers benefited from the use of the AI coach, the discrepancies between middle versus lower and higher performers prompt new questions about what might contribute to these differences. Survey data indicated that lower performers were more overwhelmed compared to the other workers. The survey also suggests that higher performers perceived higher levels of resentment towards the AI coach compared to the other workers. In the second iteration of the experiment, the researchers limited the AI feedback to lower performers and found statistically significant differences in performances with the AI coach and lower reported levels of cognitive overload for this group. In the final iteration of the experiment, researchers leveraged both AI coaches and humans to support workers. In this experiment, coaches read the AI-generated feedback and delivered it to the worker. Ultimately, this research suggests that a hybrid use of both human and AI coaches provided the best outcomes overall indicating a partnership between AI and human coaches may be the best suited towards improved performance.

In another exploration of the impact of AI coaches, Terblanche et al. (2022) made the distinction between artificially narrow intelligence (ANI) and artificial general intelligence (AGI). The researchers of this study were interested in the impact of an artificially intelligent AI coach, VICI which was specifically and narrowly built to encourage better outcomes for student goal attainment. The researchers were specifically curious about VICI's ability to influence other important psychological dimensions to include psychological well-being, resilience, and perceived stress in undergraduate business students based in the United Kingdom. Survey data was collected before, after, and 3 months following the use of VICI. The analysis revealed that only goal attainment showed statistically significant improvements. The results, however, suggest the efficacy of AI in improving specified coaching outcomes in a scalable and inexpensive manner.

AI coaches have additionally been explored for their ability to optimize team mental models within complex surgical environments introducing an overlap between the human and the computer as partners in optimizing the operational environment (Seo 2021). With the goal of mitigating any preventable errors, the AI coach was designed to evaluate and prompt team members in two simulated team-based scenarios. The AI coach sought to infer where there might be misalignment in the team's mental models during complex healthcare executions. Based on the researcher's design, the AI coach inferred misalignment and demonstrated a 75% recall for future challenges which offers a promising start toward mitigating problems within the operating room before they even happen. This use of the AI coach as a just-in-time assistive device has also been seen in cars and industrial operations and may demonstrate another role of AI coaches in providing information and guidance at a point of need within an operational environment.

Increased interest in leveraging AI coaches has prompted several papers regarding theoretical frameworks for coaching at scale which beg important questions regarding privacy, equity, and representation (Braee, Rucker, Baglioone, Ameko, & Barnes, 2020; Terblanche, 2020; Terblanche, Molyn, Haan, & Nilsson, 2022). We explore the design implications of these in the paragraphs below.

Acknowledging the challenges associated with the design of artificially intelligent coaches, Baee et al. (2020) proposed a reworked framework from data science to be leveraged in the development of these support systems. The researchers espouse that successful AI coaches must prioritize **reliability**, **fairness**, **engagement**, and **ethics**.

The construct of reliability acknowledges that there are data pieces associated with a students' or employees' profile that may not be known in the development of the AI coach. Missing data or sample bias may make recommendations from an AI coach less impactful without awareness or consideration of factors such as wealth and/or culture. Many AI coaches also rely on self reports as a means of evaluation, which can translate to errors based on faulty user inputs or lacking a common vocabulary. An additional challenge stems from those who may seek to corrupt the AI coach. Internet trolls have been known to subvert and corrupt AI chatbots with racist propaganda. Instances like Microsoft's Tay Chatbot demonstrate how bad actors can impede the development of AI coaching technologies.

The construct of Fairness seeks to address concerns regarding disparate outcomes. This is where representative sampling in the development of the AI coach becomes critical for ensuring positive experiences. For example, basing all of the user research on male audiences may bias the abilities of the AI coach toward behaviors that may not be as useful towards women. You may over-treat one population or under-treat another, without consideration for the audience you are seeking to support. Fairness is also a consideration when defining metrics associated with the AI coach's success. As Obermeyer and Mullainathan (2019) found, a focus on cost may translate to worse outcomes for one group over another.

Engagement within this framework alludes to the motivational, attitudinal, and attentional aspects of the AI coaches' design. The key consideration in engagement is to ensure that the AI coach provides enough value and is designed in a way to encourage use. For example, too many alerts may translate to cognitive overload for the end user and a perception that the coach is a nuisance. Too few may stop the user from creating a practice of using the AI coach. Gamification as well as short and long-term planning may help facilitate ongoing interaction.

Finally, ethics, or the impact of technology on society, is a critical consideration throughout all systems designs. Sample selection, privacy, data storage, data ownership and how data is reported and presented all pose important ethical questions for developers, designers, and researchers of AI coaches. Are the populations used to test the AI coach considered vulnerable? Who owns the data associated with the interactions between the individual and coach? Where is the data kept? What data might be sensitive or destructive if hacked or leaked? It is particularly important to conceive of how to frame less desirable outcomes for end users. For example, a recent interface design of Fintech brokerage Robinhood prompted 19-year-old Alex Kearns to commit suicide given his belief that he owed hundreds of thousands of dollars for stock market losses (Dokoupil et al., 2021). While all systems may have unintended consequences, we have an obligation as designers to explore how interpretation may influence human behaviors.

Role of Technology

The table below only focuses on four types of guidance in the learner-coach, mentor, or AI interaction in the PLiF framework. As we can see here, two technology classifications supported by the learner-coach, mentor, or AI coaching interaction include collaboration and communication as well as assessment and analytics tools.

Collaboration and communication tools here are essential for allowing for the 1 to 1 or the mix of 1 to 1 and 1 to N interactions. In the table below, it is notable to see how the use of the tools differs. For example, human-based interactions tend to focus on communication and collaboration technology classifications whereas AI coaching is more aligned with providing assessment and analytic capabilities. We also saw in this chapter, how researchers are beginning to experiment with a hybrid mix of AI and human coaches to leverage the scalable powers of AI while also capitalizing on the emotional intelligence of humans (Luo et al., 2021) (Figure 7.1) (Table 7.1).

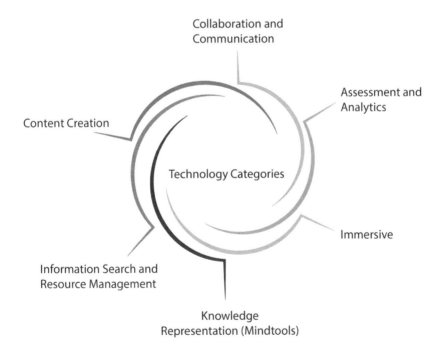

Figure 7.1 Technology Categories.

Table 7.1 Technology Recommendations Based on Type of Guidance

Type of Guidance	Technologies	Optimized For ...	Technology Classifications
Mentoring	Zoom, Microsoft Teams, Slack, SMS Text	Long-term networking relationships	Collaboration and Communication
Online/In-Person Coaching	Zoom, Microsoft Teams, Slack, SMS Text	Supporting progress toward defined goals	Collaboration and Communication
AI coaching	Cultivate, Torch.io, Cyrano.ai, Vici	Scaling coaching solutions. Bubbling up ongoing observations based on digitally based conversations, meetings, and emails.	Assessment and Analytics

Designing Coaching and Mentoring Programs Using Train the Trainer Model

The "Train The Trainer" model is a training framework intended to engage master trainers in coaching new trainers that are less experienced with a particular topic or skill, or with training overall (https://www.cdc.gov/healthyschools/trainingtools.htm). It serves as an internal training program that has the ability to help ensure that your employees are learning and acquiring all of the skills, knowledge, and insight they need to perform their jobs well and it does this through coaching and mentoring. Supportive instructional strategies are strategies typically enacted by the expert, coach, mentor, instructor, or embedded AI agent or performance support system, with the goal of modeling the desired performance, skill, or process, and observing and supporting learners during their implementation of a learning task. In this approach, coaching consists of observing or monitoring learner performance when completing a task and offering hints, feedback, and modeling to bring learner performance closer to expert performance (Collins & Kapur, 2014). So how can the train-the-trainer model support learner-coach, mentoring, and AI interactions? Let's consider this workplace training example in which an online apprenticeship program was developed to train corporate team members in the Appreciative Inquiry.

A large pharmaceutical company is transitioning to a more flexible employee development model called Appreciative Inquiry. Before transitioning to this new methodology, company employees were members of small work teams that moved through a traditional development process of identifying problems and developing solutions without much authority or influence because team members expected leaders and project managers to make final decisions. This traditional employee development curriculum did not reflect the new management style needed to cope with shifting priorities, matrixed responsibilities, and short production deadlines, hence a more flexible employee development methodology called Appreciative Inquiry was instituted at the company.

In order to redefine roles across the organization, new teams were formed so that team members could be groomed to hold the position of team leader or project manager in their respective departments. These team members were matched with online coaches and mentors to help them develop expert-level knowledge of the Appreciative Inquiry process. Multimedia resources were made available for the learners to use to observe modeled examples of the approach. Learners documented their attempts to apply the appreciative inquiry model to their work situations through online journals, and submitted role-play videos for mentor and peer critique. They also participated in developmental team projects and engaged in online discussions with their peers. The goal was to allow these team members to internalize the skills of experienced leaders and managers who can use the Appreciative Inquiry process to build and support successful productive teams.

The Train-The-Trainer model engages learners in active and constructive thinking processes through observation of expert performance, articulation, and reflective practice. It also engages learners in goal-directed and regulatory behavior as they seek to become experts in their own right. And thirdly, it engages learners in collaborative and conversational activities as they seek help, guidance, and support from experts, coaches, mentors, and peers.

Case Study/Use Case: Cyrano.ai

Named after the French play written in 1897, the original purpose of Cyrano.ai was to use AI to analyze and enhance conversations between therapists and their youthful patients. The tool was developed to address the threat of suicide, the second most common cause of death for teenagers. Built specifically with the aim to offer free psychological and mental health resources to at-risk adolescents, Cyrano.ai was designed as a scalable solution to analyze adolescent and therapist conversations to encourage more meaningful dialogue. Cyrano.ai does this by scaling data analytics for coaching and psychiatric professionals with the aim of offering free mental health resources to troubled teens. To fund this enterprise, Cyrano.ai also offers an enterprise suite of insights specifically for sales representatives to strategically leverage conversation as a mechanism for emotional change (Limon & Plaster, 2022). This, in turn, also builds a database of natural language processing (NLP) model for analysis, fueling future insights on how one might structure conversations to be the most impactful depending on the end user. As Baee et al. (2020) point out, the distinctions between young adults and salespeople will be critical to investigate and understand in order to enhance the reliability and ethics of the tool.

Founded by former Executive Director and CEO of a medical health clinic, Scott Sandland founded Cyrano.ai due to his in-depth experience with troubled teenagers. He felt that many of the existing personality-driven assessments of AI coaching were limited and did not take into account the myriad of factors that might drive behaviors. Instead, Sandland has worked with his team to develop machine learning algorithms that analyze NLP to detect an employee or client's desires, abilities, reasoning, needs, and assessed commitment. These factors help guide how messages could be crafted and what strategies might work best for the collaboration or to foster a better working relationship.

In a recorded session, a Cyrano report provides insight into the conversational commitment of different stakeholders (e.g., compelled, focused, or curious), priorities (e.g., data, instinct, community, etc.), and preferred type of communication styles (e.g., visual, auditory, or kinesthetic). In each report, the service also offers actionable suggestions on how best to communicate, follow-up, and work with the other person based on the observations the artificially intelligent analysis makes. Users of Cyrano.ai can then leverage the insights to better frame, propose, or pitch solutions enhancing collaborative partnerships and garnering enhanced business outcomes to include 26% increases in sales and 44% increases in efficiency at a Metro Honda car dealership according to their site.

References

Barrato, J. B., & Moneo, M. R. (2021). Can coaching contribute to the development of self-regulation? Similarities and differences between these two processes. *Coaching: An International Journal of Theory, Research, and Practice*, *15*(2), 166–179. https://www.tandfonline.com/doi/abs/10.1080/17521882.2021.1929362

Bersin, J. (2021). AI-enabled coaching is hot. And there's lots more to come. *Bersin Research*. https://joshbersin.com/2021/07/ai-enabled-coaching-is-hot-and-theres-lots-more-to-come/

Baee, S., Rucker, M., Baglione, A., Ameko, M. K., & Barnes, L. (2020). A framework for addressing the risks and opportunities in AI-supported virtual health coaches. *Proceedings of the PervasiveHealth Conference.*

Collins, Allan, & Kapur, Manu. (2014). Cognitive apprenticeship. In *The Cambridge Handbook of the Learning Sciences* (pp. 109–127). 10.1017/cbo9781139519526.008

Dokoupil, T., Kaplan, M., Finn, M., McDonald, C., Kamin, J., & Kaplan, R. (2021, February 8). *Alex Kearns died thinking he owed hundreds of thousands for stock market losses on Robinhood. His parents have sued over his suicide.* CBS News. https://www.cbsnews.com/news/alex-kearns-robinhood-trader-suicide-wrongful-death-suit/

Duckworth, A. L., Kirby, T. A., Gollwitzer, A., & Oettingen, G. (2013). From fantasy to action: Mental contrasting with implementation intentions (MCII) improves academic performance in children. *Social Psychological and Personality Science, 4*(6), 745–753. https://www.tandfonline.com/doi/abs/10.1080/01443410.2010.506003?journalCode=cedp20&src=recsys

Grant, A. M., Green, L. S., & Rynsaardt, J. (2010). Developmental coaching for high school teachers: Executive coaching goes to school. *Consulting Psychology Journal, 62*(3), 151–168.

Institute of Leadership and Management (n.d.). Introduction of OSCAR [YouTube Video]. YouTube. https://www.youtube.com/watch?v=DGp3whqYY1Y

Limon, D. & Plaster, B. (2022, January 25). Can AI teach us how to become more emotionally intelligent? Harvard Business Review. https://hbr.org/2022/01/can-ai-teach-us-how-to-become-more-emotionally-intelligent

Luo, X. Qin, M. S., Fang, Z., & Qu, Z. (2021). Artificial intelligence coaches for sale agents: Caveats and solutions. *Journal of Marketing, 85*(2), 14–32. 10.1177/0022242920956676

Mann, A., Fainstad, T., Shah, P., Dieujust, N., Thurmon, K., dunbar, K., Jones, C. (2022). "We're all going though it": Impact off an online group coaching program for medical trainees: A aualitative analysis. *BMC Medical Education, 22.* doi: 10.1186/s12909-022-03729-5

Marcdante, K., & Simpson, D. (2018). Choosing when to advise, coach, or mentor. *Journal of Graduate Medical Education, 10*(2), 227–228. 10.4300/JGME-D-18-00111.1

Miller, K. (2020, April 3). *What is the GROW coaching model (incl. examples)*. Positive Psychology. https://positivepsychology.com/grow-coaching-model/

Obermeyer, Z. & Mullainathan, S. (2019). Dissecting racial bias in an algorithm used to manage the health of populations. *Science, 366*(6464), 447–453. doi: 10.1126/science.aax2342

Oettingen, G. (2014, October 27). *Stop being so positive. Harvard Business Review.* https://hbr.org/2014/10/stop-being-so-positive

Oettingen, G., Kappes, H. B., Gutenberg, K. B., & Gollwitzer, P. M. (2015). Self-regulation of time management: Mental contrasting with implementation intentions. *European Journal of Social Psychology, 45*(2), 218–229. https://onlinelibrary.wiley.com/doi/abs/10.1002/ejsp.2090

Okorie, C., Ogba, F. N., Amujiri, B. A., Nwankwo, F. M., Oforka, T. O., Igu, C. N., … & Iwuala, H. O. (2022). Zoom-based GROW coaching intervention for improving subjective well-being in a sample of school administrators: A randomized control trial. *Internet Interventions, 29,* 10.1016/j.invent.2022.100549

Panchal, S., & Riddell, P. (2020). The GROWS model: Extending the GROW coaching model to support behavioural change. *The Coaching Psychologist, 16*(2), 12–25.

Reitman, A., & Benatti, S.(2021, March 26). *Mentoring vs. Coaching.* ATD. https://www.td.org/insights/mentoring-versus-coaching-whats-the-difference

Ribbers, A., & Waringa, A. (2015). *E-coaching: Theory and practice for a new online approach to coaching.* Oxon: Routledge.

Saddawi-Konefka, D., Baker, K., Guarino, A., Burns, S. M., Oettingen,G., Gollwitzer, P. M., & Charnin, J. E. (2017). Changing resident physician studying behaviors: A randomized, comparative effectiveness trial of goal setting versus use of WOOP. *Journal of Graduate Medical Education, 9*(4), 451–457. DOI: 10.4300/JGME-D-16-00703.1

Seo, S., Kennedy-Metz, L. R., Zenati, M. A., Shah, J. A., Dias, R. D., & Unhelkar, V. V. (2021). Towards an AI coach to infer team mental model alignment in healthcare. *2021 IEEE Conference on Cognitive and Computational Aspects of Situation Management (CogSIMA)* (pp. 39–44), doi: 10.1109/CogSIMA51574.2021.9475925

Seabrook, L. (2017). *Exploring teachers' perceptions of the GROW coaching model.* ProQuest Dissertations Publishing.

Terblanche, N. (2020). A design framework to create artificial coaches. *International Journal of Evidence Based Coaching and Mentoring, 18*(2), 152–165.

Terblanche, N., Molyn, J., Haan, E., Nilsson, V. O. (2022). Comparing artificial intelligence and human coaching goal attainment efficacy. *PLOS One.* 10.1371/journal.pone.0270255

van Nieuwerburgh, C. (2014). *An introduction to coaching skills: A practical guide.* Sage Publications Ltd.

Whitmore, J. (1988, 1992, 2002, 2010). *Coaching for performance: Growing people, performance and purpose.* London: Nicholas Brealey Publishing.

8
Designing for Learner–Social Network Interaction

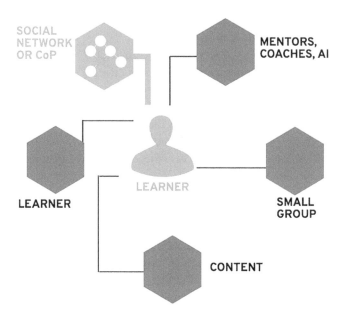

Figure 8.0 Learner to Social Network or COP Interaction.

Overview of Learner-Social Network Interaction

In Chapter 3, we defined learner-social network interaction as a type of interaction that reflects the acceptance of "the network or community of peers"

DOI: 10.4324/9781003121008-8

as a dimension of personalized learning. The term social network or social networking stems from a class of technologies known as social software, social media, or Web 2.0 technology. As described in Chapter 3, Web 2.0 technology is "read-write" technology because it allows users not only to read from the Web but also to share their own content freely, easily, and widely. More importantly, Web 2.0 has been characterized as the "The Social Web" and described as the second stage of Internet growth that is all about "connecting people" in contrast to "connecting information" (Davis, 2008). So Web 2.0 technology is more than a set of cool and new technologies and services and the so-called "network effect" that more than a billion Internet users are producing is changing the way people interact, do business, and learn (Anderson, 2007). When Web 2.0 pioneers and influencers were queried about how they would define Web 2.0 technology, different perspectives emerged as expected, however, what stood out were overarching themes such as openness, personal experience, software as a service, user-generated content, the people's Web, social networking, social media, grassroots movement, read/write Web, the wisdom of the crowds, and others (Jones, 2008).

The social side of Web 2.0 was emphasized by EDUCAUSE (http://www.educause.edu/) (a nonprofit association whose mission is to advance higher education by promoting the intelligent use of information technology) in 2007. Specifically, the concepts of user-created content and social networking were highlighted as new trends that will have a significant impact on college and university campus learning environments (Kitsantas & Dabbagh, 2010). Due in part to this emphasis, the term social software (or social media) has become more commonplace in higher education than the term Web 2.0. Additionally, educational researchers and practitioners have further delineated some of the social affordances or attributes of Web 2.0 technologies as (a) establishing group identity and personal reputations, (b) building social contexts of knowledge, (c) enabling personalization, and (d) erecting recommendation and folk knowledge systems (also called folksonomies) (Dabbagh & Reo, 2011). For example, social networking sites such as Facebook and LinkedIn enable members to post personal and professional information (e.g., a resume or CV) and to connect to other professionals and friends with similar interests and skills, forming a personalized network. Members of these social networks can also ask for endorsements or recommendations from others within their personalized network to establish personal reputation systems. Moreover, employers who become part of the network as individuals can look for specialized talent within this "folk" knowledge system that is entirely built and driven by its members (hence the word folksonomy).

Social media has also gained ground in the workplace and has been shifting learning from formal to informal, from individualistic to collectivistic, and from top-down to bottom-up (Dabbagh et al., 2016). The transfer of knowledge through social media has become more fluid between individuals in the same organization or even in the same field, resulting in virtual Communities of Practice (CoPs or vCOPs). These digital learning practices are further described as knowledge maturing, since they afford a more informal, collective sense of learning in the workplace (Freifeld, 2013; Ravenscroft et al., 2012). Different social media technologies such as blogs, microblogs, social bookmarking tools, and wikis are being used in corporate environments and their use has demonstrated a positive impact on work performance (Leftheriotis & Giannakos, 2014). Further, research has suggested that workers who use social media on the job have a higher chance of engaging in learning activities than those who do not (Puijenbroek, Poell, Kroon & Timmerman, 2014).

Overall, Web 2.0 technology and in particular social media has changed the nature of social interaction rendering the learner-social interaction dimension of the Personalized Learning framework (PLiF) a critical component of personalized learning that has major implications for higher education and workplace learning contexts. More specifically, Web 2.0 technology has enabled an unprecedented opportunity to enact the fundamental principle of *learning as a social process* which is based on the concept that knowledge is always under construction (fluid, dynamic) and acquired through enculturation into a community of practice (Dabbagh & Bannan-Ritland, 2005). As posited by Stodd and Reitz (2019):

> *Social learning (in contrast to formal learning) is a story largely written by the learners, themselves. It's about tacit, tribal, and lived wisdom that exists within distributed communities. It's often untidy, diverse, and deeply personal, as people bring their own perspectives and experiences into the learning space (p. 269).*

Another definition of social learning that is equally pertinent for this dimension of PLiF is provided by Sol, Beers, and Wals (2013) who define social learning as "an interactive and dynamic process in a multi-actor setting where knowledge is exchanged and where actors learn by interaction and co-create new knowledge in on-going interaction" (p. 37).

Given these definitions, the question becomes what are the social systems or networks that support learner-to-social network interaction? We identify two such networks for this chapter: Communities of Practice (COP) and Personal Learning Networks (PLN). We describe each social system next.

Communities of Practice

Communities of Practice or COP exemplify social networking or social interaction. The premise is that when enough people begin using a particular social software tool, or interacting (sharing and aggregating) in an online community, the value of the network increases for everyone involved and a multiplier dynamic can set in that escalates the benefits of the service for all (Dabbagh & Reo, 2011). Communities of practice are "groups of people informally bound together by shared expertise and passion for a joint enterprise" (Wenger & Snyder, 2000, p. 139). The construct has become popular in the business community and in organizations that focus on knowledge as intellectual capital.

COPs are formed when members of a community are united by a common purpose and engage in mutual activities, mediating common values, interests, and goals. Specifically, there are three main elements that must be present for COPs to develop, 1) Commitment to a shared domain, 2) Engagement as a community, and 3) A shared practice and dedication to new knowledge (Wenger-Trayner & Wenger-Trayner, 2014). COPs are successful only when these three characteristics are present and cultivated together. Thus COPs can be described as shared environments that permit sustained exploration by members enabling them to understand the kinds of problems that experts in various areas encounter and the knowledge that these experts use as tools to solve problems of practice. Web 2.0 technology has enabled the formation of COPs as social networks that include novices and experts as participants who interact with each other to build a reciprocal interchange of ideas, data, and opinions using collaboration and communication technologies. Transformative styles of communication are characteristic in a COP, which means that the contributor, the participator, and the lurker (receiver) are changed (transformed from novice to expert) as they share in the goal of learning and knowledge generation and application. The purpose of a COP is to develop members' abilities and skills and to build and exchange knowledge in a relevant and meaningful context and a supportive learning environment. The following are the instructional characteristics of COP:

- Control of learning is distributed among the participants in the community and is not in the hands of a single instructor or expert.
- Participants are committed to the generation and sharing of new knowledge.
- Learning activities are flexible and negotiated.

- The participants exhibit high levels of dialogue, interaction, collaboration, and social negotiation.
- A shared goal, problem, or project binds the participants and provides a common focus and an incentive to work together as a community.
- Diversity, multiple perspectives, and epistemic issues are appreciated.
- Traditional disciplinary and conceptual boundaries are crossed.
- Innovation and creativity are encouraged and supported.

Communities of practice are different from formal work groups or project teams in that they are defined by knowledge rather than task, and members are self-selecting rather than assigned by a higher authority. Interaction between the Learner and the COP is seen as involving peers outside of the organizational context. This offers learners the opportunity to leverage the insights of those who are dealing with similar challenges but in different use cases. Exposure to ideas outside of the employee's organizational context may offer new ideas for approaching internal problems. In a COP, learning is a shared endeavor among the members of the community rather than something that is controlled by a single instructor or expert. In this way, learning activities are collaborative, flexible, and diverse. The participants are committed to generating and sharing new knowledge for a common purpose through "high-levels of dialogue, interaction, collaboration, and social negotiation" (Dabbagh & Bannan-Ritland, 2005, p. 8). Cambridge and Suter (2005) describe COPs as "dynamic social structures that require 'cultivation' so that they can emerge and grow" (p. 1). Organizations and individuals can facilitate the formation of a COP through planned activities and by creating a community environment. However, it is the members of the community that keep it flourishing over time.

Who is Doing It

Communities of Practice are utilized in a variety of settings including, education, professional organizations, communities, governments, corporations, health and social care, and businesses (profit or non-profit) all over the world. Most organizations, whether related to business, education, or government, rely on some form of COP as a resource for collaboration and improvement (Wenger-Trayner & Wenger-Trayner, 2014). COPs work well in professional settings because there is no formal teacher-leading instruction. Instead, COPs consist of both novices and experts sharing knowledge to advance their interests or shared goal. COPs are especially useful in a professional setting because they enable practitioners to take collective responsibility for managing the knowledge they need, create a direct link between learning and performance, and are not limited by formal structures. This is especially evident in government contexts where COPs are formed to solve problems related to education, health, and security (Wenger-Trayner & Wenger-Trayner, 2014). However, in more traditional hierarchical organizations where collaboration among workers is not valued, it can be challenging to create a true COP. In education, COPs are useful in teacher training or connecting administrators to other colleagues. COPs can go beyond internal organizational communities by connecting professionals across a specific domain.

Examples of COP

A really great example of COP is professional technical organizations like the Institute of Electrical and Electronics Engineers (IEEE) (https://www.ieee.org/). According to IEEE (2022), it is the world's largest technical professional organization with a diverse membership of software engineers, computer scientists, information technology professionals, physicists, medical doctors, and of course all types of engineers (chemical, materials, mechanical, civil, electric, etc.). The common learning goal or purpose of this COP since its inception in 1884, is to support professionals in these related disciplines for the greater good of humanity.

Another great example of COP is the American Geophysical Union's (AGU) Thriving Earth Exchange (https://thrivingearthexchange.org/). Thriving Earth Exchange or TEE is an example of a successful COP whose goal is to strengthen and enhance collaboration among communities, scientists, and partner organizations so that all communities can build healthy, resilient, thriving, just, and ecologically responsible futures. The TEE (n.d.) believes that "community science" happens when citizens and scientists work together by "defining questions, designing protocols, collecting and analyzing data, and using scientific knowledge in decision-making" (about page). The Thriving Earth Exchange program "connects communities with scientists and supports them as they work together to tackle local challenges related to natural hazards, natural resources, and climate change" (about page). Through TEE, scientists are able to commit to helping local environmental projects submitted by citizens. This creates a community with a single focus to make an environmental impact and "do science together" (about page). Additionally, the TEE facilitates collaboration and interaction among community members, scientists, and sponsors. The TEE cultivates the three necessary characteristics of COP: (1) members of the TEE have a commitment to the **shared interest** of tackling local environmental issues, (b) **interact regularly** through their website, blog, webinars, Twitter, and the Community Science Exchange, and (3) are committed to **working together** scientifically to make a positive impact on a community.

Personal Learning Networks

In order to understand Personal Learning Networks (PLNs) as a social network that supports learner-to-social network interaction, we must first understand what a Personal Learning Environment or PLE is. The concept of PLE, described in chapter 2, dates back to as early as 1976 but the modern concept of the PLE dates back to 2005 with the spread of the use of social media technologies and the exploration of their possibilities to enrich the traditional Virtual Learning Environment or VLE (van-Harmelen, 2008). More specifically, a PLE can be described as a learning environment that is largely facilitated by cloud-based Web 2.0 technologies and services designed to help learners create, organize and share content, participate in collective knowledge generation, and manage their own meaning-making (Dabbagh & Castaneda, 2020). Hence, from a technological perspective, a PLE is a self-driven digital learning space that is unique to its maker, author, or initiator, and composed of one or more technological artifacts, tools, or platforms. These include experience and resource-sharing tools, social networking tools, and mobile and immersive technologies that put the "I" in user interface and the "We" into webs of social participation emphasizing the sociotechnical or socio-technological nature of the PLE (Davis, 2008). Essentially, the PLE is not a collection of new software, rather, it is a new approach to using technologies for learning (Attwell, 2007).

Dabbagh and Reo (2011) developed a three-level framework for social media use that allows learners to develop a PLE by tapping into the affordances of social media and gradually activating the features of the social media tool to enable the degree of interaction and sharing desired for learning in an e-Learning context. Level 1 of this framework is **Personal Information Management**. Level 1 is the lowest level of social interactivity in which the learner uses social media to develop and manage personal information without activating any of the social sharing or networking features the tools provide and does not have an observable presence on the "grid", so to speak. Learners may "pull in" other people's content from the cloud but the goal is to create a private learning environment rather than sharing self-generated content with others. The focus is on managing private information for personal productivity or e-learning tasks such as online bookmarks, multimedia archives, and personal journals and writing.

Level 2 of the framework is **Basic Interaction or Sharing**. This level embraces the users' capacity for communication, social interaction, and collaboration via social media. This is where learners can activate the built-in features of social media that enable social interaction through various strategies such as (a) expressing individual identity, (b) gaining awareness of the presence of others, (c) engaging in conversations, (d) establishing relationships, (e) forming groups and reputations, and (f) sharing experiences and resources publicly (Butterfield, 2003; Sessums, 2006). Collectively, this behavior helps foster a nascent culture of knowledge sharing and can spawn relatively small common interest networks and groups. **This is where the learner starts to build a Personal Learning Network or PLN.**

Level 3 of the framework is **Social Networking**. Social networking, as described earlier in this chapter, corresponds to the highest degree of social interaction. At this level of the framework, learners are using social media to foster informal learning communities based on the knowledge topics or content they are seeking, thereby extending the PLE from a personal learning space to a social learning space or **Personal Learning Network (PLN)**. The mechanism that directs this process is known as the network effect as mentioned earlier. So personal learning networks or PLNs develop as individuals freely and intentionally connect with those interested in the topic under study in order to collaborate and learn collectively, thereby establishing a personalized learner-social network interaction.

Putting it more simply, PLNs are "the people we connect to in order to learn from, collaborate with, or be inspired by" (Jackson, 2015). Jarche (2014) developed a set of processes known as Personal Knowledge Mastery (PKM) to help learners develop effective PLNs. The aim is to empower individuals to take charge of their personal and professional development through a continuous process of seeking, sensing-making, and sharing (see Figure 8.1). Similar to Dabbagh and Reo's (2011) three-level framework of social media use, Jarche's PKM has three stages. First is **seeking,** which involves finding things out and keeping up to date. In other words exploring, filtering, curating, and pulling resources (from trusted sources) related to the skill or knowledge the individual wishes to learn about. Then comes **sensing,** which is how we personalize or process information and use it. This includes reflecting on the information we gathered in the seeking phase, connecting it to our own understandings, and putting it into practice. Then comes

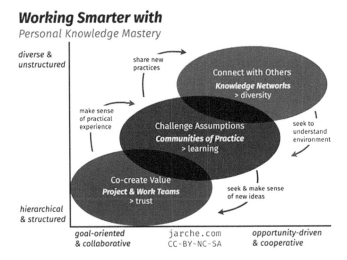

Figure 8.1 Personal Knowledge Mastery (PKM) Framework.

sharing which includes exchanging resources, ideas, and experiences with our networks as well as collaborating with our colleagues.

As illustrated in Figure 8.1, seeking, sensing, and sharing are continuous processes that can start in a PLN, extend to a COP, and result in a work team where the knowledge is applied in the organization to improve performance. The process is then continued to see how well the application worked, and how it can be improved, sharing experiences and new practices along the way. Capturing and sharing information can increase the frequency of serendipitous connections, inside and outside the organization and across disciplines where real innovation happens. As I think about how PKM processes can help an individual develop an effective PLN, an example comes to mind. Using my PLN on Twitter, I discovered a thread that talked about OpenAI's chatGPT (https://openai.com/blog/chatgpt/), a chatbot that optimizes language models for dialogue. I was browsing my Twitter feed (my PLN/social network) and saw a thread from a trusted source mentioning chatGPT and how it is going to impact the college essay. This was my "seeking" stage of PKM. I then shared this new knowledge with doctoral students in a class I was teaching and we engaged in a discussion on what this means to the teaching of writing skills. This was my "sensing" stage. Then I circled back to the "seeking" stage to seek more information on chatGPT and found out that some educators are already using chatGPT in their writing assignments in novel ways. Now I wish to circle back to the "sensing" stage to test ideas of how educators can develop formal applications that integrate chatGPT meaningfully in writing assignments. I will seek a COP that has expertise in this knowledge domain in order to test this new idea. Once this is accomplished, I can share the application with colleagues in my college or department (work team) so that we can integrate this into the curriculum.

Jarche (2014) argues that in addition to seeking, sensing, and sharing, we need to become adept at filtering information as well as discerning when and with whom to share. Like any skill, these require practice and feedback. Much of this can be provided in COPs, which Jarche considers a halfway space between work teams and social networks, where trusted relationships can form that enable people to share knowledge more openly. Connecting social networks, COPs and work teams is important for integrating learning and working in the network era.

A Personal Learning Network (PLN) can be seen as one's gateway to continuous learning, exchange of thoughts and ideas, validation of one's thoughts and insights on challenges encountered, and involvement in the process of continuous inquiry and exploration on topics that matter (Chattopadhyay, 2016). As Couros and Hildebrandt (2016) suggest, "PLNs can be critical for sustained long-term learning, for students and facilitators alike" (p. 157). In today's climate of continuous change, it is not possible for an organization to provide training for every conceivable skill that may be required, particularly when these skills are emergent (Chattopadhyay, 2016). Moreover, the rapidity of change makes ongoing efforts to reskill and retool even more critical to modern-day workers. Workers must be ready to adapt quickly to new contexts triggered by technological advancements, to reskill continuously, and to integrate learning into every facet of their jobs (Dabbagh & Castaneda, 2020). That is why it is extremely critical that individuals take control of their own professional development by developing PLEs and PLNs and using PKM to engage in continuous and lifelong learning.

Designing Learner-Social Network Interaction

Creating, developing, or designing communities of practice (COP), personal learning environments (PLE), or personal learning networks (PLN) is not an easy task given that these learning spaces are self-driven, informal, and composed of one or more technological artifacts, social media tools, or platforms. More importantly, these learning spaces place the responsibility for organizing learning on the individual. Hence learners need support, guidance, and pedagogical interventions to make the best possible use of social media to support their learning goals and effectively engage in learner-social network interaction. Instructional strategies that can be used to support the design and implementation of COPs and PLNs belong to a class of strategies known as supportive instructional strategies (Dabbagh, et al., 2019). Supportive instructional strategies are "strategies typically enacted by the expert, coach, mentor, instructor, or embedded performance support system, with the goal of modeling the desired performance, skill, or process, and observing and supporting learners during their implementation of a learning task" (Dabbagh et al., 2019, p. 29). Supportive instructional strategies include scaffolding, modeling and explaining, and coaching and mentoring.

Scaffolding can support learner to social-network interaction in the following ways: first the interaction between the learner and the instructor, mentor, expert, coach, or instructional system is collaborative and conversational; second, the learner's intentions are at the forefront of the learning task supporting goal-directed behavior; third, the learner is challenged to perform beyond his or her comfort zone enabling active and constructive learning; and fourth, scaffolding eventually enables the learner to independently complete the learning task promoting self-directed and self-regulated learning. Stodd and Reitz (2019) propose a "scaffolded social learning" approach or design methodology that creates a loose structure within which learning communities carry out "sense making" activities while engaging with both formal and informal social knowledge. This design methodology involves creating learning experiences across all modalities of the learning spectrum to include formal, social, and individual learning, and using a range of learning facilitators to include community managers, storytellers, coaches, and social leaders. Distributing learning modalities and learning facilitators helps maintain the momentum of social learning and drives up engagement.

Modeling and explaining is another supportive instructional strategy that can be used to support learners in COPs or PLNs. Modeling and explaining are time-tested instructional strategies made most evident in apprenticeship learning. Apprenticeship learning emphasizes "showing and telling" where showing is the modeling strategy and telling is the explaining strategy. Essentially, modeling shows how a process unfolds, while explaining involves giving reasons why it happens that way. Integrating both the demonstration and explanation during social learning interactions is very useful for the learner to see how a process is handled. This has become increasingly easier to implement given video technology. Modeling and explaining support social learning in the following ways: first it engages learners in active listening and questioning; second it presents concepts and domain knowledge at their level of complexity through the use of authentic processes and contextualized examples; and third it engages learners in constructive thinking through observation, articulation, and reflection.

Coaching and mentoring can also be used to support learner-social network interaction in COPs or PLNs. Coaching and mentoring are supportive instructional strategies that are closely related. Coaching consists of observing or monitoring learner performance when completing a task and offering hints, feedback, and assistance to bring the performance closer to expert performance (Collins & Kapur, 2014), while mentoring is providing expert advice and support to assist learners in attaining goals and overcoming barriers and challenges, and serving as a role model. When implementing coaching and mentoring strategies, it is important not to stifle learner exploration or goal-directed behavior. This can easily happen when coaches or coaching systems provide too much guidance too quickly. As Collins (2012) posited, a coach should only provide assistance when real difficulties are encountered by the learner. In a coaching relationship, the learner is responsible for setting the agenda and content that will be covered during a coaching session and the coach is responsible for managing and facilitating the session and helping the learner use their own skills and resourcefulness to solve specific problems and overcome challenges. Hence, coaching should be perceived as a collaborative process that supports not only the enhancement of the learner's performance or mastery of skill but also the enhancement of the learner's ability for self-directed learning, self-confidence, and personal growth (Mihiotis & Argirou, 2016). Table 8.1 provides a snapshot of how supportive instructional strategies can be implemented using learning technologies.

It goes without saying that **dialogic instructional strategies** are the core for designing learner-social network interaction. Dialogic instructional strategies promote "dialogic" or "conversational" instruction. In other words, instruction that uses "talk" or discourse (dialogue) to support and effectuate learning. Dialogic instruction is centered on dialogue (communication and interaction) between teachers and learners, learners and learners, and learners and the professional community. Dialogue can be verbal, written, or audiovisual (e.g., using VoiceThread or similar) and can take the form of a discussion, debate, argumentation, or questioning. Dialogue in online learning environments is sometimes referred to as digital or electronic discourse. The goal of dialogic instruction is to allow different stakeholders in the teaching and learning process to express their opinions and understandings of the content they are teaching or learning, explain and clarify ideas, exchange and develop ideas, ask questions, provide feedback or commentary, demonstrate how

Table 8.1 Supportive Instructional Strategies Mapped to Learning Activities and Technologies (borrowed from Dabbagh et al., 2019)

Instructional Strategies	Example Learning Activities	Categories of Learning Technologies
Designing for Scaffolding	• Demonstrations • Explanations • Performance Support Systems (PSS) • Individualized Guidance	• Content Creation Tools (e.g., LMS tools, performance support tools and systems, infographics, microlectures) • Knowledge Representation Tools (e.g., KWL charts)
Designing for modeling and explaining	• Demonstrations • Explanations • External modeling of thought processes	• Content Creation Tools (e.g., job aids, video, animations, slideshows, screencasts)
Designing for coaching & mentoring	• Interaction with instructor and experts • Novice coaching • Feedback processes	• Collaboration & Communication Tools (e.g., videoconferencing, animated agents, shared online spaces, chats, Twitter, discussion forums) • Knowledge Representation Tools (e.g., PowerPoint templates)

knowledge learned can be applied in a variety of contexts, and provide evidence-based arguments that advance and expand knowledge of the content domain (Dabbagh et al., 2019).

Instructional strategies that support dialogic learning include articulation, collaboration and social negotiation, and reflection. **Articulation** involves providing opportunities for learners to make their tacit knowledge explicit by overtly explaining it to others. This allows learners to refine their understanding through reasoning, argumentation, and problem-solving, share multiple perspectives, and generalize their knowledge so that it is applicable in different contexts (Collins, 2012). **Collaboration and Social Negotiation** involve working together as a community towards a common goal such as collectively solving problems, creating products, or completing learning tasks. More specifically, collaboration is the act of fostering interaction, conversation, and joining of resources by two or more learners to complete any number of learning activities, and social negotiation encompasses the interrelations and dialogue between two or more individuals to arrive at a mutually beneficial outcome. Collaboration and social negotiation build upon the importance of the social environment and interactions with others to provide information and opinions, which may conflict with their own understanding. It is within the resolution, or negotiation, of these conflicts in which knowledge is constructed and learning occurs (Schunk, 2011). **Reflection** or reflective thinking includes a process of analyzing and making judgments about what has happened to give a situation new meaning. Promoting reflection or reflective thinking involves asking learners to review what they have learned, analyze their performance, and compare it to that of experts and peers (Collins & Kapur, 2014). Reflection is an intentional behavior with the goal of analyzing one's actions, comparing it to others, and ultimately forming expert knowledge on the topic or skill.

Table 8.2 demonstrates how supportive and dialogic instructional strategies can be used to design a COP. The table shows the pedagogical alignment across five instructional design components, including (a) the instructional characteristics of a COP presented earlier in this chapter, (b) the instructional strategies that support the design of a COP (primarily supportive & dialogic), (c) the learning outcomes of the COP, (d) the learning activities the COP participants will engage in, and (e) the assessment (how the effectiveness of the COP will be assessed). The COP represented in Table 8.2 was designed to address the learning problem facing new teachers fresh out of college having had little experience in the classroom. These teachers, upon getting their first teaching job, are usually thrown into a "sink or swim" situation where they don't know what to do. Most schools assign a mentor to a new teacher however mentors' abilities can range from great to poor, and even with an assigned mentor, many new teachers have moved to a new city or state and don't know anyone, and consequently feel isolated from the professional teaching community. This makes it hard to ask questions or to collaborate with their peers. The problem is there is no easy, open way for teachers to communicate past the peers closest to their classroom. A COP will allow new and veteran teachers from different schools and school districts across the state and beyond a place to discuss issues, trends, and other topics that will help them in their profession.

Technologies that Support Learner-Social Network Interaction

Since social networking is heavily based on social media technologies and their learning affordances, we classify social media into the following five

Designing for Learner–Social Network Interaction 159

Table 8.2 A COP to Enculturate New Teachers into the Profession

Characteristics of a CoP	Instructional Strategies	Learning Outcomes	Learning Activities	Assessment
Control of learning is distributed	Collaboration/Social Negotiation Multiple perspectives Articulation	Participants will gain skills in collaboration, critical thinking, and problem-solving. Participants will identify strategies to improve their teaching practice.	Participants will take on roles to maintain the CoP (e.g., administration and maintenance). Participants will decide on future topics to cover.	Participants volunteer for roles to maintain the COP. Participants suggest future topics in a survey, or post questions/ problems to discuss.
A shared goal	Collaboration/Social Negotiation Articulation Multiple Perspectives Scaffolding	Participants will gain strategies for creating lesson plans, classroom management, and other skills relevant to the teaching practice (to be determined as the COP grows)	Participants will join the COP because they share the goal of improving their practice through collaboration, discussions, and shared resources. Participants will establish a sense of community where people feel safe to discuss issues relevant to themselves or others.	A sense of community will be reflected in the continued use of the COP. Teachers take skills/ strategies learned in COP back to their classroom. "Success Stories" and resources will be shared with the community (posted to COP website).
Participants generate and share new knowledge Learning activities are flexible and negotiated	Collaboration/Social Negotiation Problem Solving Reflection Articulation Modeling/Explaining		Participants will discuss/ collaborate through email, forums, chat windows, etc. to solve classroom mgt. problems, create/ collaborate on lesson	Participants self-assess their participation, and participate weekly. Survey on the effectiveness and usefulness of the COP, including how they use the COP.

(Continued)

Table 8.2 (Continued)

Characteristics of a CoP	Instructional Strategies	Learning Outcomes	Learning Activities	Assessment
Participants exhibit high levels of dialogue, interaction, collaboration, and social negotiation	Coaching Scaffolding		plans including new strategies and ideas, and propose future strategies to gain and problems to solve. Participants will reflect on their own practice and experiences as they share personal stories and experiences. Participants will mentor and coach other teachers. Participants will add to the collective knowledge and resources of the COP.	"Success Stories" & "Resources" will be posted to the COP website. Teachers take skills/strategies learned on COP back to their classroom. Evidence of mentor/coach/collaboration/problem solving/critical thinking can be seen on discussion boards. Participants are ranked on "People" page by years of experience, and subject matter is listed.
Multiple perspectives	Collaboration Articulation Modeling/Explaining Coaching Multiple Perspectives Exploration Reflection		Participants will discuss/collaborate through email, forums, chat windows. Participants will reflect on their own practice and experiences as they share personal stories and experiences. Participants will mentor and coach other teachers.	Evidence of cross-curricular collaboration can be seen on discussion boards. Participants suggest future topics in a survey, or post questions/problems to discuss. Reflection will be evident in stories & advice shared on discussion boards.

Traditional disciplinary and conceptual boundaries are crossed		
Innovation and creativity are encouraged and supported	Exploration Articulation Problem Solving Collaboration	Participants will have a variety of experience and knowledge and will collaborate in discussions, chat to create new ideas. Participants will be encouraged to collaborate and engage in discovering/creating new ways to solve problems. Participants will engage in cross-curricular collaboration.

categories to provide a better understanding of the types of social media technologies that can be used to support learner-social network interaction:

1. Communication Tools (e.g., Web 2.0–enabled e-mail applications such as Outlook and Gmail; Web conferencing tools such as Zoom, MS Teams, and Google Meet)
2. Experience- and resource-sharing tools (e.g., blogs, microblogs, & wikis such as WordPress, Twitter, PBWiki; media-sharing tools such as Flickr and YouTube; social bookmarking tools such as Zotero; file-sharing tools, such as Google Docs and Dropbox)
3. Social networking tools (e.g., LinkedIn, FaceBook, Twitter, WhatsApp)
4. Gaming (e.g., social gaming, casual games, MMORPG)
5. Web or online office tools (e.g., Google Apps, Microsoft Teams)

Another way of classifying social media technologies is by functionality. Figure 8.2 provides six functions of social media. These include:

- Publishing
- Sharing
- Messaging
- Discussing
- Collaborating
- Networking

Figure 8.2 Social Media Landscape 2020.

Bower and Torrington (2020) also developed a typology of free Web 2.0 technologies providing educators and designers with a list of 226 social media technologies arranged into 40 types and 15 clusters that can be used via a browser or mobile app to promote more productive and interactive learning. Figure 8.3 illustrates the 15 clusters as text-based tools, image-based tools, video tools, website creation tools, knowledge organization and sharing tools, data analysis tools, 3D modeling tools, coding tools, social networking systems, learning management systems, assessment tools, audio tools, multimodal production tools, digital storytelling tools, and web conferencing tools.

As you can see from the various classifications of social media highlighted in this section, and the examples provided in the visuals, all the technology categories presented in chapter 4 of this book are applicable to designing learner-to-social network interaction. Figure 8.4 shows the six initial technology categories used throughout this book to guide the digital design of the dimensions of the Personalized Learning Interaction Framework.

The MOOC as a Use Case of Learner-Social Network Interaction

Massive Open Online Courses (MOOCs) are a popular trend in the online learning landscape with roots in the ever-expanding repertoire of Open Educational Resources (OER) and online learning technologies (Dabbagh et al., 2016). The term MOOC was coined in 2008 by Dave Cormier to describe the Connectivism and Connective Knowledge (CCK08) course and highlight the key characteristics of this new pedagogical model. For reference purposes, the term MOOC stands for the following:

- Massive - there is no limit on attendance;
- Open - free of charge and accessible to anyone with internet connection;
- Online - delivered via the internet; and
- Courses - structured around a set of goals in a specific area of study

There are two types of MOOCs stemming from two different pedagogical approaches: cMOOCs and xMOOCs. cMOOCs are based on connectivism, which emphasizes interaction with a distributed network of peers, learning artifacts, and learning technologies. Participants are encouraged to utilize different social media and technology platforms to pursue their personal goals, self-organize their participation, and generate and share knowledge with their networks. Social networks and collaborative learning are essential

164 Designing for Learner–Social Network Interaction

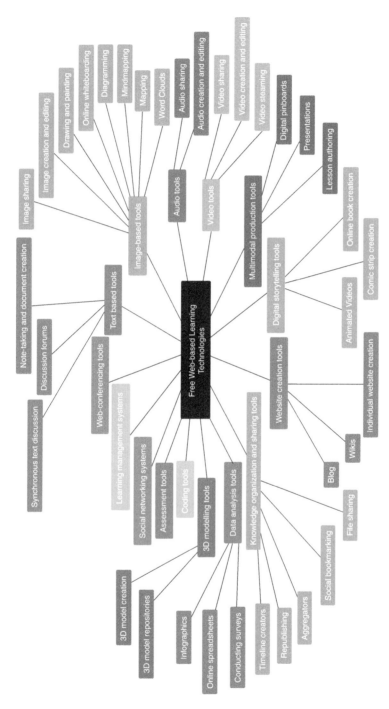

Figure 8.3 Typology of Free Web-Based Learning Technologies.

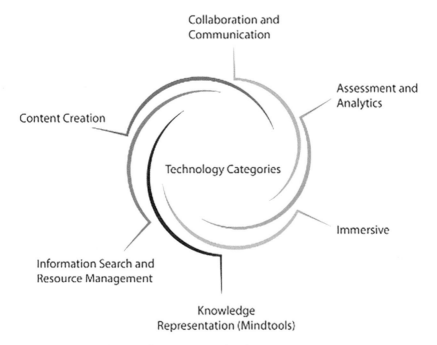

Figure 8.4 Six Classes of Learning Technologies.

elements of a cMOOC. xMOOCs on the other hand are based on a cognitive-behaviorist approach hence xMOOCs are more structured and centralized, and emphasize individual learning through video lectures and regular assessments. xMOOCs are usually offered by prestigious universities using platforms such as Coursera, Edx, and Udacity. cMOOCs are more aligned with learner-social network interaction hence the use case provided here is a cMOOC.

A prime example of a cMOOC in higher education is the Connectivism and Connective Knowledge course, which was offered through the Learning Technologies Center and Extended Education at the University of Manitoba and facilitated by George Siemens and Stephen Downes. The goal of this MOOC was to explain and enable the understanding of the principles of connectivism as a learning theory of the digital age. The MOOC was offered for credit to 25 paying students from the university and was also open for registration at no cost to those interested in participating without credit, which brought the total number of participants to over 2000 across 81 nationalities. This MOOC spanned 12 weeks, each of which included an introductory video, a synchronous session, and suggested readings and activities through the course wiki. Collaboration and discussion were encouraged through different online venues such as discussion forums, Twitter, and blogs. Because the course emphasized learner autonomy, participants were encouraged to set their own personal goals, participate in the course using other social media tools, and decide on their level of participation in the different activities. Interestingly, the open nature of the course and its emphasis on autonomy and diverse networks enabled participants to develop their own sessions and learning venues such as Second Life meeting areas, Google and Facebook groups, and a course page on Twine (Downes, 2008; McAuley et al., 2010). In other words, the MOOC enabled the creation of Personal Learning Networks (PLNs) within the larger social network.

References

Anderson, P. (2007). What is Web 2.0? Ideas, technologies, and implications for education. JISC Technology and Standards Watch, February 2007. Retrieved July 14 2008 from http://www.jisc.ac.uk/media/documents/techwatch/tsw0701b.pdf

Attwell, G. (2007). The personal learning environments: The future of eLearning? *eLearning Papers*, *2*(1), 1–8.

Bower, M., & Torrington, J. (2020). Typology of free web-based learning technologies, Available from https://library.educause.edu/resources/2020/4/typology-of-free-web-based-learning-technologies

Butterfield, S. (2003, March 24). An article complaining about 'social software' … Sylloge. Retrieved February 10, 2006, from http://www.sylloge.com/personal/2003_03_01_s.html#91273866

Cambridge, D., & Suter, V. (2005, January 1). Community of Practice Design Guide: A Step-by-Step Guide for Designing & Cultivating Communities of Practice in Higher Education. Retrieved March 31, 2022, from https://library.educause.edu/resources/2005/1/zcommunity-of-practice-design-guide-a-stepbystep-guide-for-designing-cultivating-communities-of-practice-in-higher-education

Chattopadhyay, S. (2016). *Why Build Personal Learning Networks*. eLearning Industry. Available from https://elearningindustry.com/build-personal-learning-networks

Collins, A. (2012). What is the most effective way to teach problem solving? A commentary on productive failure as a method of teaching. *Instructional Science*, *40*(4), 731–735.

Collins, A. & Kapur, M. (2014). Cognitive Apprenticeship. In R. K. Sawyer (Ed.), *The Cambridge handbook of the learning sciences* (pp. 109–127). Cambridge: University Press.

Couros, A., & Hildebrandt, K. (2016). Designing for open and social learning. In G. Veletsianos (Ed.), *Emergence and innovation in digital learning* (pp. 143–162). AU Press.

Dabbagh, N., & Bannan-Ritland, B. (2005). *Online learning: Concepts, strategies, and application*. Upper Saddle River, NJ: Prentice Hall, Pearson Education.

Dabbagh, N., Benson, A., Denham, A., Joseph, R., Al-Freih, M., Zgheib, G., Fake, H., & Guo, Z. (2016). Learning technologies and globalization: Pedagogical frameworks and applications. *SpringerBriefs in Educational Communications and Technology*. Springer.

Dabbagh, Nada, & Castaneda, Linda. (2020). The PLE as a framework for developing agency in lifelong learning. *Educational Technology Research and Development, 68*, 3041–3055. 10.1007/s11423-020-09831-z

Dabbagh, N., Howland, J., & Marra, R. (2019). *Meaningful online learning: Integrating strategies, activities, and learning technologies for effective designs*. New York, N.Y.: Routledge.

Dabbagh, N., & Reo, R. (2011). Back to the future: Tracing the roots and learning affordances of social software. In M. J. W. Lee, and C. McLoughlin (Eds.), *Web 2.0-based e-Learning: Applying social informatics for tertiary teaching* (pp. 1–20). IGI Global.

Davis, M. (2008). *Semantic wave 2008 report: Industry roadmap to Web 3.0 & multibillion dollar market opportunities (executive summary)*. Washington DC: Project 10X. Retrieved June 16, 2008 from http://www.project10x.com/

Downes, S. (2008). Places to go: Connectivism & connective knowledge. *Innovate: Journal of Online Education, 5*. Retrieved from http://bsili.3csn.org/files/2010/06/Places_to_Go-__Connectivism__Connective_Knowledge.pdf

Freifeld, L. (2013). Dive Into 2013 Training. *Training, 50*(1), 8.

Jackson, N. (2015). Seek, Sense, Share: Understanding the Flow of Information Through a Personal Learning Network. Available from https://www.lifewideeducation.uk/blog/seek-sense-share-understanding-the-flow-of-information-through-a-personal-learning-network

Jarche, H., (2014) The Seek > Sense > Share Framework Inside Learning Technologies January 2014, *Posted Monday, 10 February 22 014* http://jarche.com/2014/02/the-seek-sense-share-framework/

Jones, B. (2008). *Interviews with 20 Web 2.0 influencers: Web 2.0 heroes*. Wiley.

Kitsantas, A., & Dabbagh, N. (2010). *Learning to learn with Integrative Learning Technologies (ILT): A practical guide for academic success*. Information Age Publishing. Available from http://infoagepub.com/products/Learning-to-Learn-with-Integrative-Learning-Technologies

Leftheriotis, I., & Giannakos, M. N. (2014). Using social media for work: Losing your time or improving your work?. *Computers in Human Behavior, 31*, 134–142. DOI: 10.1016/j.chb.2013.10.016

McAuley, A., Stewart, B., Siemens, G., & Cormier, D. (2010). The MOOC model for digital practice. Retrieved from: www.elearnspace.org/Articles/MOOC_Final.pdf

Mihiotis, A., & Argirou, N. (2016). Coaching: From challenge to opportunity. *The Journal of Management Development, 35*(4), 448–463.

Puijenbroek, T. V., Poell, R. F., Kroon, B., & Timmerman, V. (2014). The effect of social media use on work-related learning. *Journal of Computer Assisted Learning, 30*(2), 159–172. DOI:10.1111/jcal.12037

Ravenscroft, A., Schmidt, A., Cook, J., & Bradley, C. (2012). Designing social media for informal learning and knowledge maturing in the digital workplace. *Journal of Computer Assisted Learning, 28*, 235–249. 10.1111/j.1365-2729.2012.00485.x

Sessums, C. (2006, January 21). Notes on the significance of the emergence of blogs and wikis. Available from http://eduspaces.net/csessums/weblog/6172.html

Schunk, D. H. (2011). *Learning theories: An educational perspective* (6th edition). Boston, MA: Pearson Education, Inc.

Sol, J., Beers, P. J., & Wals, A. E. J. (2013). Social learning in regional innovation networks: Trust, commitment and reframing as emergent properties of interaction. *Journal of Cleaner Production, 49*, 35–43. DOI: 10.1016/j.jclepro.2012.07.041

Stodd, J., & Reitz, E. (2019). Social learning. In J. J. Walcutt and S. Schatz (Eds.), *Modernizing learning: Building the future learning ecosystem* (pp. 269–284). Washington DC: Government Publishing Office. License: Creative Commons Attribution CC BY 4.0 IGO

van Harmelen, M. (2008). Design trajectories: Four experiments in PLE implementation. *Interactive Learning Environments, 16*(1), 35–46. DOI: 10.1080/10494820701772686

Wenger, E. C., & Snyder, W. M. (2000). Communities of practice: The organizational frontier. *Harvard Business Review, 78*(1), 139–146.

Wenger-Trayner, E., & Wenger-Trayner, B. (2014, April 15). Communities of practice: A brief introduction. https://wenger-trayner.com/wp-content/uploads/2013/10/06-Brief-introduction-to-communities-of-practice.pdf

Evaluating Personalized Learning Designs 9

Evaluating Strategies for PL

The importance of measuring learning and business outcomes goes without saying. Enhancing a competitive edge, positive impacts to return on investment and equity, increased employee motivation, commitment, and satisfaction are but a few of the many benefits associated with Training and Development programs (Jasson & Govender, 2017; Pelster et al., 2016; Sahinidis & Bouris, 2008; Thompson et al., 2018). Many business executives expect a return on their training investment; however, evidence suggests that learners retain less than 10% of what's learned in formal training courses where the focus is solely on the transmission of content and what is remembered (Jasson & Govender, 2017). This data point may be one of the myriads of reasons to explore other training and development strategies like the PLiF (Thompson et al., 2018).

It's also important to acknowledge that PL metrics, assessment, and evaluation may be dependent on the programs put into place. An assessment of the effectiveness of individualized program implementations toward achieving learning outcomes is different from the assessment of the effectiveness of programmatic level evaluation. As Dabbagh, Howland, and Marra (2018) specify, **assessment** focuses on the measurement of whether or not instructional objectives are met whereas **evaluation** is the process of determining the worth or value of an instructional program. In this chapter, we will explore both the measurement of learning outcomes via assessment as well as programmatic value via evaluation.

DOI: 10.4324/9781003121008-9

And as we mentioned earlier in the book, the PLiF framework is intended to be a holistic strategy. In this, it is imperative to reemphasize that **personalization evolves from the incorporation of each interaction collectively within the framework and not the individual interactions.** Therefore, defining the scope of the overall assessment of learning and programmatic evaluation is necessary for understanding the impact training programs have on an organization overall. In this chapter, we will begin by exploring data points that may be leveraged to personalize learning. Next, we will outline the variety of techniques that might be used to assess the learning happening in the PLiF on an interaction level with acknowledgment that each interaction (e.g., learner-content, learner-learner, learner-small group, learner-mentor, coach, and AI, learner-community of practice), may benefit from its own assessment of metrics and analysis. Finally, we will explore how we can evaluate the effectiveness of the PLiF by adapting Kirkpatrick's Levels of Evaluation to account for a PLiF implementation.

Data Sources to Personalize Learning

As mentioned early, data sources to personalize the learning experience vary depending on the evaluation method defined. These include ***Learner Defined Data*** (e.g., learner preferences, personalized learning plans, learner goals, desired learning activities, learner profiles, and espoused interests); ***Behaviorally Defined Data*** (e.g., implicitly defined interests, information consumption behaviors, navigation preferences, behavioral logs, motivational level); ***Contextually Defined Data*** (e.g., location, time, organizational role, type of task, language, instructor input); ***Relationship Driven Data*** (e.g., content relationships and community relationships); and ***Performance Data*** (e.g., learner performance, existing expertise or prior mastery, completions, academic outcomes, self-report metrics, and level of proficiency).

While certain data sources can personalize an experience, learner perceptions of how useful those personalized learning approaches vary among stakeholders. According to a survey on personalized learning in a Massive Open Online Course, there were considerable differences in perspectives between employees, managers, and teachers or trainers on how learning *should* be personalized (Betts & Sephton, 2018). For example, while 44% of employees found personalizing content based on role or job function desirable, 78% of managers and 61% of trainers and teachers saw the benefit of personalizing in that manner. Similar discrepancies were observed based on personalizing based on previous learner activity with only 55% of employees stating the practice would be useful for their purposes compared to 86% for managers and 78% for teachers or trainers.

Our research suggests both managers and trainers saw personalizing based on certain identifying factors (e.g., role or job function and previous learning activity) as more desirable compared to employees in general (Fake, 2018). While personalizing based on the employee's identifying factors may drive efficiency, this research indicates that a sizable population of employees may feel that these types of approaches to personalizing learning are not as helpful potentially as others. Behavioral metrics may be informative (e.g., is there any increase in training usage with programs account for an employee's job role or previous learning activity?). This, however, may flavor employee perceptions of the Workforce Training and Development Programs and impact the interaction between the employee and the program. The tensions between organizational needs and individual desires are apparent here. It's also important to acknowledge that the motivations for training may differ between the individual learner and the organization. Whereas an organization may seek a particular outcome from training and development programs, an individual may be motivated by another factor altogether, including changing jobs, evolving their personal skillset, or addressing an ongoing, however, less acknowledged organizational need. Perhaps a solution to this tension is to make the needs of an organization explicit so that learners can elect which problems they are most compelled to solve, propose other solutions, and identify training and development programs to solve the problems brought forth by the organization.

Additional research is needed to understand which aspects of personalized learning offerings are most useful to stakeholders. Questions emerge regarding the differences between employee, managers, and leadership perceptions of how helpful different personalized learning data sources are in creating an effective learning experience.

The larger question here is who should set the data analytics that personalizes the learning experience. Do learners define the metrics associated with their training and development? Should it be training and development professionals? A third-party? We explore this further below in a discussion about the types of assessments proposed by experts.

Measuring Effectiveness of Learning Through Assessment

The types of assessment mentioned in expert responses included "ongoing self-assessments", "strength and weaknesses analyses", and "360 reviews". In addition to the aforementioned assessments, experts discussed using more "objective diagnostics" while also embedding evaluations of the individual's "proficiency level". Those who advocated for self-assessments seemed to support the individual identification of growth goals with support through community, network, or mentor-based interactions. Those who proposed objective assessments or proficiencies were more likely to define the learning goals upfront and then provide flexible learning pathways or resources for learners to achieve those goals.

These approaches to personalized learning emphasize different aspects of ownership over the learning process. On the one hand, for experts who advocated for self-assessment, it was important that learners develop and identify their personal learning goals. On the other hand, a contingent of experts felt that competencies should shape the define the learning goals and that learners should instead pursue the flexible learning paths available to them in order to achieve those goals. The effectiveness of each approach may be an interesting area for future research and experimentation.

Measuring the Learning in PLiF: Types of Assessments

When it comes to how one might measure the impact of personalized learning programs and the impact of the PLiF, experts focused on consistent or variable assessment according to the learners' needs, the use of **individual reflective assessment** (self-reflection and self-evaluation which can be both formative and summative), **collective reflective assessment** (e.g., 360 evaluations, performance reviews, peer or managerial scores, and/or feedback from others which can be both formative and summative), **internal objective assessment** (e.g., knowledge check, objective formative feedback), and **external objective assessment** (e.g., competency-based tests, exams, etc.) to assess the achievement of their learning goals. In the following paragraphs, we will explore the types of assessment to use and circumstances where one might wish to leverage reflective or objective assessments, which data sources to use, as well as how these assessments may be structured, sequenced, and built upon.

Individual Reflective Assessments

According to experts, self-assessment was mentioned as a means of encouraging personalized learning practices in Workforce Training and Development Programs (Fake, 2018). Andrade (2018) points out that most definitions of self-assessments tend to be broad, however, the practice should offer feedback to "inform adjustments to processes and products that deepen learning and enhance performance". The act of reflection, therefore, must evolve as the learner evolves.

In designing self-assessments and evaluations, Andrade (2018) emphasizes that formative models tend to offer students more ability to honestly assess their performance. For example, in circumstances where performance outcomes were judged by a self-assessment, learners often overestimated their abilities. For example, Tejeiro et al. (2012), found higher education students tended to rate their performance at a higher level compared to faculty ratings when the self-reflection counted towards their final grade.

The study additionally suggests that self-assessment is most impactful when areas of focus are defined and that student perceptions are more positive when they are involved in developing the criteria for self-assessment. Andrade (2018) indicates that this is also true when learners are offered a flexible rubric or checklist to guide their assessment when revising work. This finding suggests that learner ownership and buy-in to the rubric, checklist, or make-up of the self-assessment may increase positive perceptions regarding the practice. Therefore, while templates may be useful, offering flexible self-assessments may increase the adoption and use of this technique.

The Association for Talent and Development (ATD, 2022) currently leverages a self-assessment as a mechanism to prioritize where one might wish to focus across three domains of practice to include developing professional capability, impacting organizational capability, and building personal capability. These three defined domains represent 23 knowledge and skill areas wherein the ATD recommends practitioners focus time and attention in order to respond to the demands of the modern talent and development profession (2022). After reviewing 189 statements regarding one's perception of skills and abilities on a scale from "exploring" to "expert", the ATD assessment unlocks a report and a proposed learning plan to identify areas of strength, weakness, potential gaps, and offer existing resources to support continuous training and development opportunities for industry professionals.

Collective Reflective Assessments

Collective reflective assessments are a common means of conducting performance reviews in the industry. As the Society of Human Resource Management (SHRM) defines, performance appraisals are "periodic evaluations of an employee's job performance against a set of expectations or goals" (SHRM, 2022). Collective reflective assessments may also be leveraged in MOOCs or leveraging peer review techniques within higher education (Chan & King, 2017).

Of the collective reflective assessments, one approach popular in industry is the 360 review (Zenger & Folkman, 2020). According to their Harvard Business Review article, 360 reviews succeed when a variety of factors are considered. To begin, the leader should have a role in defining who should conduct the assessment and encourage those they select to be candid in their feedback. Next, anonymity may foster greater candid feedback across participants. When the report is presented to the individual, other supporting factors involve the interpretation from a trusted individual with a consideration of the context in which the feedback was provided. Ultimately, the feedback should be presented in a manner that offers guidance and the next steps in the form of a customized development plan. Finally, Zenger and Folkman (2020) recommend the learner continue ongoing touchpoints with training or coaching professionals to provide a sense of accountability.

In these best practices, we continue to see the importance of the learner's ownership over their evaluation process as a key theme in the effectiveness of assessment implementation and impact.

Combining Individual and Collective Reflective Assessments

A combination of self-assessment and input from peers could foster the development of a personalized learning plan for each person to enable their personal growth and development. For example, Managers who want to move into leadership roles could be encouraged to leverage a self-assessment to reflect on the abilities they already have in these areas. In the self-assessment process, the manager would be encouraged to consult with peers, reporting employees, supervisors, or leadership to get feedback either in-person, via email or chat, which they can then use to shape their own, unique learning goals that address their individual deficits and identify room for improvement elicited from their reflections and the feedback they received. In the example mentioned above, self-assessment and peer feedback are used to document areas for growth and improvement as well as set future learning goals.

Internal Objective Assessments

Whereas individual reflective and collective assessments may be more subjective and dependent on the perception of the individual within their own personal and communal spheres, Internal Objective Assessments are leveraged to measure progress compared to a standard or competency as defined by a third party. This type of assessment can be useful when demonstrating competencies across organizations and beyond an organizational or institutional realm. As Carnegie Mellon's Eberly Center defines, formative assessment is intended to "monitor student learning to provide ongoing feedback that can be used by instructors to improve their training and by students to improve their learning" (2022). These types of assessment can be leveraged to help students identify areas of strength and weakness in a skill or knowledge-based domain wherein success metrics within the field have been defined. For example, credentialing exams such as the AWS Cloud Practitioner Exam seek to monitor proficiency based on knowledge, skills, and abilities as defined by Amazon. This is also true for standardized testing for other domains. Practice tests, knowledge checks, and practice sessions all serve as examples of internal objective assessments.

Formative assessments may also be used in active learning classrooms to provide student feedback prior to submitting a deliverable. For instance, Adkins (2018) leveraged formative assessments in a User-Centered Design course to encourage active learning and adjust the course to do a better job of meeting student needs. In this, Adkins leveraged formative assessment not only to assess the learning in the classroom, but also to optimize the environment for future students by conducting a formative assessment on the actual course.

As mentioned earlier, the other approach advocated by experts involves conducting internal objective assessments that evaluate individual proficiencies towards defined competencies. For example, the assessment used in a leadership training scenario could offer an objective assessment of the learner's skill sets that would then help the learner formulate a training plan. The learner could complete a series of daily assessments delivered through a responsive design adaptive platform (i.e., no longer than 10 minutes) in which managers are required to answer questions. The assessments are directly aligned with key competencies derived from each training goal. Mentors and mentees receive an automated report each week with system-recommended actions for improvement based on the desired leadership model. Then, mentors meet with assigned participants once a week to debrief on the results. Here, competencies seem to be defined for the learner, but flexible learning pathways and support structures have been built to accommodate the learner's experience.

External Objective Assessments

External Objective Assessments, or summative assessments define and evaluate student learning at the end of instruction and compare it against a standard or benchmark. Examples include high-stakes final exams, competency-based assessments, and final program evaluations. These point-in-time assessments tend to emphasize the timeliness of the learning and whether or not set standards or benchmarks are achieved by the learners.

The added pressure of benchmarks and standards may see more impact in high-demand fields such as medicine. As Raupach et al. (2013) discovered, summative assessment significantly increased the odds of correctly identifying 3 out of 5 electrocardiogram examinations compared to formative assessments. In this model, the high stakes associated with the summative exam corresponded to the high stakes of accurately identifying a diagnosis. Therefore, a takeaway for practitioners may be to marry the severity of the domain to the seriousness of the assessment. Whereas some domains may have wiggle room, the inaccurate diagnosis of an ailment may lead to death. Therefore, a summative assessment may be more aligned with the outcomes necessary to measure the success of the learner.

Combining Multiple Forms of Assessment

One might argue that a hybrid approach may be best suited toward leveraging the collective strengths and weaknesses of personalized learning assessments. For example, a personalized learning and development program could begin with an internal reflective assessment (e.g., self-assessment) and follow up with an objective diagnostic to see what learning objectives and content are most needed and align the content delivery toward those individual needs. These reflective and objective assessments could then be revisited on an ongoing basis to support continued growth and development and to identify what needs more work and what can be considered accomplished.

The table below specifies the different forms of assessment, their definition, the perspective they espouse, and potential use cases wherein the assessment may be applicable (Table 9.1).

Evaluating Personalized Learning Designs 177

Table 9.1 Application of Assessments in Personalized Learning

Type of Assessment	Definition	Perspective	Potential Use Cases
Individual Reflective Assessment	An individual conducts a self-assessment to identify strengths, weaknesses, opportunities, and gaps in proficiency	The individual is capable of assessing their current level of proficiency	A learner leverages or helps define a rubric or existing syllabus to determine if they understand gaps in their current understanding of a topic.
Collective Reflective Assessment	An individual requests feedback from the collective with regard to their proficiency	The collective is best suited to assessing the individual's current level of proficiency	A learner gathers feedback from others to assess the effectiveness of their presentation or communication skills
Internal Objective Assessment (formative)	A formative assessment the learner elects to measure their performance against a standardized metric	A third-party set of competencies or standards is best to assess the individual's current level of proficiency	Learners complete a practice test on a topic of interest to identify areas they need to focus on more.
External Objective Assessment (summative)	A summative assessment the learner uses to measure their performance in order to achieve collective acknowledgment of their proficiency	A third-party set of competencies or standards is best to assess the individual's current level of proficiency	Learners take an exam to demonstrate proficiency at a particular standard. Particularly useful when operating in a cross-organizational context (e.g., Government contracting)

It is important to acknowledge the specific stressors associated with demonstrating and assessing the value of programs in a Workforce Training and Development environment wherein the focus may be centered on the return of the training's investment rather than the specific achievement of specified learning outcomes. The hope is that measuring the effectiveness of these types of learning interventions will bolster an argument to the leadership of other positive training outcomes beyond the bottom line.

Tools to Assess Personalized Learning Environments

Technologies that are used to assess personalized environments can include rubric generation, rubric banks, analytic tools, test and quizzing tools, digital portfolio systems, learner response systems, and immersive learning environment-generated products/results to name a few (Dabbagh, Howland, and Marra, 2018). In addition, many HR platforms offer performance reviews for employees. The alignment of these tools to the respective forms of assessment is explored below (Table 9.2).

Evaluating the Return on Investment of Your PL Program Overall

Despite potential ongoing critique and adaptation, Kirkpatrick's (1993) four levels of evaluation remains a commonly referenced model for determining the ROI of Training Programs in Workforce Training and Development Programs (Dabbagh & Bannan-Ritland, 2005; Downes, 2016; Jasson & Govender, 2017). The model defines **Level 1** as measuring the reaction of how learners perceive the training; **Level 2** is associated with the successful measurement of the learning based on changes to attitudes, knowledge, or skill; **Level 3** is associated with behavioral outcomes; and **Level 4** presents business results or changes that have occurred on an organizational level due to the training. Experiencing many iterations over time, Phillips (2013) proposed Return on Investment as the 5th dimension, Kaufman and Keller (1994) split Level 1 into two sections to include input (or learning materials) and process (or delivery), and Jasson and Govender (2017) sought to account for risk in further enhancing the impact of the model.

Given the popularity and general acceptance of this model in the industry, evaluation leveraging Kirkpatrick's is proposed to evaluate the effectiveness of

Evaluating Personalized Learning Designs 179

Table 9.2 Aligning Tools to Types of Personalized Learning Assessments

Tools	Example Technology	Types of Assessment Supported
Digital portfolio systems	Weebly Wix Wordpress Google Sites	• Individual Reflective Assessment • Collective Reflective Assessment
Performance management*	UltiPro UKG Pro Workday	• Individual Reflective Assessment • Collective Reflective Assessment
Analytics tools	Google Analytics LMS Specific Reports xAPI powered interfaces	• Internal Objective Assessment • External Objective Assessment
Test and Quizzing Tools	Kahoot Zoom Polls/Questions Slideswith.com QuizStar Articulate Quizmaker ProProfsQuizmaker	• Internal Objective Assessment • External Objective Assessment
Learner response systems	Kahoot Zoom Polls/Questions Slideswith.com Poll Everywhere	• Collective Reflective • Internal Objective Assessment

(*Continued*)

Table 9.2 (Continued)

Tools	Example Technology	Types of Assessment Supported
Immersive learning environment generated-products	Figment AR Experience Real History Google Expeditions Minecraft Light Up Learning Horizon Workrooms	• Individual Reflective Assessment • Collective Reflective Assessment • External Objective Assessment
Rubric generation tools & Rubric Banks	iRubric Rubistar EssayTagger	• Individual Reflective Assessment • Collective Reflective Assessment • Internal Objective Assessment • External Objective Assessment

Note
* There may be instances where objective assessment is leveraged or designed within the instruction.

personalized learning. Assuming the application of the PLiF model, we demonstrate proposed questions, example methods, and measures for PLiF in the list below.

- **Level 1 - Reaction: How do learners perceive the PLiF?**
  - **Questions:** What are learner perceptions of training relevancy? Employee satisfaction? Perceived organizational loyalty? Perceptions of learning opportunities?
  - **Example Methods/Measures:**
    - Workforce Training and Development Survey
    - Employee Satisfaction Survey
    - Interviews
- **Level 2 - Learning: What are the learning outcomes associated with the application of the PLiF?**
  - **Questions:** What is the performance of learners based on the assessments? How does this performance change over 3 months? 6 months? 12 months? What learning outcomes are observable?
  - **Example Methods/Measures:**
    - Pre/post performance analysis of a randomly assigned test and control group
    - Interviews
    - Overarching assessment based on collective results from the collection of reflective and objective assessments mentioned earlier in this chapter to measure the acquisition of knowledge, skills, and abilities
    - Completions of certifications
- **Level 3 - Behavior Change: What are the observable behavior changes associated with the PLiF?**
  - **Questions:** How are learners approaching new learning tasks? What self-directed learning behaviors do they exhibit? What training interactions do they actively leverage? What new organizational relationships and networks have stemmed from program implementation?
  - **Example Methods/Measures:**
    - Pre/post performance analysis of randomly assigned test and control groups compared to measurement of newly adopted behavior
    - Adoption, engagement, and sustained use of available interaction types
    - Data analytics associated with supported learning technologies

- **Level 4 - Business Results:** How do the business outcomes of individuals applying the PLiF framework differ from their coworkers? How do the business outcomes compare before and after the application of the program?
  - **Questions:** Does the PL training program support organizational outcomes and goals?
  - **Example Measures:**
    - Organizational capabilities prior to and after the installment of PLiF over time.
    - Reduction of customer complaints and time to task completion
    - Increases in responsiveness, customer satisfaction, net promoter score, employee satisfaction, cross-team collaboration, employee engagement, and employee retention
- **Level 5: Return on Investment:** What is the cost and benefit of the PLiF program?
  - **Questions:** What are the hard (e.g., materials, development hours, systems) and soft costs (employee hours) of the new programs? How do business results compare prior to the PLiF program? After 3 months? 6 months? 12 months?
  - **Example Measures:**
    - Increase in net profit, productivity, inter-organizational collaboration, client or student retention rates, revenue growth rate, average revenue per user
    - Projected value of the new organizational capability
    - Assessed competitive advantage

Your Blueprint to Assess Your Organization's PLiF Offerings

To support the development of the PLiF in your workforce or organizational learning environment, it is first recommended to conduct a holistic audit of your existing training programs. In this process, training and development managers or instructional designers will identify what programs currently support learner-to-content, learner-to-learner, learner-to-small group, learner-to-coach, mentor, or AI, and learner to the community of practice interactions. An example inventory can be found in Table 9.3 below.

In this exercise, the types of programs, what is being personalized (e.g., content, delivery, assessment, etc.); who is involved (individuals, groups, stakeholders, etc.); where the program occurs (specific location, remotely,

Evaluating Personalized Learning Designs 183

Table 9.3 Example Inventory for Assessing Current Personalized Learning Offerings

Interaction Type	Types of Programs	Who (Stakeholders)	How	Data Sources
Learner to Content	Udemy/LinkedIn Learning Class Access Reimbursement for Class materials	Learner IT support Admin	1:1 and Mix	Learner Defined Behavioral Performance
Learner to Learner	Peer Coding Peer Projects 1:1 Walks Donut.io Buddy Programs	Learner Peer Project Management	1:1	Learner Defined Relationship-Driven
Learner to Small Group	Lunch and learn Project Focused Tiger Teams Internal Project Work	Learner Managers Project Management	1:1 and Mix	Behavioral Contextually Defined Relationship-Driven Performance
Learner to Mentor, Coach, or AI Assistant	Coach Check-ins Elected Use of AI Assistant Intra-preneurships	Learner Coach HR Team Managers Leadership	1:1	Learner Defined Behavioral Contextually Defined Relationship-Driven Performance
Learner to Social Network or CoP	Internal messaging groups External Messaging Groups Meet-up Groups Committee or Community Involvement External Conferences Fellowship Programs Company Vlogs	Learner External Resources	1:1 and Mix	Learner Defined Performance

asynchronously, etc.); when the learning happens, what types of engagements (e.g., 1:1 or a mix of 1 to N and 1:1); and how the program success is measured can all be charted on the inventory. Once the types of programs have been identified, it becomes easier to see where there might be opportunities or gaps in the existing offerings.

References

Adkins, J. (2018). Active learning and formative assessment in a user-centered design course. *Information Systems Education Journal, 16*(4), 34–40.

Andrade, H. L. (2018). A critical review of research on student self-assessment. *Frontiers in Education, 4*. https://www.frontiersin.org/articles/10.3389/feduc.2019.00087/full

Betts, B., & Sephton, E. (2018). We need to talk about … Personalized learning. Results from our global survey report. *HT2Labs*. Retrieved from https://www.ht2labs.com/personalized-learning-survey-report/

Chan, H. P., & King, I. (2017). Leveraging social connections to improve peer assessment in MOOCS. *WWW '17 Companion: Proceedings of the 26th International Conference on World Wide Web Companion*, 341–349, 10.1145/3041021.3054165

Dabbagh, N., & Bannan-Ritland, B. (2005). *Online learning: Concepts, strategies, and application*. Upper Saddle River, NJ: Prentice Hall, Pearson Education.

Dabbagh, N., Howland, J., & Marra, R. (2019). *Meaningful online learning: Integrating strategies, activities, and learning technologies for effective designs*. New York, N.Y.: Routledge.

Downes, S. (2016). New models of open and distributed learning. In M. Jemni, K. Khribi, and M. Koutheair (Eds.), *Open education: From OER to MOOCs* (pp. 1–21). Berlin, Germany: Springer.

Eberly Center (2022). *What is the difference between formative and summative assessment?* Carnegie Mellon University https://www.cmu.edu/teaching/assessment/basics/formative-summative.html#:~:text=The%20goal%20of%20formative%20assessment,target%20areas%20that%20need%20work

Fake, H. (2018). *Personalized learning within online workforce environments*. Fairfax, Virginia, United States: Manuscript in preparation, College of Education and Human Development, George Mason University.

Jasson, C. C., & Govender, C. M. (2017). Measuring return on investment and risk in training – A business training evaluation model for managers and leaders. *Independent Research Journal in the Management Sciences, 17*(1). 10.4102/ac.v17i1.401

Kaufman, R., & Keller, J. M. (1994). Levels of evaluation: Beyond Kirkpatrick. *Human Resource Development Quarterly, 5*(4), 371–380. 10.1002/hrdq.3920050408

Kirkpatrick, D. L. (1993). *How to train and develop supervisors*. New York: AMACOM.

Pelster, B., Johnson, D., Stempel, J., & van der Vyver, B. (2016, February). *Careers and learning: Real time, all the time* [Research Report]. Retrieved from Deloitte Insights: https://www2.deloitte.com/insights/us/en/focus/human-capital-trends/2017/learning-in-the-digital-age.html?id=us:2el:3dc:dup3818:awa:cons:hct17#endnote-4

Phillips, P. (2013). *The bottom line on ROI. How to measure the ROI in learning and development, performance improvement, and human resources*. ROI Institute. https://roiinstitute.net/

Raupach, T., Brown, J., Anders, S., Hasenfuss, G., & Harendza, S. (2013). Summative assessments are more powerful drivers of student learning than resource intensive teaching formats. *BMC Medicine, 11*(61). 10.1186/1741-7015-11-61

Sahinidis, A. G., & Bouris, J. (2008). Employee perceived training effectiveness relationship to employee attitudes. *Journal of European Industrial Training, 32*(1), 63–76. https://isedj.org/2018-16/n4/ISEDJv16n4p34.pdf

Society for Human Resource Management (2022). *Managing employee performance.* SHRM. https://www.shrm.org/resourcesandtools/tools-and-samples/toolkits/pages/managingemployeeperformance.aspx

Tejeiro, R. A., Gomez-Vallecillo, J. L., Romero, A. F., Pelegrina, M., Wallace, A., & Emberley, E. (2012). Summative self-assessment in higher education: Implications of its counting towards the final mark. *Electronic Journal of Research in Educational Psychology, 10*(2), 789–812. http://investigacion-psicopedagogica.org/revista/articulos/27/english/Art_27_707.pdf

The Association for Talent and Development (2022). *Access the capability model.* ATD. https://www.td.org/capability-model/access

Thompson, L., Pate, D., Schnidman, A., Lu, L., Andreatta, B., & Dewett, T. (2018). *2017 workplace learning report: How modern L&D pros are tackling top challenges.* Retrieved from https://learning.linkedin.com/blog/learning-thought-leadership/introducing-the-2017-workplace-learning-report–top-trends—cha

Zenger, J. & Folkman, J. (2020, December 23). *What makes a 360-Degree review successful?* Harvard Business Review.

Empowering Learners to Engage in Personalized Learning Experiences

10

Introduction

In this book, we presented the Personalized Learning Interaction Framework (PLiF) as a learner-centered approach for supporting personalized learning in workforce training and development programs as well as in higher education contexts. The PLiF was a result of a Delphi study (Fake & Dabbagh, 2021) whose goal was to seek expert knowledge on the educational concept of personalized learning, its dimensions (e.g., who should conduct personalized learning, what can be personalized, where it can be personalized, and how personalization should occur), and its application (i.e., how these dimensions should be applied given different education and training case studies). The research resulted in five types of interaction that support personalized learning: (1) learner-content interaction, (2) learner-learner interaction, (3) learner-mentor, coach, or Artificial Intelligent (AI) Assistant interaction, (4) learner-small group interaction, and (5) learner-social network or community of practice interaction. We described each type of interaction of the PLiF, and how it can be implemented using technology along with examples and best practices in Chapters 4, 5, 6, 7, and 8 (Figure 10.1).

In this chapter, we extend our discussion of the PLiF beyond its five dimensions of interaction to focus on the learner who is at the center of this framework and the situational context of PLiF within the larger learning ecosystem of the organization. Specifically, we focus on how to empower

DOI: 10.4324/9781003121008-10

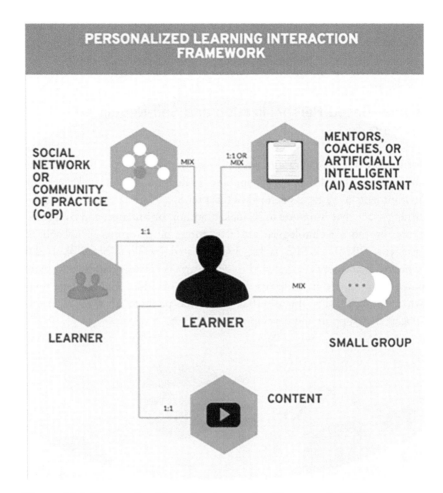

Figure 10.1 Personalized Learning Interaction Framework (PLiF).

learners to take charge of their own learning and engage in personalized learning experiences that strategically inform and guide their learning goals and help them pursue meaningful, adaptive, and flexible education pathways to accommodate their work, and life goals, and become successful agents and curators of their own learning over their lifetimes. First, it is important to note that the PLiF is based on "learner-based personalization" and not "systems-based personalization" as discussed in Chapter 2 of this book. **Learner-Based Personalization** refers to a learning experience wherein the learner (versus the system) drives the choice of what, how, when, where, and why the learning is personalized. A common approach that captures learner-based personalization is the construct of Personal Learning Environments or PLEs, which is briefly discussed in Chapter 2 and Chapter 8 of this book. We elaborate on the concept of PLEs next and its role in supporting self-regulated learning.

Learner-Based Personalization and Self-Regulated Learning

Learner-Based Personalization which is at the core of the PLiF can be achieved through the development and evaluation of Personal Learning Environments or PLEs. As defined in Chapter 8, a PLE is a self-driven digital learning space that is unique to its maker, author, or initiator, and composed of one or more technological artifacts, tools, or platforms (Dabbagh & Castaneda, 2020). A PLE is largely facilitated by cloud-based Web 2.0 technologies and services designed to help learners create, organize and share content, participate in collective knowledge generation, and manage their own meaning-making. Figure 10.2 shows the plethora of Web 2.0 technologies that support the development of a PLE.

Figure 10.2 Web 2.0 Technologies that Support PLE.

A PLE can also be described as a learning environment designed around each learner's goals or learning approach. The PLE helps learners organize the influx of information and resources that they are faced with on a daily basis into a personalized digital learning space or experience (Dabbagh, 2015). The underlying principle of a PLE is that the student (learner) is put in charge of pedagogically designing their own learning environment, hence it is learner-based personalization at its finest. In a PLE, the student develops an individualized digital identity through the perceptual cues and cognitive affordances that the personalized learning environment provides such as what information to share and when, who to share it with, and how to effectively merge formal and informal learning experiences.

> In the 21st century, PLEs have been steadily gaining ground as an effective platform for student learning and have been described by scholars such as Brigid Barron, Stephen Downes, Tom Haskins, Scott Wilson, and Mark van Harmelen as individual educational platforms, self-initiated and interest-driven learning environments, unique creations of individual learners that help shape their knowledge and understandings, self-directed learning systems, and methods and tools that help students organize and self-manage their learning.
>
> (Dabbagh, 2015, p. 573)

The rise of the PLE is also, in part, a reaction to the use of the Learning Management System (LMS) in higher education contexts. LMSs are primarily controlled by the institution's faculty and administrators, leaving little room for students to create, manage, and maintain a personalized learning space that supports their own learning activities as well as connections to peers and social networks across time and place. Hence learner control and learner-based personalization are often absent in the institutional LMS. Contrastingly, in a PLE, the locus of control shifts away from the institution to individual students, helping them take control of their own learning and build a personal cyberinfrastructure and learning ecosystem that extends learning beyond the boundaries of the classroom, institution, or organization, using distributed and portable tools. In a PLE, the student chooses the tools that match their learning preference and pace, and the student decides how to organize and manage the content to learn effectively and efficiently. Consequently, PLEs can be perceived as a single student's educational or e-learning platform, allowing collaboration with other students, experts, instructors, mentors, coaches, etc., and coordination of such interactions across a wide range of systems and learning communities. Given this description of

PLEs, the question becomes, are students (learners, individuals) ready to take this on? Are learners ready to drive their own learning using the PLE approach? Do learners possess the strategies and skills needed to develop and maintain an effective and ever-evolving PLE for a lifetime of learning?

In fact, there is strong evidence that PLEs coupled with the affordances of social media can foster Self Regulated Learning (SRL) which is critical for developing and maintaining a PLE (Dabbagh & Kitsantas, 2012). SRL is defined as the learner's ability to independently and proactively engage in self-motivating and behavioral processes that increase goal attainment (Zimmerman, 2000). More specifically, SRL can be regarded as a set of skills that enable learners to set learning or task goals, identify learning or task strategies needed to achieve those goals, and reflect on the efficacy of the strategies and processes that helped them achieve their goals (Dabbagh & Kitsantas, 2012). SRL skills can be compared to Personal Knowledge Management (PKM) skills, defined as "the act of managing one's personal knowledge through technologies" (Cigognini et al., 2011, p. 127), ranging from creating, organizing, and sharing digital content and information, to higher order or more complex PKM skills such as connectedness, critical ability, creativity, and the ability to balance formal and informal learning contexts. PKMs were discussed briefly in Chapter 8 as a set of processes (seeking, sensing, sharing) that help learners develop effective Personal Learning Networks (PLNs) (Jarche, 2014). The focus of this chapter is on SRL skills and how they can be fostered through the development of PLEs.

The relationship between PLEs and SRL is intuitive and interdependent and social media technologies have pedagogical affordances that can foster this relationship. Specifically, PLEs can be perceived as a pedagogical approach that facilitates SRL through the deliberate and strategic integration of formal and informal learning using social media technologies (Dabbagh & Kitsantas, 2012). PLEs require the development and application of SRL skills because PLEs are built bottom-up starting with personal goals, information management, and individual knowledge construction, and progressing to socially mediated knowledge and networked learning through PLNs and COPs.

Kitsantas and Dabbagh (2010) posit that social media have pedagogical affordances that can help support and promote student self-regulated learning by enabling the creation of PLEs, and that the relationship between PLEs and SRL is synergistic requiring the simultaneous, progressive, and transformative development and application of self-regulated learning skills using social media. However, when students (learners) are put in charge of developing a PLE, they need pedagogical guidance and support, particularly if they do not possess SRL skills. With insufficient guidance, students may not be able to create a PLE that cultivates their independent learning skills and helps them achieve their learning goals. This is where the role of faculty (including instructors, trainers, coaches, mentors, AI assistants, etc.) becomes crucial. Faculty need to scaffold students on how to manage and navigate the content they create in a PLE and how to become effective organizers, analyzers, evaluators, and synthesizers of information as they gradually assume more responsibility for their own learning (Dabbagh, 2015). Dabbagh and Kitsantas (2012, 2013) developed a scaffolding framework (Table 10.1) to assist faculty in scaffolding student PLE development using social media technologies to support SRL. The framework is based on the pedagogical affordances of social media, namely the three levels of interactivity that social media enable: personal information management, social interaction and collaboration, and information aggregation and management (see Figure 10.3).

As illustrated in Table 10.1, level 1 of the scaffolding framework, **personal information management**, is used to scaffold learners to create a private learning space using social media technologies such as blogs and wikis and to populate this space with self-generated content for personal productivity or organizational learning tasks. This could include creating online bookmarks and media resources surrounding course topics and personal journals and calendars related to course assignments and learning tasks. These activities engage students in acquiring and applying the SRL skills of goal setting and time management. **This level also aligns with the PLiF dimension of Learner-Content Interaction.**

Level 2 of the scaffolding framework, **social interaction and collaboration**, is used to scaffold learners to engage in social interaction and collaboration by sharing the content and task organization they created in level 1 with their peers and course instructors, thereby extending the PLE from a personal learning space to a social learning space or personal learning network (PLN). For example, learners can enable the commenting and collaborative editing features of blogs or wikis, inviting instructor and peer feedback and informal knowledge sharing. Such activities promote the SRL processes of self-monitoring and help-seeking, and prompt students to identify strategies needed to perform more formal learning tasks. **This level aligns with the PLiF dimensions of Learner-Learner Interaction, Learner-Small Group Interaction, and Learner-Coach/Mentor/AI Assistant Interaction.**

Level 3 of the framework, **information aggregation and management**, is used to scaffold learners to engage in content aggregation and synthesis using various social media tools and features prompting student reflection and evaluation of their overall learning experience and leading to further

Table 10.1 Scaffolding Framework to Assist Faculty in Supporting Student PLE Development

Social media Levels of Interactivity PLiF Interaction Type	(Level 1) Personal information management Learner-content interaction	(Level 2) Social interaction and collaboration Learner-learner Interaction Learner-small group interaction Learner-instructor interaction (mentor/coach/AI) Interaction	(Level 3) Information aggregation and management Learner-social network interaction
Social media experience and resource sharing tools (e.g., blogs, wikis, youtube)	Instructor encourages students to use a *blog* as a private journal to set learning goals and plan for related course tasks Instructor encourages students to use a *wiki* as a personal space for content organization and management	Instructor encourages students to activate the blog sharing and commenting features to allow peer and instructor feedback Instructor encourages students to activate the wiki's commenting and collaborative editing features to invite feedback and participation in organizational tasks	Instructor demonstrates how to configure a blog to pull in additional content and how to add the blog to RSS aggregation services Instructor demonstrates how to review the wiki's history to promote self-reflection and self-evaluation of learning across time
Cloud-based technologies (e.g., Google Calendar)	Instructor encourages students to use a cloud-based calendar for personal time management of course tasks and learning goals	Instructor encourages students to use the cloud-based calendar collaboratively to manage course-related team projects, activities, and tasks	Instructor demonstrates how to archive personal and group calendars to promote self-evaluation and self-reflection on time management

| Social networking sites (e.g., Facebook, LinkedIn) | Instructor encourages students to create a profile on Facebook or LinkedIn related to their academic and career goals | Instructor encourages students to link to communities and groups related to their learning goals and professional interests and to engage in relevant discussion | Instructor encourages students to reflect on their social networking experience and restructure their profile and manage their social presence accordingly |

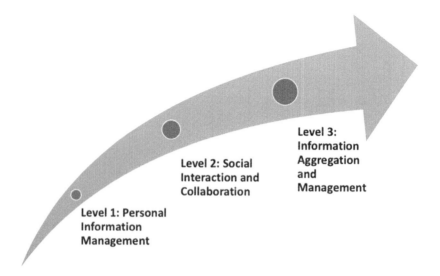

Figure 10.3 Three Levels of Social Media Interactivity.

customization and personalization of the PLE around their learning needs. These activities support the SRL skills of self-reflection and self-evaluation and help students become better prepared for future educational and professional pursuits. **This level aligns with the PLiF dimension of Learner-Social Network Interaction**. Figure 10.4 provides a snapshot of Table 10.1 showing the three levels of the scaffolding framework and the use of social media technologies to support self-regulated learning skills in PLE development.

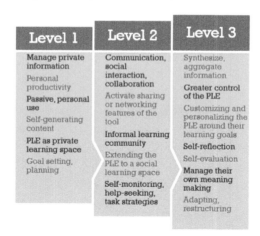

Figure 10.4 Scaffolding SRL in PLE Development.

Research on Social Media, SRL, and PLEs

Now that we have connected the PLiF to the scaffolding framework that supports the development of a PLE using SRL, let's examine the research on social media, SRL, and PLEs to see if PLEs are indeed enablers of SRL through the use of social media. Most of the research conducted on how PLEs can support self-regulated learning using social media has been in higher education contexts since this is where the construct of PLEs was conceptualized and tested. As defined earlier in this chapter, PLEs can be described as new-generation learning environments that embody the Web 2.0 characteristics of openness, personalization, collaboration, social networking, social presence, and user-generated content (Dabbagh & Kwende, 2021). PLEs enable personal and social learning experiences that empower learners to direct their own learning and develop lifelong learning skills, crossing institutional and organizational boundaries and evolving over time and place, making competencies and capabilities visible and attainable in education and workplace contexts. The research presented in this section validates these PLE principles and characteristics.

In a series of studies (Dabbagh & Fake, 2017; Dabbagh & Kwende, 2021) that examined college students' perceptions of PLEs and what social media tools students use to structure their PLEs, participants (who were part-time students and full-time workers) were asked to document in a blog post what tools they use for learning and what their ideal PLE might look like. Findings revealed that students perceived PLEs as a digital learning platform that allowed (a) collaboration with other students and instructors; (b) the use of technology as tools for discovery learning and experimentation; and (c) the curation and management of educational resources. Additionally, participants reported that their ideal PLE would include opportunities for discussion, collaboration, and interaction; tools for organizing, planning, and resource management; experiential learning strategies; and the use of effective technology to support a personalized learning experience. Overall, participants in these two studies perceived PLEs as making their learning experience more personal, connected, social, and open (Tu et al., 2012). Another interesting finding of these studies is that participants perceived PLEs as physical spaces intersecting with or augmenting digital spaces. Participants reported that physical spaces provide comfort, peace, and serenity that enable personalized learning.

In a case study (Dabbagh et al., 2015) that examined how students create PLEs using social media and the extent to which they engage in the SRL process, findings revealed that PLE development engages students in the SRL processes of goal setting, task strategies, self-monitoring and self-evaluation. Participants also reported being intrinsically motivated in using social media to create their PLE. It can be inferred here that when learning is driven by the student's internal needs, interests, motivations, and preferences, as is the case in PLEs, personalization becomes intrinsic to the learner and learning becomes a personal endeavor (Ito et al., 2013). Moreover, the goal of the learner shifts from a recipient of information and participator in a learning experience that is designed and facilitated by the instructor, to a collector, organizer, and designer of one's own learning experience.

In a qualitative study that examined personalized learning within workforce education contexts (Fake & Dabbagh, 2021), leaders in training and development were interviewed to uncover how they defined personalized learning in the workplace and how it might be implemented as a training approach in workforce online programs. The findings revealed a multitude of perspectives regarding how learning should be personalized (e.g., in multimodal formats from a delivery, informational, and device perspective), who should be conducting the personalized learning (individuals, managers or supervisors, training departments, online communities of peers, or adaptive technologies), and what parameters should be used in personalizing learning (e.g., by learner preferences, personalities, role, level of proficiency, task). These differences in perspectives suggest a lack of clarity regarding what personalization is, and how it might be designed, implemented, or evaluated as an approach for training and development in the organization. In fact, it was this lack of clarity that led to the Delphi study that resulted in the PLiF which formed the basis of this book.

The results of the Fake and Dabbagh 2021 study also revealed that the majority of participants described personalized learning as involving the learner with input from a wide range of social relationships, social networks, and collaborative technologies suggesting that an individualized as well as a social element to personalized learning was important to workforce leaders. Other research has come to similar conclusions demonstrating the power of social media in supporting the creation of personalized learning experiences (Dabbagh & Kitsantas, 2012). ***A key takeaway of this research is that personalized learning requires connections to social networks and communities of practice within and outside the organization. Thus enabling ongoing engagement with peers or others on a variety of domains and organizational topics, using the PLiF, may need to become a priority for those implementing personalized learning in the workforce.***

To understand how the findings of this research scales to a large audience, Dabbagh, Fake, and Zhang (2019) examined student perspectives on the value and effectiveness of *technology use for personal learning* in higher education. Six hundred and twenty-two college students (N = 622) in a large public university in the U.S. were surveyed regarding what technologies (hardware and software) they use most frequently for learning, what technologies they value for learning, and how effective they perceive technology in supporting their learning. The results revealed that technology use and value were closely aligned, with laptops and smartphones reported as most frequently used for learning and highly valued underscoring the importance of mobile and portable devices in supporting anytime anywhere learning. In terms of software used for learning, search engines, file-sharing tools, digital libraries, YouTube videos, and wikis were ranked highest, suggesting that social media use is enabling self-directed learning approaches that place students at the center of their learning process reinforcing the concept of **Learner-Based Personalization**, which is the principle underlying the PLiF.

Overall, the majority of participants in this study perceived technology as effective in fostering discussion, collaboration and interaction; enabling experiential learning; supporting organization, planning, and resource management; and facilitating a personalized learning experience. The results of this study confirm the results of the studies in higher education contexts mentioned earlier in this section and suggest that traditional learning management systems (LMS) may no longer serve as the best means for organizing or facilitating learning in organizations and institutions given that learners are embracing tools and resources that extend beyond the traditional LMS and designing their own PLEs using social media technology.

Jane Hart, Founder of the Centre for Learning & Performance Technologies (C4LPT) – one of the world's leading websites on learning trends, technologies, and tools – and author of the online resource Modern Workplace Learning 2023, conducts a yearly survey on the top 100 tools used for personal learning (PPL), workplace learning (WPL), and education (EDU). The results of the 16th Annual Tools for Learning Survey revealed that the top 10 tools used for personal learning (PPL) were YouTube, PowerPoint, Google Search, MS Teams, Zoom, Google Docs/Drive, LinkedIn, Word, Canva, and Wikipedia. These technologies fall into the categories of collaboration and communication tools, content creation tools, and information search and resource management tools (see Chapter 4 for the classification of learning technologies) further solidifying the research on what tools learners use for learning and validating the intensifying evidence that traditional LMSs are no longer sufficient for supporting learning in the 21st century. Figure 10.5 shows the 2022 top 100 tools for learning across the personal, workforce, and education contexts. This can also be accessed here https://www.toptools4learning.com/.

198 Empowering Learners to Engage

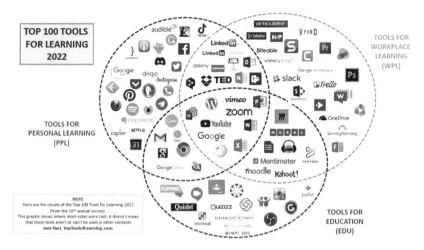

Figure 10.5 Top 100 Tools for Learning.

Personalized Learning as a PLE Ecosystem

Given the potential of a PLE to support learner-based personalization by integrating the dimensions of the PLiF and capitalizing on the affordances of social media technology and SRL as illustrated so far in this chapter, the next step is to envision what this might look like in the larger context of a learning ecosystem. An ecosystem "is comprised of interconnected parts, with the behaviors of many individual agents affecting one another as well as the environment's overall holistic pattern" (Walcutt & Schatz, 2019, p. 227). So a **learning** ecosystem can be defined as "a system of people, content, technology, culture, and strategy, existing both within and outside of an organization, all of which has an impact on both the formal and informal learning that goes on in that organization" (Eudy, 2018).

The term **learning ecosystem** is not just a catchy word or phrase, rather it helps us think about all the components that make up a learning system and how these components interact with each other. It also helps consider a holistic view of the learning environment to include people/learners, training content, technology, learning culture, and business strategy, and examine the complex relationships among these components. Just like when we think about living ecosystems, whether they are self-sustaining or endangered; healthy or sick; nurtured or threatened; thinking about learning ecosystems in this way makes us aware of what is going on inside and outside the organization from a learning and development perspective and how this will impact organizational performance and the bottom line. Walcutt and Schatz (2019) suggest that the future learning ecosystem is a substantive re-imagination of learning and development due to the need to recognize that learning can no longer be viewed as a single event, nor a series of events, but rather learning must be viewed as a lifelong experience of continual growth. Walcutt and Schatz also suggest that future learning ecosystems must provide personalized pathways for learners to progress through, and that deep learning that expedites the transfer of learning from practice to real-world settings must be strongly emphasized.

The concept of a learning ecosystem transcends the traditional approach to designing instruction which generally assumes a given target population (a particular individual or cohort) as well as a specific setting and set of conditions (e.g., specific objectives, subject matter). When we envision learning across lifetimes this linear approach to designing instruction no longer suffices. We need instructional design models that encompass diverse learning experiences, various media, diverse populations, cultures, and contexts, many of which fall outside the instructional designer's purview. Consequently, we need an updated instructional or learning design approach that (Walcutt, Bannan, & Dabbagh, 2019, p. 226):

- facilities learning as a gestalt derived from the collective sum of all learning events and experiences;
- recognizes learning outcomes are increasingly self-directed and stitched across different contexts, networks, and communities; and
- actively incorporates technology to enable learning - not only as an instructional delivery mechanism but also as the "glue" to connect learning events to one another.

In other words, we need a multidimensional model of instructional design that integrates traditional micro-level interventions as well as macro- and meta-level interventions; considers learners' own agency in the learning process, and actively connects experiences across the crisscrossing landscape of the learning ecosystem.

Having established the concept of a learning ecosystem and the need for updated instructional models to support the design, development, implementation, and evaluation of a learning ecosystem, let's consider how we might envision the PLE as a learning ecosystem. The PLE can be considered a freely assembled ecosystem consisting of any set of communication and collaboration channels, cloud resources, web apps, and social media technologies that enable learner agency in creating educational pathways to achieve learning, work, and life goals. In fact, EDUCAUSE, the nonprofit association whose mission is to advance higher education through the use of information technology, defines PLEs as *tools, communities, and services that constitute the individual educational platforms learners use to direct their own learning and pursue educational goals* (2009). However in order to extend the pedagogical and technological concept of the PLE to a future learning ecosystem based on the principles and characteristics of learning ecosystems outlined in this section, we envision PLEs as the core of a learning ecosystem where individuals are able to create personalized learning interactions that strategically inform and guide their learning goals and education pathways; enable the selection of different education providers to achieve those goals; and attain recognition for lifelong learning skills with the help of digital and stackable credentials. The overarching vision of this learner-driven PLE ecosystem is a more diverse, personalized, social, adaptive, dynamic, integrated, and transparent system configured of education providers, open education resources (OER), learning communities, and social and professional networks in which learners can select and combine in their PLEs different education providers (e.g., LinkedIn Learning) to achieve learning goals targeted for specific job skills, and providers can "compete" for learners who are paying for competency-based credit or discrete components of a degree or certification rather than the degree itself (Dabbagh & Castaneda, 2020). Figure 10.6 provides a snapshot of what the PLE as a future learning ecosystem might look like.

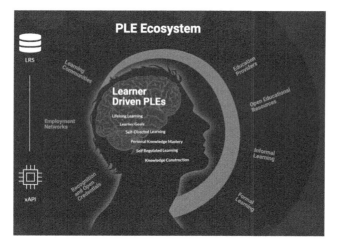

Figure 10.6 PLE ecosystem.

As you can see from the figure, PLEs are learner-driven and vary from person to person. Learners choose their education pathways based on their learning needs, goals, and interests. They can seek formal or informal learning opportunities to advance their knowledge on a topic; choose to participate in learning communities related to their field of study; become members of employment networks searching for new employment opportunities; or, seek micro-credentials through badging. These are just a few of the opportunities that are available for learners as they build their personal learning environments.

The proposed future learning ecosystem aligns with the ten principles put forth by the U.S. Department of Education's Office of Educational Technology in January 2017 for a "student-centered higher education ecosystem" that (a) guides students toward education that enables them to achieve their goals, is suitable to their needs, and aligns with their interests; (b) allows students to build meaningful education pathways incrementally; (c) allows students to document their learning in ways that can be applied to further education or meaningful work; and (d) enables the creation of a network of learning that supports students as peers, creators and entrepreneurs, and agents of their own learning.

Implementing the PLE as a Future Learning Ecosystem

In order to achieve the vision of a learner-centered ecosystem that is premised on the concept of PLEs and PLiF, several pilots/phases need to take place. First, we need to ensure that there is a transparent and equitable process for learners to create PLEs across all learning contexts. Although there are numerous known platforms and technologies that enable the design of PLEs (e.g., Evernote, Known, and e-portfolios), a PLE can be created in any technology or set of technologies or tools that support the following six components: personal profiler, aggregator, editor, scaffolds, recommender, and services (Kop & Fournier, 2014). Most Web 2.0 technologies (e.g., blogs, wikis, social bookmarking tools, tags, aggregation services) support these six components. In fact, learning in the context of Web 2.0 technologies has become highly self-motivated, autonomous, and informal, as described earlier in this chapter.

However creating PLEs is not just about the Web 2.0 technologies, it is also about the process that guides the effective design of PLEs which involves using the PLiF and its five interactions to progressively support self-regulated learning strategies and skills such as goal setting, task strategies, help-seeking, time management, self-monitoring, and self-evaluation. This process is depicted in the three-level framework for scaffolding SRL through the use of social media and PLiF interactions to develop evolving and sustainable PLEs (see Table 10.1). We propose testing this framework using three phases as follows:

Phase 1: Scaffolding PLE Development with Human Coaches Using the 3-Level Framework

The three-level framework will be tested with college students at (at least) six institutions worldwide to ensure that the sample population is diverse, cross-cultural, and inclusive of students of various ethnicities and socio-economic status. This first phase will involve human coaches who will coach students/learners on how to develop PLEs using the three-level framework. As indicated in Table 10.1, this involves supporting learners in creating learner-content interaction, learner-learner interaction, learner small group interaction, learner-mentor/coach interaction, and learner social network interaction, per the PLiF.

Phase 2: Designing an AI Coach to scaffold PLE Development Using the 3-Level Framework

The second phase will involve designing and testing an AI coach or personal assistant that scaffolds the development of PLEs. The use of AI in education is empowering intelligent tutoring systems which may evolve into "lifelong learning companions" that can gather data and support learners as they grow and develop their knowledge. The AI coach will be modeled on the human coaching interactions that occur in the first phase and will target the six essential technological components of a PLE mentioned earlier. The AI coach will scaffold learners in creating a PLE by helping them identify learning goals, link to social networks or learning communities around shared goals, and determine learning pathways that lead to recognition and credentialing of competencies acquired. This personalized learning experience is based on the three-level framework depicted in Table 10.1 and aligns with the PLiF interactions. Design-based research (DBR) will be used to evaluate the effectiveness of the AI coach in supporting PLE development and the degree to which students acquire SRL skills.

Phase 3: Embed an LRS into the Learning Ecosystem Infrastructure to Capture Learning Analytics and Optimize the PLE Ecosystem

The third pilot or phase will involve embedding an LRS (Learning Record Store) in the learning ecosystem infrastructure (which could be the university's LMS if this is what is being used to test the ecosystem or similar platform) to collect data on the learning ecosystem. An LRS enables modern tracking of learning experiences, achievements, and job performance (if needed) across multiple platforms and applications through the use of xAPI technology. The LRS is the heart of any technology-enabled ecosystem and the data collected from a range of learning activities (learning analytics) can be used to support personalized learning experiences and evaluate the effectiveness of the learning ecosystem in achieving its goals. In order to accomplish phases 2 and 3 of this pilot, we will need a machine learning expert to assist with the development of the AI coach and LRS/xAPI experts in order to ensure that learning data is shared responsibly across platforms, applications, and stakeholders.

In terms of beneficiaries, the PLE ecosystem would benefit college students and their future workplaces as well as college faculty, education providers, and learning resource providers. Personalized learning would be supported and promoted. A university setting is ideal for testing this future learning ecosystem given the diversity of the student population across global institutions and the resources available to faculty and students to achieve teaching and learning goals. Risks include the degree to which students are willing to take control of their learning, preparing faculty to transform their teaching practice to accommodate the concept of a PLE, ensuring seamless transitions between the components of the PLE ecosystem, and keeping the PLE ecosystem open and secure. Additional challenges in the workplace include corporate leadership buy-in, scaling PLEs across the organization, learner privacy considerations, and creating cultural norms surrounding the use of social media technologies.

Extending the Dimensions of PLiF

As we envision future learning ecosystems that require new instructional design models, we will also need to acquire new learning theories that embrace learner-based personalization interactions. One such theory that has come to the forefront in the digital age is Sociomaterial Entanglement Theory or SET. SET is proposed as a theory that embodies the socio-material entanglement with which people learn and the technosocial reality we live in as well as an approach that enacts contemporary ideas about how people learn (Dabbagh & Castaneda, 2020). SET was conceptualized to battle the prevailing tendency of traditional learning theories to limit conceptions of the "social" to interactions between persons rather than between persons and things (Malafouris & Renfrew, 2010). Specifically, traditional learning theories that are grounded in constructivism, social constructivism, situated cognition, cognitivism, or behaviorism, have remained oblivious to the "medium" or "material" that shapes human interaction and agnostic of its affordances and how they influence the manner in which people act, perceive, or think. Enter connectivism.

Connectivism is a result of the intense use of technology in education functioning more as a philosophy of education rather than a learning theory. In his classical article, Siemens (2005) discussed the limitations of behaviorism, cognitivism, and constructivism as theories of learning because they do not address learning that occurs outside people (i.e., learning that is stored and manipulated by technology) and within organizations (Mattar, 2018). At its heart, connectivism is the thesis that knowledge is distributed across a network of connections (to humans and things), and therefore learning consists of the ability to construct and traverse those networks (Downes, 2007). The PLE can be perceived in a similar vein. The relationships between the elements that configure the PLE, human and non-human, and their role in facilitating learning are symbiotic in that they impact each other in a reciprocal way (Dabbagh & Castaneda, 2020). Hence, the PLE elements are entrenched in what some scholars call a socio-material entanglement (Carvalho and Yeoman 2019; Decuypere & Simons 2016; Fenwick et al., 2011).

In other words, the intersection of the technical (material) and the social (human) through thought and action, also known as multiagent socio-technical systems, means that humans and "things" are ontologically inseparable and are observable through intra-action and through the relationships with the other elements of the learning ecosystem in the context of their contribution to the learning activity (Frauenberger, 2020, p. 21). SET builds on the socio-material entanglement phenomenon and multiagent socio-technological systems. SET is not an explanatory theory, but rather an approach or framework with a broad spectrum of applications that are able to integrate some of the most naturalistic ideas about how people learn in the digital environment. SET embraces "connected learning" or "networked learning" as depicted in connectivism and "connectivist pedagogy" (Downes, 2022). Given this discussion, we propose adding a sixth dimension to the Personalized Learning Interaction Framework (PLiF) which forms the basis of learner-based personalization and the enabler of the PLE learning ecosystem. We propose calling this sixth dimension: **Learner-to-Internet**

of Things (IoT) Interaction. The Internet of things (IoT) describes physical objects (or groups of such objects) with sensors, processing ability, software, and other technologies that connect and exchange data with other devices and systems over the Internet or other communications networks (Brown, 2016; Hendricks, 2015; ITU, 2022; and Shafiq et al., 2022). Some of the most common IoTs that are used commercially include home automation, such as Amazon's Alexa or Google Home, and wearable technology, such as Apple Watch.

Within the PLiF framework, the Learner-Internet of Things interaction references data inputs within the multiple technological systems. The array of data inputs from the multiple devices may be collected on a dashboard and serve as a mechanism to cultivate a reaction or hypothesis by the learner which then can be used to test new learning actions, behaviors, or approaches. The sensors, apparati, or tools used to collect these insights, therefore, become a reflection and observation of the existing PLE learning ecosystem. This allows the learner to consider the output and decipher their next learning actions, enabling a data-driven approach toward future learning and action. The possibilities extend to many collaborative and cross-functional operational environments. For example, the government, higher education, non-profits, and industrial partners have used sensors to chart and optimize traffic patterns in downtown areas of Chicago (Array of Things, 2021). In another study, Bannan et al. (2020) leveraged IoT to chart and optimize cross-team collaboration in simulated law enforcement emergency scenarios. As Kurzweill and Baker (2016) argue, the increased connectivity of devices fosters the possibility of more dynamic interventions, advanced instructional techniques and may free the instructor or trainer to focus on facilitating learning based on the data elicited from interconnected devices.

In conclusion, learning can no longer be understood by focusing solely on cognition, development, or the behavior of individual learners; neither can it be understood without reference to its situated, sociocultural and lifelong nature, the tools through which learners construct meaning, and the context in which these tools are used.

References

Bannan, B., Dabbagh, N., & Walcutt, J. J. (2019). Instructional strategies for the future. In J. J. Walcutt and S. Schatz (Eds.), *Modernizing learning: Building the future learning ecosystem* (pp. 223–242). Washington, DC: Government Publishing Office. License: Creative Commons Attribution CC BY 4.0 IGO.

Bannan, B., *Torres, E. M., Purohit, H., *Pandey, R., & Cockroft, J. L. (2020). Sensor-based adaptive instructional systems in live simulation training. In R. Sottilare and J. Schwarz (Eds), *Adaptive Instructional Systems. HCII 2020. Lecture Notes in Computer Science, vol 12214* (pp. 3–14). Cham: Springer. 10.1007/978-3-030-50788-6_1

Blaschke, L. M. (2012). Heutagogy and lifelong learning: A review of heutagogical practice and self determined learning. *The International Review of Research in Open and Distributed Learning, 13*(1), 56–71. 10.19173/irrodl.v13i1.1076

Blaschke, L. M. (2013). E-learning and self-determined learning skills. In S. Hase & C. Kenyon (Eds.), *Self determined learning: Heutagogy in action* (pp. 55–68). Bloomsbury Academic.

Brown, E. (2016, September 20). 21 Open Source Projects for IOT. Linux.com. Retrieved December 22, 2022, from https://www.linux.com/NEWS/21-OPEN-SOURCE-PROJECTS-IOT/

Carvalho, L., & Yeoman, P. (2019). *Connecting the dots: Theorizing and mapping learning entanglement through archaeology and design*. British Journal of Educational Technology. 10.1111/bjet.12761

Cigognini, M. E., Pettenati, M. C., & Edirisingha, P. (2011). Personal knowledge management skills in Web 2.0-based learning. In M. J. W. Lee and C. McLoughlin (Eds.), *Web 2.0-based e-Learning: Applying social informatics for tertiary teaching* (pp. 109–127). IGI Global.

Computation Institute (2021). Array of things technology [YouTube Video]. Array of Things. https://www.youtube.com/watch?time_continue=166&v=pFL5QNwgs6A&feature=emb_logo

Dabbagh, N. (2015). Personal Learning Environments (PLEs). In M. J. Spector (Ed.), *SAGE encyclopedia of educational technology* (pp. 572–575). Thousand Oaks, CA: Sage Publications.

Dabbagh, N., & Castaneda, L. (2020). Beyond personalization: The PLE as a framework for lifelong learning. *Educational Technology Research and Development, 68*(6), 3041–3055. 10.1007/s11423-020-09831-z

Dabbagh, N., & Fake, H. (2017). College students' perceptions of personal learning environments through the lens of digital tools, processes and spaces. *Journal of New Approaches in Educational Research (NAER Journal), 6*(1), 28–36.

Dabbagh, N., Fake, H., & Zhang, Z. (2019). Student perspectives of technology use for learning in higher education. *The Iberoamerican Review of Digital Education (RIED), 22*(1), 127–152.

Dabbagh, N., & Kitsantas, A. (2012). Personal Learning Environments, social media, and self-regulated learning: A natural formula for connecting formal and informal learning. *The Internet and Higher Education, 15*(1), 3–8.

Dabbagh, N., & Kitsantas, A. (2013). The role of social media in self-regulated learning. *International Journal of Web Based Communities (IJWBC), Special Issue, Social Networking and Education as a Catalyst Social Change, 9*(2), 256–273.

Dabbagh, N., Kitsantas, A., Al-Freih, M., & Fake, H. (2015). Using social media to develop Personal Learning Environments (PLEs) and self-regulated learning skills: A case study. *International Journal of Social Media and Interactive Learning Environments, 3*(3), 163–183.

Dabbagh, N., & Kwende, M. (2021). Personal Learning Environments as digital spaces that are collaborative, adaptive, and autonomous: College students' perceptions of

Personal Learning Environments. *Proceedings of the Technological Ecosystems for Enhancing Multiculturality (TEEM '21) Conference.* 10.1145/3486011.3486507

De Laat, M., & Dohn, N. B. (2019). Is networked learning postdigital education? *Postdigital Science and Education, 1*(1), 17–20. 10.1007/s42438-019-00034-1

Decuypere, M., & Simons, M. (2016). Relational thinking in education: Topology, sociomaterial studies, and figures. *Pedagogy, Culture & Society, 24*(3), 371–386. 10.1080/14681366.2016.1166150

Downes, S. (2007). Models for sustainable open educational resources. *Interdisciplinary Journal of E-Learning and Learning Objects, 3*(1), 29–44.

Downes, S. (2007). What Connectivism is. Half an Hour (weblog). https://halfanhour.blogspot.com/2007/02/what-connectivism-is.html

Downes, S. (2022). Newer Theories for Digital Learning Spaces. In: *Handbook of Open, Distance and Digital Education.* Singapore: Springer. 10.1007/978-981-19-0351-9_8-1

Drexler, W. (2010). The networked student model for construction of personal learning environments: Balancing teacher control and student autonomy. *Australasian Journal of Educational Technology, 26*(3), 369–385.

EDUCAUSE Learning Initiative (ELI) (2009). The seven things you should know about … Personal Learning Environments. Retrieved from http://net.educause.edu.mutex.gmu.edu/ir/library/pdf/ELI7049.pdf

Eudy, R. (2018). What is a learning ecosystem? and how does it support corporate strategy? HSI. (n.d.). Retrieved December 22, 2022, from https://hsi.com/blog/what-is-a-learning-ecosystem-and-how-does-it-support-corporate-strategy

Fake, H., & Dabbagh, N. (2021). The personalized learning interaction framework: Expert perspectives on how to apply dimensions of personalized learning in workforce training and development programs. *Proceedings of the Technological Ecosystems for Enhancing Multiculturality (TEEM '21) Conference.* 10.1145/3486011.3486503

Frauenberger, C. (2020). Entanglement HCI the next wave? *ACM Transactions on Computer-Human Interaction, 27*(1), 1–27.

Fenwick, T., Edwards, R., & Sawchuk, P. (2011). *Emerging approaches to educational research: Tracing the sociomaterial* (1st ed.). Abingdon: Routledge. Frauenberger, 2020

Gillis, A. S. (2022, March 4). *What is IOT (internet of things) and how does it work? - definition from techtarget.com.* IoT Agenda. Retrieved December 22, 2022, from https://www.techtarget.com/iotagenda/definition/Internet-of-Things-IoT

Goodyear, P. (2005). Educational design and networked learning: Patterns, pattern languages and design practice. *Australasian Journal of Educational Technology, 21*(1), 82–101.

Hart, J. (2022). Top 100 Tools for Learning 2022 - Results of the 16th Annual Survey. Top 100 Tools for Learning 2022. Retrieved December 22, 2022, from https://www.toptools4learning.com/

Hendricks, D. A. (2015, August 10). *The trouble with the internet of things – london datastore.* London Datastore News. Retrieved December 22, 2022, from https://data.london.gov.uk/blog/the-trouble-with-the-internet-of-things/

ITU. (2022). *Internet of things global standards initiative.* Retrieved December 22, 2022, from https://www.itu.int/en/ITU-T/gsi/iot/Pages/default.aspx

Ito, M., Gutiérrez, K., Livingstone, S., Penuel, B., Rhodes, J., Salen, K., Schor, J., Sefton-Green, J., & Watkins, S. C. (2013). Connected learning: An agenda for research and design. Irvine, California. Retrieved from http://dmlhub.net/sites/default/files/ConnectedLearning_report.pdf

Jarche (2014) (this comes from here so I need help citing it) https://jarche.com/2014/02/the-seek-sense-share-framework/

Kitsantas, A., & Dabbagh, N. (2010). *Learning to learn with Integrative Learning Technologies (ILT): A practical guide for academic success*. Greenwich, CT: Information Age Publishing.

Kop, R., & Fournier, H. (2014). Developing a framework for research on Personal Learning Environments. *E-learning in Europe Journal, 35*, 13–17.

Kurzweil, D., & Baker, S. (2016). *The internet of things for educators and learners*. Educause. https://er.educause.edu/articles/2016/8/the-internet-of-things-for-educators-and-learners

Malafouris, L., & Renfrew, C. (2010). *The cognitive life of things: Recasting the boundaries of the mind*. Cambridge: McDonald Institute for Archaeological Research.

Mattar, J. (2018). Constructivism and connectivism in education technology: Active, situated, authentic, experiential, and anchored learning. *RIED. Revista Iberoamericana de Educación a Distancia, 21*(2), 201–217. doi: 10.5944/ried.21.2.20055

Rahimi, E., van den Berg, J., & Veen, W. (2015). Facilitating student-driven constructing of learning environments using Web 2.0 personal learning environments. *Computers & Education, 81*, 235–246. 10.1016/j.compedu.2014.10.012

Shafiq, M., Gu, Z., Cheikhrouhou, O., Alhakami, W., & Hamam, H. (2022). The rise of "internet of things": Review and open research issues related to detection and prevention of IOT-based security attacks. *Wireless Communications and Mobile Computing, 2022*, 1–12. 10.1155/2022/8669348

Siemens, G. (2005). Connectivism: A learning theory for the digital age. *International Journal of Instructional Technology and Distance Learning, 2*(1). Available from http://www.itdl.org/Journal/Jan_05/article01.htm

Taraghi, B. (2012). Ubiquitous personal learning environment (UPLE). *International Journal of Emerging Technologies in Learning, 7*(2), 7–14.

Torres-Kompen, R., Edirisingha, P., Canaleta, X., Alsina, M., & Monguet, J. M. (2019). Personal learning environments based on Web 2.0 services in higher education. *Telematics and Informatics, 38*, 194–206.

Tu, C. H., Sujo-Montes, L., Yen, C. J., Chan, J. Y., & Blocher, M. (2012). The integration of personal learning environments and open network learning environments. *TechTrends, 56*(3), 13–19. 10.1007/s11528-012-0571-7

U.S. Department of Education, Office of Educational Technology (2017). *Reimagining the role of technology in higher education: A supplement to the national education technology plan*. Washington, D.C., 2017.

Walcutt, J. J., & Schatz, S. (2019). Modernizing learning. In J. J. Walcutt and S. Schatz (Eds.), *Modernizing learning: Building the future learning ecosystem* (pp. 223–242). Washington, DC: Government Publishing Office. License: Creative Commons Attribution CC BY 4.0 IGO.

Zimmerman, B. J. (2000). Attainment of self-regulation: A social cognitive perspective. In M. Boekaerts, P. Pintrich, and M. Zeidner (Eds.), *Self-regulation: Theory, research, and applications* (pp. 13–39). Orlando, FL: Academic Press.

Index

Note: **Bold** page numbers refer to tables and *italic* page numbers refer to figures.

ADL *see* Advanced Distributed Learning
Advanced Distributed Learning 36
AGI *see* Artificial General Intelligence
AGU *see* American Geophysical Union's
AI coaches 129–130, 135–138
AIR *see* American Institute of Research
American Geophysical Union's 150
American Institute of Research 18
American Psychological Association 18
andragogy 54–55
ANI *see* Artificially Narrow Intelligence
APA *see* American Psychological Association
appreciative inquiry 140–141
articulation 157
Artificial General Intelligence 137
Artificially Narrow Intelligence 137
Association for Talent and Development 173
asynchronous instructional delivery *78*
ATD *see* Association for Talent and Development
augmented reality (AR) experiences 10

backwards design 80, *80*
basic interaction/sharing 152
behaviorally defined data 94, 170
better together 134
bichronous instructional delivery *79*
blended approach 20

blended personalized learning 33; in higher education 35–36; in K-12 contexts 33–35; research on 33; in workforce training and development 36–39

C4LPT *see* Centre for Learning & Performance Technologies
CAI *see* Computer Assisted Instruction
California State University, Los Angeles 83
CBI *see* Computer-Based Instruction
CCK08 *see* Connectivism and Connective Knowledge
CDOL *see* Center for Distance and Online Learning
Center for Distance and Online Learning 83
Centre for Learning & Performance Technologies 197
Chief Learning Officer 110
Circumstances, Thoughts, Feelings, Action, and Results 134
CLO *see* Chief Learning Officer
COACHE *see* Collaborative on Academic Careers in Higher Education
coaching 129
coaching programs, design 130–133
collaboration and social negotiation 157
collaborative brainstorming *see* Design thinking
collaborative learning 108

Collaborative on Academic Careers in Higher Education 122
collective reflective assessment 172, 174–175
Communities of Practice 123, 147–151
Computer Assisted Instruction 5
computer-automated learner-to-learner interaction 94
Computer-Based Instruction 8
Connectivism and Connective Knowledge 163
content creation and delivery 69–71
content delivery 69–71; technology of 67–69
contextually defined data 94, 170
cooperative learning 108
COP see Communities of Practice
CPS see creative problem solving
creative problem solving 115
CTFAR see Circumstances, Thoughts, Feelings, Action, and Results
Cyrano.ai 141

Dalton Plan, structural pillars 2
DBR see design-based research
Delphi Method 44–46
Denver Public Schools 30
Design Thinking 114–117
Design-based research 202
Dewey, John 1–2
DFM see Distinguished Faculty Mentors
dialogic instructional strategies 156
Distinguished Faculty Mentors 124
Donut 103
DPS see Denver Public Schools
DT see Design Thinking

e-coaching 130; programs of 133–135
EDU see education
education 197
EDUCAUSE 146
engagement 137
entangled pedagogy 12
ethics 137
E-Time 28
external objective assessment 172, 176

Faculty Mentoring Communities 122, 123
fairness 137
FMC see Faculty Mentoring Communities
folksonomies 146

Game-Based Learning 76
GBL see Game-Based Learning
George Mason University 122
GMU see George Mason University
GROW model 131

iCivics 82, *82*
IEEE see Institute of Electrical and Electronics Engineers
immersive learning environments: games as 76; simulations and virtual reality as 75
immersive learning, technology 71–75
individual reflective assessment 172, 173
Information Communication Technologies 9, 29
Institute of Electrical and Electronics Engineers 150
instructional delivery modality 77
Instructional Systems Designers 49
intelligent machines 3–5
internal objective assessment 172, 175–176
Internet of things 205
IoT see Internet of things
ISD see Instructional Systems Designers

Jigsaw method 117

knowledge-building communities 123

LACOE see Los Angeles County Office of Education
LEAP Innovations 34
learner agency 13–14
learner defined data 170
learner to community of practice 52–53
learner to content interaction 50
learner-based approach 20
learner-based personalization 7, 20, 26–27, 30, 32, 187–194, *188*, 197; research on 26–27
learner-based personalized learning 26; in higher education contexts 29–30; in K-12 contexts 27; workforce training and development contexts 30–33
learner-centered teaching strategies 1
learner-content interaction 47, *60*; use case of 82–83
learner-defined data 94
learner-learner interaction 47, *87*; design of 90

learner-small group interaction *106*, 106–108; design 111–114
learner-social network interaction 194; coaching and mentoring 156; communities of practices 148–151, 154; COP interaction *145*; designing of 154–158, **157**; massive open online courses 163–166; network effect 146; overview 145–147; personal learning environment 151, 154; personal learning networks 151–154; technologies 158–163, **159–161**, *162*, *164*, *165*
learner-teacher instructor 47
learner-to-Internet of Things interaction 204–205
learner-to-learner interaction 50–51; categories of peer learning 95–97
learning ecosystem 198–199
Learning Experience Designers 49
Learning Management System 31, 38, 62, 69, 83, 119, 189
Learning Record Store 203
LED *see* Learning Experience Designers
LMS *see* Learning Management System
Los Angeles County Office of Education 83
LRS *see* Learning Record Store
lunch and learn 121

Massive Open Online Communities/ Courses 10, 91, 163–166, *164*, *165*
means of expression 133
mental contrasting 132
mentoring 129
mobile learning 10
MOOCs *see* Massive Open Online Communities/Courses
multiagent socio-technical systems 204
multimedia design principle 62–66
multimedia learning 61

National Center for Faculty Development and Diversity 124
NCFDD *see* National Center for Faculty Development and Diversity
new faculty members 122
NFM *see* new faculty members

O'Connor, Sandra Day 82
OER *see* Open Educational Resources

Office of Information Technology 100
OIT *see* Office of Information Technology
OLPC *see* One Laptop Per Child
One Laptop Per Child 17
Open Educational Resources 163, 200
OSCAR 132

Parkhurst, Helen 2, 3
PBL *see* Problem-Based Learning
peer collaboration 95, 109–110, 117–118, 124–125
peer facilitation 95, 110–111, 120–122, 125
peer feedback 95
peer interaction 95
peer learning 88–89
peer response 95, 110, 118–120, 125
peer tutoring 88
peer-to-peer learning 88
performance data 170
performance data 94
PERLS *see* Pervasive Learning System
personal information management 151, 191
Personal Knowledge Management 190
Personal Knowledge Mastery 152–153, *153*
personal learning 197
Personal Learning Environment Manager *see* PLEM
Personal Learning Environment 10, 27, 30, 31, 151, 195–198
Personal Learning Networks 147, 151–154, 166, 190
Personal Professional Learning Plan 30
Personalized Learning 1, 17, 18; continuum of 5–7, *6*; efforts 17–19; intelligent machines and 3–5; learner-centered teaching strategies 1–3; role/ influence of technology 7–13
personalized learning designs: assessing tools 178, **179–180**; assessment, measuring effectiveness 172; collective reflective assessment 172, 174–175; data sources 170–171; evaluating ROI 178–182; evaluating strategies 169–170; external objective assessment 172, 176; individual reflective assessment 172, 173; internal objective assessment 172, 175–176; multiple forms 176–178, **177**; organizational PLiF offerings 182–184, **183**

Personalized Learning Interaction Framework 46–50, *48*, 61, 147, 186, *187*; dimensions of *194*, 203–205; implementing PLE 201–203; learner-based personalization 187–194, *188*; PLE ecosystem 198–201, *200*; research on 195–198
Pervasive Learning System 36
PKM *see* Personal Knowledge Management
PKM *see* Personal Knowledge Mastery
PLATO Project, the 4–5
PLE *see* Personal Learning Environment
PLEM 27
PLiF *see* Personalized Learning Interaction Framework
PLNs *see* Personal Learning Networks
PPL *see* personal learning
PPLP *see* Personal Professional Learning Plan
pre-internet technology *8*
Pressey, Sidney L. 3
Problem-Based Learning 109, 121
programming tutoring system 23
protus *see* programming tutoring system
proximity 133

reflection 158
relationship driven data 94, 170
reliability 137
Return on Investment 178–182
ROI *see* Return on Investment
rotated selection 94

SAMHSA *see* Substance Abuse and Mental Health Services Administration
scaffolded social learning 155
scaffolding framework 191, **192–193**, *194*
SDL *see* Self-Directed Learning
Self Regulated Learning 190–191, 195–198
Self-Directed Learning 31
Self-Regulated Learning 30

self-selection 93
semantic 11
SHRM *see* Society of Human Resource Management
social affordances/attributes 146
social learning 147
social media 146
social networking 152
social software 146
social web 9, 146
Society of Human Resource Management 174
SRL *see* Self Regulated Learning
Substance Abuse and Mental Health Services Administration 83
supportive instructional strategies 155
synchronous instructional delivery *77*
systems-based approach 20
systems-based personalization 20; in higher education 23–24; in K-12 21–23; research on systems 20–21; workforce training and development programs 25–26
systems-based personalization 7, 20–23

TEE *see* Thriving Earth Exchange
Thriving Earth Exchange 150
time 133
"train the trainer" model 140–141

vCOPs *see* virtual Communities of Practice
virtual Communities of Practice 147
Virtual Learning Environment 151
visibility 133
VLE *see* Virtual Learning Environment

Web 1.0 Technologies *9*
Web 2.0 Technologies *10*, 11, 146
Web 3.0 technologies 11
workplace learning 197
WPL *see* workplace learning